THE WEHRMACHT IN RUSSIA

BY BOB CARRUTHERS

© Coda Books Ltd
ISBN: 978-1-906783-39-6

C✜DA
BOOKS LTD

Published by Coda Books Ltd,
Unit 1, Cutlers Farm Business Centre, Edstone,
Wootton Wawen, Henley in Arden,
Warwickshire, B95 6DJ
www.codabooks.com

Printed and bound in Great Britain by Lightning Source Books
Chapter House, Pitfield, Kiln Farm, Milton Keynes, MK11 3lW

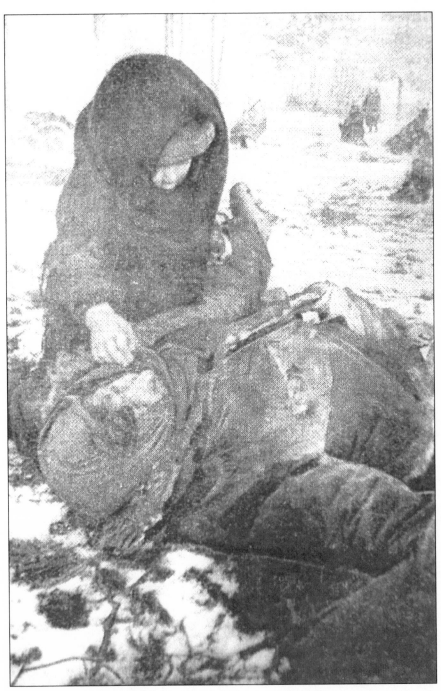

The agony of suffering endured by the Russian people was experienced on an unimaginable scale. 70,000 towns and villages were destroyed and 30 million perished.

CONTENTS

The Führer is photographed here with his two most sycophantic staff officers, Wilhelm Keitel and Alfred Jodl, Hitler managed to extract a number of concessions from Stalin in the year before the launch of Barbarossa. After the war both were hanged as war criminals for their part in the events described in this book.

CHAPTER 1
THE ROAD TO WAR

There are almost too few superlatives to describe the terrible war fought between the two great dictators of the twentieth century. It involved the most participants, caused the highest casualties, saw the largest tank battles, and encompassed the longest battle front. The years between 1941 and 1945 saw overwhelming triumphs and terrible disasters as the conflict see-sawed backwards and forwards from Poland, almost to Moscow, on to the Volga and then right back to Berlin.

It was fought in an unforgiving environment where conditions could swing from searing summer sun to a freezing winter with temperatures as low as minus forty degrees below zero then just as quickly change to an ocean of mud as the snows melted and the rains came.

The real figure will never be known but as many as thirty million may have given their lives in the fight to the death which saw Hitler stand at the very gates of Moscow before the exhausted Red Army managed to claw its way back to wrestle a victory from the threshold of annihilation.

With typicial arrogance, which dispensed with any suggestion of caution, Hermann Goering ominously summarised German policy toward the Soviet Union when he made a typically sinister speech in 1941:

"Many tens of millions in the industrial areas will become redundant and will either die or have to emigrate to Siberia."

In little more than one year, Goering's promise had been made good. Hitler's armies had reduced vast areas of western Russia to dust and rubble and subjected the Soviet peoples to unimaginable horror. Russia experienced an agony of brutality as she was dragged through a nightmare of slaughter to the very edge of extinction.

The launch of Operation Barbarossa, the invasion of the Soviet Union on the 22nd June 1941, was Germany's most desperate gamble of the Second World War. However it was a gamble Hitler felt compelled to take if his ambition of the complete subjugation of Europe were to become a reality. Hitler simply had to overcome Stalin sooner or later and 3,500,000 German troops were initially committed to what was to become the most appalling conflict in the history of warfare, in the course of the next four years as casualties mounted to unheard of levels, she would need to find 3,500,000 more.

The successful conquest of Russia would have provided Germany with the agricultural and industrial infrastructure to ensure Hitler's mastery of Europe; it would also have conveniently rid him of the only military power capable of challenging his domination of Europe. To the warped minds of the ruling elite running Nazi Germany, the deaths of tens of millions of Russians was not simply an economic necessity; their destruction would pave the way for the 'Grossraum', an arrogant concept developed by Heinrich Himmler as the culmination of Hitler's call for 'Lebensraum' or living space. The Grossraum was envisaged as a gigantic Germanic state stretching from the Atlantic Ocean in the west, to the mountains of the Ural in the east.

The Grossraum would be ruled by the master race of Germans served by the more acceptable of the untermensch sub-humans within its borders namely the Slavs. The Jews, who were deemed too decadent to be allowed to survive, were to be eliminated in an extended final solution which was predicated on the fittest being worked to death with the remiander perished by other means.

Once established, this superstate would provide Hitler with the ideal platform for his ultimate aim: complete domination of the world. Hitler's nightmarish vision was of a world in which nationalism would cease to exist, replaced by a universal society of masters and slaves.

Standing between Hitler and the realisation of his vision for the east were the armies of the Union of Soviet Socialist Republics, a fighting force whose state of disorganisation was mirrored by the paranoia of its political leadership. The disarray in the ranks of the Red Army was a direct result of the excesses of Stalin's totalitarian state. Ironically, it was the mechanism of Hitler's totalitarian state which equipped Germany with the best fighting machine in the world.

Like Stalin, Hitler had dispensed with his internal political opponents during his 'night of the long knives', but unlike his rival, Hitler had industriously cultivated the leadership of Germany's armed forces. Stalin meanwhile, was busily destroying the Russian officer corps. In 1936, Tukhachevski, Chief of Staff of the Russian army was executed for treason following a trial which lasted only a single day. Six of the eight generals forming the court-martial which condemned him were themselves to follow suit soon after. By the end of the purge, the Russian army had lost three of the five remaining Marshals of the Soviet Union; all eleven deputy Ministers of Defence; seventy five of the eighty members of the Military Soviet; all the commanders of the military districts; thirteen of the fifteen army commanders; more than half the corps commanders and approximately thirty per cent of the officers below brigade level.

Despite the turmoil in his armed forces, to the outside world, it still appeared that Stalin nonetheless held the balance of power in Europe. When a German-Soviet non-aggression pact was announced in August 1939, the civilised world was naturally shocked. By cynically ignoring their ideological differences, national socialist Germany and communist Russia agreed to take no military action against one another for the next ten years. The existence of this pact was bad enough but it hid a sinister understanding between the two powers. By means of a secret additional protocol, Hitler and Stalin also agreed to divide the independent states of eastern Europe between them.

With the secret protocol in place, Stalin was, for the time being at least, freed from the need to placate Hitler. The Soviet Union moved quickly and threatened the Baltic states with invasion unless they allowed Soviet armies to be stationed within their borders. The citizens of Latvia, Estonia and Lithuania had little option but to comply. Rigged plebiscites gave a gloss of legitimacy to what was effectively a military invasion.

The German invasion of western Poland in September 1939 was the signal for a simultaneous thrust into eastern Poland by Stalin's Red Army. Like two rampaging bullies in an overgrown playground, the two dictators divided the spoils between them, while the western allies mobilised but did nothing. By 1940, in addition to eastern Poland, Stalin also controlled Lithuania, Latvia and Estonia.

Only Finland had the courage and strength to resist Stalin and the hard fought winter war of 1939-1940 brought home the harsh truth that Stalin's purges had been

Molotov is met by Ribbentrop during the negotiations which led to the non-aggression pact and the accompanying secret protocol, which was signed in the early hours of 24th August 1939.

disastrous for the Soviet military machine. Had Hitler proved to be a man of his word all might have been well for Stalin. In the nine years of peace provided by the Treaty, the Red Army could have been brought back to full efficiency. Hitler, of course, had his own ideas, and the Treaty was to prove short lived.

Despite the non-aggression pact with Hitler, Stalin was wise enough to remain wary of his sinister neighbour to the west. The expansion of Soviet territory was considered necessary to Stalin's overall military strategy, which required the creation of a deep barrier of Russian-held territory between the Soviet Union and Nazi Germany. The occupation of the Baltic states had helped create such a barrier. From behind this defensive wall he planned to allow the western allies and Germany to fight a mutually destructive war in the west as they had done for four years during the Great War.

Less than one year later, however, Stalin's hopes of a protracted war evaporated with the brilliant success of Hitler's 1940 campaign in the west, which saw Denmark, Norway, Holland, Belgium, and France fall in rapid succession. The lightning campaign through the Balkans and Greece in 1941, could only produce more grounds for disquiet.

The great offensive against Russia, code-named Barbarossa, had long been fermenting in Hitler's mind. Firmly rooted in the crazed framework of National Socialist ideology was the conviction that Germany's destiny lay in the east. Once more Hitler needed a quick war. Once more he needed it soon. His political instinct told him that Germany would never stand so strong as she stood in 1941. His gambler's instinct told him that if he delayed, even for one year, the crowds that cheered the latest successes so fervently might no longer be willing to follow him into so hazardous an undertaking, and there was surely no greater military adventure than the invasion of Russia.

An invasion of Britain had been postponed indefinitely, but it would still be at least four years before Britain would be capable of mounting an attack on the mainland of Europe. The German submarine blockade of her shores and the relentless bombing of British war industries might delay such preparations even further.

As early as the autumn of 1940, the invasion of Britain had no longer appeared to be a real prospect. Ironically, the failure of the Luftwaffe in the Battle of Britain only made the Russian adventure more likely, but in Germany there was even a measure of demobilisation in response to the general feeling of euphoria which accompanied the widely-held belief that the real war had ended with the capture of France.

Sections of the German military were clearly opposed to the venture. After the war, General Guenther Blumentritt, who was Chief of Operations Staff from January 1942 onwards, recorded his own frustration as to why Hitler had refused to accept the advice of his staff officers. Obviously, there is the danger that Blumentritt, in company with many others, was simply trying to shift the blame on to the convenient shoulders of

Jodl and Keitel, but his account is remarkably consistent with the other senior officers who were mostly in agreement that the attack on Russia should not have been allowed to proceed.

Following the spectacular victories in Poland, Norway, France and the Balkans, the German forces assembled for Barbarossa expected to fight a short campaign which would secure their victories throughout Europe. Hitler became convinced that he could crush the Red Army as easily as he had defeated his other enemies. Blumentritt recalled that Hitler was impervious to all warnings, and there were plenty of them. Hitler had spent the great war in the trenches on the western front. In Hitler's experience the eastern front was considered the easy option, where, in contrast to the grinding horror of the trenches, a war of movement was still possible. In spring of 1941, Field-Marshal von Rundstedt, who had spent most of the First World War on the Eastern Front, had the temerity to ask Hitler outright if he knew what it meant to invade Russia. The Commander-in-Chief, Field-Marshal von Brauchitsch, and his Chief of the General Staff, General Halder, also counselled Hitler against the invasion. So too did General Koestring, who had lived in Russia for years and knew both the country and Stalin intimately. It was all to no avail as Hitler simply refused to give in.

According to those around him, it seems that Hitler first seriously contemplated an attack on Russia during the summer of 1940. As far as can be drawn from the workings of his unique personality his motives were two-fold: first, to get in his blow before the Russians could attack him; and secondly, to conquer new living-space, or 'lebensraum', for the expanding population of Germany. Hitler appeared to accept that the plan was, to a certain extent, dependent on his securing peace with Britain, as he knew that he could only carry out his intentions in the east successfully if his western front was secure. A two-front war had always led to disaster for Germany, but even when it became quite clear that Britain would never make peace with Germany, Hitler still did not abandon his eastern adventure.

The German military, of course, had no way of predicting the sinister workings of the Führer's own warped logic. Hitler's manic gaze stayed firmly focused on Russia. The first Barbarossa directive ominously stated that the USSR might be invaded even before the war with Great Britain was over.

Hitler and Ribbentrop sought to suggest that the massive German military build up was, in fact, merely a form of coercion to force Stalin into a negotiating position. In this they seem to have been successful. On June 14th 1941, Stalin made this perfectly plain by the famous Tass statement, which effectively declared that the Russians were well aware of German troop concentrations, but that there was still nothing to prevent a settlement of Soviet/German relations.

The formal face of the Red Army was carefully calculated to project an aura of power. In reality there was confusion and inefficiency at all levels. These weaknesses were apparent in the disastrous winter war of 1939-1940 with Finland. They were more cruelly exposed in June 1941.

Though Stalin accepted that war was now almost inevitable, in 1941 he certainly did not expect to be attacked. He decided Russia had at least until the spring of 1942 to prepare herself. His explosive denials of all contrary information were so fierce that vital intelligence concerning German preparations was kept from him by subordinates fearful of the violence of his reaction.

As the German build-up toward Operation Barbarossa continued, Stalin's attempts to pacify Hitler grew more desperate. He had already stated in an interview with Pravda in November 1939, that it was not Germany who had attacked Britain and France, but Britain and France who had attacked Germany. Stalin now forbade any criticism of Germany to be printed in the newspapers. In 1940 he increased Russian supplies to Germany and withdrew recognition of the Norwegian and Belgian governments in exile.

In the following year, when Hitler successfully invaded Greece and Yugoslavia, Stalin quickly expelled the Yugoslavian ambassador to Moscow and refused a request to recognise the Greek government in exile. Stalin felt he was continuing to buy time with these unrequited concessions, but his use of the breathing space which he had already obtained was totally devoid of any worthwhile attempt to remedy his military disadvantages. With the opening of Barbarossa a certainty, the principal strategic dilemma facing the Wehrmacht was exactly how Russia could be defeated.

In this vast theatre of operations, within the limited time available to them, the Germans knew that, should the Russians succeed in withdrawing behind the Dnieper and Dvina rivers, the Germans would be confronted with the same problem that had faced Napoleon in 1812.

Hitler's primary objectives were dictated by his economic agenda. He wanted the rich grain lands of the Ukraine, the industrial area of the Donetz basin and the Caucasian oil fields.

Brauchitsch and Halder saw the campaign from a different point of view. They felt the Wehrmacht should eliminate the Red Army first and go for the economic prizes only when that had been achieved. However, both Hitler's plans and those of his top military advisers did coincide in one respect. They all agreed that the bulk of the German forces should be committed north of the Pripet Marshes. In the north, two army groups, North and Centre, would attack; the stronger was Army Group Centre. Their joint task was to send forward their armour on the two flanks, to encircle the enemy west of the Upper Dnieper and Dvina, and to prevent any Russian escape eastward. Meanwhile other elements of Army Group North were to capture Leningrad, link up with the Finns and eliminate all Russian forces in the Baltic region. Only then, was Moscow to be attacked from the west and north simultaneously. South of the Pripet Marshes, Army Group South was to launch a frontal attack and advance eastwards. Not surprisingly, it was this smaller force which made the slowest initial progress.

Further planning was pointless, since the development of the campaign would ultimately depend on the success of these initial operations. For that reason, the differences between Hitler's point of view and that of the Army High Command remained unresolved when the battle began. This was to be the cause of much friction later in the summer, with the most unfortunate consequences.

By May 1940, one hundred and seventy Soviet divisions were stationed in newly occupied territories in the Baltic States and Poland, with the result that over half the Red Army were occupying positions whose fortifications and rearward communications were incomplete. By June 1941, with a German attack imminent, the situation had deteriorated and the Western Special Military District was little short of a shambles.

Many divisions were between six to seven thousand men short of wartime establishment. Levies of experienced personnel had been hived off to build new tank and aviation units. Only one of the six mechanised corps had received their full complement of equipment. Three of the four motorised divisions had no tanks, and four out of every five vehicles in the tank fleets were obsolete. Four of the corps could only deploy one quarter of their designated motor vehicles, and in another four, one in three motor vehicles needed repairs.

From even a cursory analysis, although the opposing forces had amassed vast amounts of weaponry along their common borders, the Soviet Red Army and the German Wehrmacht were anything but equal adversaries.

In the western part of Russia, the Red Army consisted of about five million men. Although the tank strength of the Red Army on the 21st June 1941 was an impressive 23,108 machines, only 8,000 were battle ready and in good condition.

The Soviet forces clearly had the numerical advantage over the three and a half million Germans, who were equipped with only 3,800 tanks, but in terms of combat experience, readiness and leadership, the Germans enjoyed an overwhelming advantage.

The powerful German forces, which the one hundred and seventy understrength divisions of the Red Army faced, were divided into three large army groups. These consisted of one hundred and forty eight fully manned and equipped divisions, of which nineteen were panzer and fifteen panzer grenadier divisions.

Army Group South was commanded by Field Marshal Gerd von Rundstedt, and was charged with seizing Kiev and taking control of the Ukraine as far as the river Dnieper. Field Marshal von Bock's Army Group Centre was to strike towards Smolensk. Army Group North, under Field Marshal von Leeb, was to attack through the Baltic states and seize Leningrad.

The three German army groups were supplemented by five hundred thousand Finnish troops advancing from their homeland in fourteen divisions, and one hundred and fifty thousand Romanians attacking along the Black Sea towards Odessa.

These forces were well supported by the Luftwaffe, which had devoted two thousand, seven hundred and seventy aircraft, some eighty per cent of its operational strength, to the build up. In total, the German forces engaged in Operation Barbarossa, fielded over three thousand, three hundred and fifty tanks, over seven thousand artillery pieces, sixty thousand motor vehicles and six hundred and twenty-five thousand horses.

The Soviet army still clung to its peace time structure. Should war occur, then each military district would be transformed into army groupings similar in structure to the German army groupings. In most respects they were the mirror image of German intentions.

The North Soviet Front was to repel any German advance through the Baltic states and defend Leningrad from Finnish attack. The North West, West and South West Fronts were to engage the three main German army groups, and the Southern Front would deal with any advance towards Odessa.

Behind these similarities, the contrast between the warring nations could not have

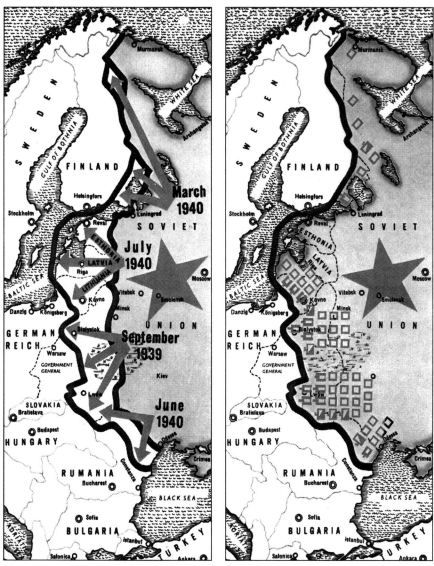

Two maps from the pages of 'Signal', the German war time propaganda magazine, which were intended to justify war by demonstrating the Soviet aggression in Eastern Europe and the subsequent build-up of Russian forces on Germany's borders. Hitler certainly used the perceived Russian build-up to justify what he claimed, was a pre-emptive strike against Russia. Whether he genuinely believed this or merely used it as a convenient excuse must remain a matter of conjecture.

French volunteers for the Wehrmacht. The proliferation of nationalities in the German armed forces did produce serious communication problems which reduced the fighting efficiency of many foreign based divisions.

been greater. While Germany boasted one of the finest industrial infrastructures in the world, Russia had still not completed her industrial revolution.

Stalin had declared in 1931 that, "one feature of old Russia was the continual beatings that she suffered for falling behind, for her backwardness... for military backwardness, for agricultural backwardness. We are fifty or a hundred years behind the advanced countries. We must make good this distance in ten years. Either we do it or they crush us."

By 1941, a generation of upheaval had left its mark economically and psychologically. Revolution and civil war had been followed by the wholesale destruction of the peasantry and enforced collectivisation. Whole segments of the population had been uprooted and transported to work in the new industries set up in the mineral rich regions of Siberia, the Urals and Kazakstan.

The firm grip of the party on the state meant that the Russian people were deprived of any suspicion of the huge build-up along their borders. The state controlled media was devoid of any mention of the increasingly anti-Soviet rhetoric employed by Hitler. Ordinary Soviet citizens were totally unprepared for the latest disaster which was about to descend on them.

Despite the many positive signs there appears to have been a number of genuine concerns among the men of the Wehrmacht. Field-Marshal von Rundstedt, the commander of Army Group South, was forthright in his views on the forthcoming battle. In May of 1941, he shared his reservations with Guenther Blumentritt who, after the war, recalled von Rundstedt's conversation with him.

"This war with Russia is a nonsensical idea, to which I can see no happy ending. But if for political reasons, the war is unavoidable, then we must face the fact that it cannot be won in a single summer campaign. Just look at the distances involved. We cannot possibly defeat the enemy and occupy the whole of western Russia, from the Baltic to the Black Sea, within a few short months. We should prepare for a long war and go for our objectives step by step. First of all a strong Army Group North should capture Leningrad and the area around it. This would enable us to link up with the Finns, eliminate the Red Fleet from the Baltic, and increase our influence in Scandinavia. The central and southern army groups should for the time being advance only to a line running Odessa - Kiev - Orsha - Lake Ilmen. Then, if we should find that we have sufficient time this year, Army Group North could advance south-east from Leningrad towards Moscow, while Army Group Centre move eastwards on the capital. All further operations should be postponed until 1942, when we should make new plans based on the situation as it then is."

Despite some of the reservations of men like von Rundstedt Hitler pressed on with his plans. At last, at 04.00 on the 22nd June 1941, the code word 'Dortmund' crackled down the wires and the full force of Operation Barbarossa was unleashed. As they had come to expect, the German armies sliced through the opposition on every front. Faced by the results of his own intransigence in military matters, Stalin panicked. While his army headquarters desperately tried to piece together the most rudimentary picture of what was happening, he ordered an immediate counter-offensive on all fronts. As the first reports of the devastation he had helped to create filtered through, Stalin was close to breaking point.

"All that Lenin created we have lost forever" he declared, before retreating to his dacha not to emerge until the 3rd July.

What really stunned the Red Army commanders was that this massive German assault had proceeded long after it had left its artillery support behind. The Red Army command had expected that there would be conventional meeting engagements, and opening actions. The perceived wisdom was that these would develop over days or even weeks. Next would come a large series of complex frontier engagements and then the real war would begin. In reality the German advance was so swift that within hours of the launch of Barbarossa, Army Group North panzer columns were approaching Riga, some fifty miles behind the front.

This extended Blitzkrieg technique, especially the bold use of armour, came as an extraordinary and disorientating surprise to the Russians, even to the senior Soviet commanders. Within forty-eight hours, general staff reports made it perfectly plain they had lost control of the situation. They were in complete chaos, and many did not know where their troops were or what was happening. They certainly did not have accurate reports of German movements, and there was no real intelligence, so they were not even sure where the German thrusts were aimed. All that they did know was that to the south, the German Army Group South under von Rundstedt was being slightly delayed. But in the north west and in the west, there was total collapse. In consequence, Stalin operated his usual practice. He took out most of the front commanders and shot them.

At the front, the rapier thrusts of the German panzer divisions were skewering through the chaotic Russian defenses. The panzer groups created deadly breaches in the Soviet line, forcing the Red Army forces into isolated pockets. The supporting German divisions then moved forward in encircling advances which surrounded these islands of defenders. The ferocity and effectiveness of the panzer attacks was so great that some of the pockets were gigantic. Groups of up to fifteen Russian divisions were surrounded and then mercilessly pounded into surrender by an ever-tightening ring of steel.

As a consequence of the confusion which raged throughout the army, many of the Red Army divisions simply broke up and formed very large pockets of leaderless troops. Within a matter of four or five days, Army Group Centre had managed to encircle 350,000 Red Army soldiers at Bialystock. That was only the first of a number of huge encirclements.

Von Leeb's Army Group North scythed into the Baltic states capturing Riga, the Latvian capital. Only in the south were the German forces limited to relatively shallow

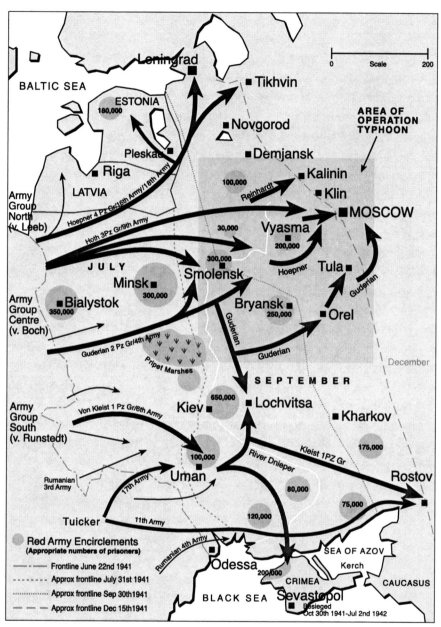

The following labels appear on the map:

BALTIC SEA

Leningrad
■ Tikhvin

ESTONIA
180,000

Pleskau
■ Novgorod

△ Demjansk

AREA OF
OPERATION
TYPHOON

■ Riga

LATVIA

■ Kalinin

100,000

Reinhardt

■ Klin

Army
Group
North
(v. Leeb)

Hoepner 4 Pz Gr/16th Army/18th Army

Hoth 3Pz Gr/9th Army

■ MOSCOW

J U L Y

30,000

Vyasma ■

200,000

300,000 ■

Minsk ■

Smolensk ■

Hoepner

Tula ■

Army
Group
Centre
(v. Boch)

■ Bialystok
350,000

300,000

Bryansk ■

250,000

Guderian

Orel ■

Guderian 2 Pz Gr/4th Army

Guderian

Pripet Marshes

Guderian

December

S E P T E M B E R

Army
Group
South
(v. Runstedt)

Von Kleist 1 Pz Gr/6th Army

650,000

Kiev ■

■ Lochvitsa

■ Kharkov

175,000

100,000

River Dnieper

Kleist 1PZ Gr

Rumanian
3rd Army

17th Army

Uman ■

80,000

Rostov ■

Tuicker

11th Army

75,000

Red Army Encirclements
(Appropriate numbers of prisoners)

120,000

—·—·— Frontline June 22nd 1941
·········· Approx frontline July 31st 1941
············ Approx frontline Sep 30th 1941
— — — Approx frontline Dec 15th 1941

Rumanian 4th Army

Odessa ■

200,000

SEA OF AZOV

Kerch

CRIMEA

CAUCASUS

BLACK SEA

Sevastopol

Besieged
Oct 30th 1941–Jul 2nd 1942

0   Scale   200

The German operation-plan for the Barbarossa offensive envisaged a four pronged assault by four separate Panzer armies which would threaten Leningrad, Moscow and Rostov. Incredibly no firm overall objective was specified with the final choice being reserved for Hitler.

advances toward Lvov and Rovno.

The number of prisoners taken, and the war material captured or destroyed by Army Group Centre since the opening of hostilities was assuming astronomical proportions. The same story was repeated in the sectors of Army Groups North and South. It is hardly surprising that Hitler, his commanders and the troops themselves, now believed that the Red Army must be nearing the end of its resources both in manpower and in weapons. Prisoners confessed that the German attack had been completely unexpected. Moscow, it seemed, was certain to fall into German hands. Great optimism prevailed in Army Group Centre. Hitler, indeed, had already set up a special engineer command whose task was to be the demolition of the Kremlin. The Propaganda Ministry saw fit to make a bombastic statement announcing that the war in the East was won and the Red Army practically annihilated.

In the skies, the Soviet airforce was faring worse than the land army, if that were possible. The early Russian fighters were far slower than the German Messerschmidt 109s, and they were constantly out fought. Many of them never even got the opportunity of aerial combat. The Luftwaffe claimed to have destroyed fifteen hundred aircraft on the ground during the first day of Barbarossa. On the second day, the commander of a Russian bomber group committed suicide after twelve German fighters had accounted for six hundred of his aircraft. Without radar, without ground control and often without sufficient fuel, the Russians were driven to desperate tactics, in a few instances even using their aircraft to ram German planes.

On the ground chaos reigned. The Luftwaffe were pulverising the road and rail links behind the Russian lines. Many officers abandoned caution and were not even using code in their desperate radio pleas for instructions from their headquarters. Naturally these messages were intercepted by German listening stations and used against their desperate senders. Struggling masses of uncoordinated troops were being slaughtered by the German troops as they attempted to obey Stalin's orders to counter-attack. Others were machine-gunned by their own military police for fleeing from positions which were worse than hopeless.

The reality of the first week of Barbarossa was that the Soviet forces were left leaderless. They had no orders. Sometimes they had guns but no ammunition, they had tanks but no fuel, they had vehicles which broke down with no prospect of repair, or they simply had orders which were contradictory. The usual situation was that if in doubt, Red Army commanders would simply order an advance.

Leaving the prisoners to be rounded up, the panzer forces scythed through hopelessly disorganised opposition and moved rapidly onwards. The well honed Blitzkrieg pattern was being repeated and the Soviet defenses whirled away like chaff in the wind. The number of prisoners taken seemed too immense to be true. But it was - and the scale of destruction was terrifying. As the news of Barbarossa reverberated around a stunned and disbelieving world, even Germany was awestruck.

By July 3rd, the battle for the frontiers was over. The German armies had advanced along a line from the river Dvina in the north, to the Dnieper in the south. General Halder, Chief of the German General Staff declared that the war against the Soviet Union had taken only fourteen days to win, Halder was wrong, German intelligence had totally under-estimated the reserves which Russia could command.

Not all the German generals joined the celebration. General Heinz Guderian, who led the 2nd Panzer Group, had been concerned about the headlong advances against widely dispersed and far-flung objectives. Nevertheless, he made his objections known, and though full of apprehension, he continued to do his duty. Guderian was acutely aware that the guiding principle of Blitzkrieg was the concentration of maximum force against a single objective. This had already been neglected, and where there should be convergence, there was now divergence. As the army groups advanced, they would move further away from one another instead of coming closer.

Moreover, Guderian was not being allowed to develop the deep penetration technique he had exploited so masterfully in France. Audacious though he undoubtedly was, even Hitler balked at the thought of his precious armoured units racing too far or too deep into the Soviet hinterland, against any one of the tempting targets which now lay at their mercy. He settled instead for a compromise with the more traditional grand strategy of envelopment.

By the end of July, the two Panzer Groups from Army Group Centre had joined near Minsk to complete a huge encirclement. The encirclement of Minsk by the two pincers of Army Group Centre, led by Hoth in the north and Guderian in the south, yielded three hundred thousand prisoners, two thousand five hundred tanks and fourteen hundred artillery pieces. Thirty-two of the forty-three Russian divisions were emasculated within the first week and the road to Moscow penetrated to a depth of three hundred kms (see page 11). By mid August, Army Group North was approaching Leningrad. The Germans continued to achieve extraordinary success as the Wehrmacht surged on with undiminished impetus. Incredible numbers of prisoners were taken and huge quantities of tanks and guns captured or destroyed.

Despite this sustained progress, Guderian was increasingly conscious of grounds for unease in the development of the campaign. The unending immensity of the land depressed many soldiers. Lack of mobility, particularly of tracked vehicles, was a severe drawback. There continued to be a huge haul of prisoners, but the German pincers were often closing too slowly, allowing large numbers of Red Army troops to get away.

Confidence and smiles, these men had no way of knowing the full scale of the horrors which awaited them.

Those that were encircled fought stubbornly and the Red Army appeared to command endless reserves. Communications were also difficult as most roads were of dirt, which, with the sudden rains, quickly turned to mud, halting entire columns.

Writing for his American captors after the war, the German General, Erhard Rauss, recalled the first signs of the impending mechanical failures, which would eventually engulf the panzer formations.

"Right at the beginning of the Russian campaign, we experienced the havoc which dust can cause in motor vehicles. Tanks sustained severe damage from the dust they stirred up while crossing vast sandy regions, many tanks had no dust filters, and on those which were equipped, the filters soon became thoroughly clogged. Quartz dust was sucked into engines, which became so ground out that many tanks were rendered unserviceable. In other tanks the abrasive action of dust reduced engine efficiency and increased fuel consumption. In this weakened condition, they entered the autumn muddy season which finally destroyed them.

The many sand roads greatly slowed, but did not stop tanks or trucks. Staff cars, with their narrower wheels, stuck easily in sand. Huge dust clouds raised by convoys frequently provoked air attacks by the surviving aircraft of the Red Airforce which resulted in serious losses of men, vehicles and horses."

Despite all of these exertions, Russia was still not defeated. By the end of August, 5,300,000 men had been mobilised. Stalin had emerged from his isolation to broadcast a message of patriotism and resistance to the nation. For once, the Russian people were told the truth - disaster was near but it could be avoided. Stalin now took direct control of the Red Army, as the pre-war complacency, which he himself had done so much to foster, had now rapidly to be undone.

In Leningrad, when news of war reached the factories, the general consensus was that it would be over within the week. "Well, it would not necessarily be over in a week," one Russian worker was reported as saying, "It will take them three or four weeks to get to Berlin" but in 1941, the attacks were all coming the other way and the general mobilisation of Russian troops failed to curtail the German advance.

Meanwhile Hitler was vacillating. Having failed to completely annihilate the Red Army, his interest turned towards securing the economic prize of the Ukrainian oil wells in preference to Moscow or Leningrad.

In common with others in the German High Command, von Kluge had a completely different agenda to Hitler. Von Kluge is a typical example of the disagreement between Hitler and his generals over the correct ground strategy.

"Moscow is both the head and the heart of the Soviet system. Besides being the capital, it is also an important armaments centre. It is, in addition, the focal junction of the Russian rail network, particularly for those lines that lead to Siberia. The Russians are bound to throw in strong forces to prevent our capture of the capital. Therefore it is my opinion that we should advance, with all the strength at our disposal, straight along the Moscow road via Minsk, Orsha and Smolensk. If we can capture this area before winter sets in, we'll have done quite enough for one year. We'll then have to consider what plans to make for 1941."

While the fortifications of the frontier districts left much to be desired, there were still extensive fortifications to be overcome deep within Mother Russia. Although they did not form a solid unbroken line of fortifications like the French maginot line, the heavily defended Stalin line was a formidable series of prepared defenses. [See Appendix One]

Areas of great importance were surrounded with heavy fortifications. For instance, the German armoured units driving for Leningrad encountered fortification systems up to six miles in depth, including numerous earth and concrete bunkers with built-in guns and other heavy weapons. There were also concrete pillboxes with disappearing armoured cupolas for artillery and machine guns. A speedy elimination of these strong defenses with the means available in mobile warfare was extremely difficult.

This was a typical example of the Russian method of defending an important fortified zone, and its capture was later described by Erhard Rauss. His account is reproduced at length here, as it gives a full flavour of the operational difficulties encountered by the German forces attempting to overcome stiffening Russian resistance from August 1941 onwards.

"The forward edge of one such defence system was situated behind an anti-tank ditch several miles long and up to twenty feet wide and twelve feet deep. Embedded in the rear wall of this ditch were dugouts housing the riflemen with their defence weapons. A second and third anti-tank ditch frequently were located in the depth of the system, and were connected by a cross ditch, so as to prevent enemy tanks that had penetrated the position from rolling it up. A machine gun or anti-tank bunker in every bend of the anti-tank ditch afforded flank protection. It was not unusual to encounter dammed-up watercourses close to fortified positions. They were up to a hundred yards wide and several yards deep, and presented an obstacle which was difficult to overcome. The Russians eliminated all favourable approaches to their front, including forests, underbrush and tall grain fields by laying extensive mine fields.

Outposts were located ahead of the fortified position wherever possible. These outposts always had engineers attached whose mission was to block routes of approach with mines or other obstacles."

The area of Krasnogvardeysk, south of Leningrad, had been developed according to these principles, and was effectively turned into an outlying fortress for the defence of Leningrad. During early September 1941, it presented great difficulties to the advance of several German corps.

Krasnogvardeysk blocked all highways and railroads leading to Leningrad from the south, and constituted the main bulwark of Russian resistance. The Russians defended it persistently. Repeated attacks by several infantry divisions were repulsed. It was only taken in the course of a general attack on the Leningrad Line, and after bitter pillbox fighting in the area immediately surrounding Krasnogvardeysk.

"The defence system around Krasnogvardeysk had been prepared long in advance, and consisted of an outer belt of concrete and earth bunkers, with numerous intermediate installations which were interconnected by trench systems that could easily be defended. There were tank-proof watercourses or swamps almost everywhere in front of the outer defence belt. Where this natural protection was lacking, wide anti-tank ditches had been dug.

At a distance of one thousand to three thousand yards behind the outer defence belt, there was an inner one consisting of a heavily fortified position encircling the periphery of the town. Just north of the town ran the continuous Leningrad Line, into which the defence system of Krasnogvardeysk was integrated. It constituted, simultaneously, the rear protection of the town, and the covering position in case the town should have to be evacuated. Beyond the open, elevated terrain immediately west of Krasnogvardeysk lay an extensive forest zone. Within that zone, a few hundred yards from its eastern edge, ran the western front of the outer defence belt. At that point it consisted of wood and earth bunkers, trenches, and strong points - all approaches to which were barricaded by extensive mine fields, abatis, and multiple rows of barbed wire. Located from two to three miles further west were mobile security detachments. Attached to these were engineer units used to lay scattered mines.

The cornerstone of this position was the heavily fortified and mined village of Salyzy, located at the southern end of the forest zone. It covered a road leading to Krasnogvardeysk from the west, and another one which branched off the former to the north within Salyzy. The latter road served as supply route for all the troops situated in the forest position. It crossed the dammed-up Ishora River via a bridge located in front of the Leningrad Line, traversing the line in a northwesterly direction. At that point the line consisted of four trench systems, one behind the other, with numerous machine-gun, anti-tank gun, and artillery bunkers.

The German 6th Panzer Division, advancing on Krasnogvardeysk from the west via Salyzy, had the mission of breaking through the Leningrad Line in this area, and

The Wehrmacht was by no means the armoured juggernaut of popular imagination. For logistical support the forces assembled for Barbarossa were dependent on 625,000 horses.

23

attacking Krasnogvardeysk from the rear. Following a plan of attack based on precise aerial photos, the division decided to push with concentrated force through the outer defence belt at Salyzy, to follow through with a northward thrust, break through the Leningrad Line, and then to roll up the latter to the east. The main body of the division attacked on the road and along the edge of the forest running parallel to it, and took the anti-tank ditch after a brief engagement, and during the night hours, also captured the village of Salyzy after having stormed a large number of bunkers. A bunker at the edge of the forest continued to offer resistance until late afternoon.

Immediately after breaking into the village, the armoured elements of the division, supported by a artillery battalion, advanced through the rear of the enemy-occupied forest position against the Leningrad Line. Under cover of tank fire, the engineers took the undamaged bridge in a coup de main and removed prepared demolition charges. About four miles north of Salyzy, the panzer grenadiers following the tanks penetrated the anti-tank ditch, and formed a bridgehead. During the evening the main body of the division cleared the surrounding forests of Red forces, and assembled in the woods for a northward thrust to join the forces at the bridgehead, which meanwhile had been cut off by the enemy. On the evening of the same day, a German panzer grenadier battalion succeeded in breaking through the inner defence ring located east of Salyzy behind a river arm, in the area of the neighbouring SS Police Division, which had been stalled along its entire front. The bridgehead thus established by the battalion opened a gateway to Krasnogvardeysk for the SS Police Division.

On the second day of attack, the bulk of the 6th Panzer Division advanced along the road to the armoured units in the northern bridgehead. Some of its elements mopped up enemy forces on the plateau west of Krasnogvardeysk, while others rolled up the Russian forest position which was pinning down a unit that had been detached as a flank guard on the previous day. During the forenoon, the entire attack area south of the Leningrad Line was cleared of the enemy. Along the northern wing of the position on the forest edge, forty thousand Russian mines were picked up and disarmed. Then, battalion after battalion was pushed through the bridgehead into the two mile long anti-tank ditch which ran up to a forest area. These battalions were pushed so far to the north that the four parallel defence systems of the Leningrad Line could be rolled up simultaneously from the flank by one battalion each. A desperate enemy attempt to repel the advance of the battalions and tanks by a cavalry attack was easily foiled. The anti-tank ditch, four yards wide and deep, had made it possible to change the attack front of the entire division by ninety degrees at one stroke. Under cover of flank and rear protection, bunker after bunker, and strong point after strong point, was blasted by Stukas, medium artillery, anti-tank and anti-aircraft guns and captured. Step by step

An officer of the Waffen SS prepares to join an attack with a hand grenade. During the coming months the Waffen SS were responsible for many instances of bravery, but they were also associated with unbridled brutality.

the trenches and nests of resistance were cleared out. All of our artillery was still in the old front, south of the Leningrad Line, and its fire thus formed a complete flanking curtain in front of the attacking battalions.

The railroad running through the attack area was reached on the second day of battle, and the Krasnogvardeysk-Leningrad highway on the third day. There, our forces took a group of artillery pillboxes equipped with disappearing armoured cupolas. At that point the division stood directly in the rear of the town. The enemy, forced to retreat hurriedly, had only one side road available for a withdrawal, and that road lay under the effective artillery fire of the panzer division. With serious losses, the Russian divisions poured back over this road and the adjoining terrain. The attempt of the motorised medium artillery, the first of the Red forces to disengage, to escape on the wide asphalt road via Pushkin, failed. The road was already blocked by German armour. All the Russian artillery, as well as all the other motor vehicles, was set afire by our armour when it attempted to break through at this point. During the following night the Russians, although badly mauled, managed to evacuate the town and escape. They then re-established themselves with strong rear guards on high terrain between

Men of the Red Army prepare to leave for the front in 1941. Over five million men like these would fall into German hands, three million of them were captured in the first year of the war.

Krasnogvardeysk and Pushkin.

The next day, pursuing German infantry divisions stalled before these heavily fortified positions, where the enemy had employed the most modern system of field fortifications ever encountered on the Eastern Front. All of the fortification installations were underground. The defence was carried out in subterranean passages, which were established along terrain steps and were equipped with well-camouflaged embrasures. The heavy weapons, likewise, were in subterranean emplacements which were invisible from the outside. There were also subterranean rooms quartering ten to twenty men each, ammunition dumps, and medical and supply installations. All installations were interconnected by underground communication passages. The entrances were situated several hundred yards farther to the rear, well-camouflaged by shrubbery and groups of trees, and protected by open squad trenches and several standard bunkers which could only be recognised from nearby. Neither the best ground nor air reconnaissance could spot this fortification system even at close range. Not even after its guns had opened fire could it be located, as a result of which it proved very difficult to neutralise. All frontal assaults of the infantry were unsuccessful.

Not until two days later was it possible to clarify the situation and to capture the position. By that time the 6th Panzer Division, committed as an encircling force manoeuvring via Pozyolok Tantsy, was pivoting into the hands of the division. The previous evening strong reconnaissance patrols had advanced into the high terrain. Suddenly encountering the rearmost outlying bunker of the position, the patrols took it by storm without orders. With the captured garrison was a Russian military engineer, the builder of this fortification system. He had with him the plans of all the installations, and when they fell into our hands, it was easy to plan the attack for the next day.

However, the attack of the lead-off panzer grenadier regiment had hardly begun when a new difficulty arose. The Russians had recognised the danger to their frontally impregnable position, and launched an attack from Pushkin against the rear of the 6th Panzer Division. A long column of tanks, the end of which could not even be seen in the dust, rolled against the German rear guard unit. The first of the Russian tanks had already passed a narrow strip between swamps and turned against the defended elevations. However, except for one 88mm flak battery and the anti-tank guns of the rear guard panzer grenadier battalion, the German division had at that moment only one panzer battalion with light Czech tanks available for its defence. The heavy flak guns were already thundering. Flames from tanks that had sustained hits rose straight toward the sky. The vanguard of Red tanks consisting of fifty-four KV-Is spread out, but kept moving ahead. Suddenly they were attacked and destroyed from very close range by a hail of fire from the tank destroyer battalion which had just arrived with twenty-seven heavy anti-tank guns. Fourteen columns of black smoke announced to the main body of the enemy the destruction of his vanguard. Thereupon the main body suddenly stopped and no longer dared to pass the narrow swamp. Rear elements fanned out and disappeared into the adjoining terrain. Heavy tank fighting indicated that our panzer regiment, which had been summoned by radio, had gone into action. Soon the din increased. The panzer regiments of the neighbouring 1st and 8th Panzer Divisions had also been summoned, and attacked the flank and rear of the Red forces. The Russians realised their precarious situation and felt themselves no longer equal to the task. Their losses and their retrograde movements bore evidence to the fact. Even the heavy tanks, only fourteen of which had been destroyed by the heavy Flak guns, turned and retreated. The enemy had avoided a showdown. The threat to the rear of the panzer division had thus been eliminated.

In the meantime, however, a German panzer grenadier attack, supported by a panzer battalion, continued according to plan. In heavy fighting, the bunkers and squad trenches, which protected the enemy's rear, were taken one by one, and the entrances to the subterranean defence system reached. During the fighting for the first entrance, the crew resisted from an inner compartment with fire and hand grenades. In this action three Russian medical corps, women in uniform, who defended the entrance with hand-grenades, were killed. When their bodies were removed, several hand grenades were found on them.

Mopping up the subterranean passages was time-consuming and difficult. It had to be carried out by specially trained shock troops with hand grenades and machine pistols. German attempts to clear out the strong bunker crews led to bitter underground hand-to-hand fighting, with heavy losses on both sides. The enemy defended itself to the utmost. The attack stalled. Only after engineer demolition teams had succeeded in determining the location of the subterranean bunkers by noting the sparser growth of grass above them, could these bunkers be blown up by heavy demolition charges from above, and taken. But the closer the shock troops came to the front position of the enemy's defence system, the more serious became the losses. The engineer demolition teams and all the other units were advancing above the Russian defence system, into the heavy artillery fire supporting the frontally attacking German infantry divisions of the neighbouring army. Only when roundabout telephone communications had been established and the devastating fire ordered to cease, was it possible to take the entire subterranean defence system. A junction was then effected with the infantry on the other side. Subsequently, German forces also occupied Pushkin.

With that, the most tenacious Russian defensive battles of 1941 between Krasnogvardeysk and Leningrad, came to an end. Only the flexible leadership of battle-tested armoured forces, attacking with elan, made it possible to overcome the defence zones which had been set up in an all-out effort of the latest Russian defence techniques. Within a week the German 6th Panzer Division had had to break through and roll up twelve positions, repel several counter-attacks, and take more than three hundred heavily fortified bunkers."

While Rauss and his colleagues were engaged in the desperate battles to the north, four reserve armies of thirty seven divisions were dispatched to bolster Russian defenses in the west front in the general area of Smolensk where Army Group Centre continued to make progress.

The Germans countered with yet another encirclement, and the panzer groups of generals Hoth and Guderian smashed through the Soviet line and manoeuvred three hundred thousand Russian troops into an indefensible pocket at Smolensk. Another one hundred and fifty thousand prisoners, two thousand tanks and two thousand artillery pieces also fell into German hands in a similar operation shortly afterwards.

Drunk with anticipation, Goebbels announced that, "the eastern continent lies like a limp virgin in the mighty arms of the German Mars."

In many respects Goebbels was correct. A bold concerted thrust would probably have led to the fall of Moscow, but Hitler had other ideas. The capture of the Russian capital would have been a profound psychological shock for the Soviets, but to Guderian's dismay, he was diverted from his plan to drive hard and fast for Moscow. Instead, he was ordered south to the Ukraine to link up with von Kleist. There his divisions still

German troops move into position before Barbarossa.

performed outstandingly, helping to take well over half a million prisoners and nearly a thousand tanks in a great encirclement behind Kiev, but these victories served only to disguise the fact that the crucial moment of the campaign had already passed.

Spurred on by the successful actions of their comrades, the men of Army Group South finally broke through the Russian South West Front, and another pocket centred on Uman yielded a further toll of one hundred thousand prisoners.

The devastating speed of the German advance was due to the power and tactical brilliance of the panzer divisions. Despite the fact that the Versailles Treaty forbade the Germans to own a tank force, the concept of an integrated armoured force had intrigued the German military since the close of the First World War. By the early thirties, ten prototype tanks had been designed and built in secret. Ironically, the initial development of what would become the most technically accomplished and effective tank programme ever seen, took place at the German-Soviet tank school at Kazan in Russia.

Russian armoured warfare was inhibited by Stalin's disenchantment with tank divisions, which had led him in the late thirties to decree that in future, armour would only be utilised in the support of infantry formations. After witnessing the German successes with their armoured divisions on the western front in 1940, Stalin changed his mind, but the reorganisation of Russian armour was not completed before the launch of Barbarossa. Even though Russian tanks outnumbered German tanks two to one at the front and six to one overall, tactical ineffectiveness, obsolete models and widespread disrepair tipped the advantage overwhelmingly in favour of Germany during the first stages of the conflict.

But it was not just the quality of the German tanks, it was the capability of the panzer commanders to control their armour that was essential. They had excellent command control facilities, and very good support and logistical facilities. Such was the haphazard and untrained manner in which the Russians handled their armour, that the Germans soon learned to defeat them even with inferior armour and guns, but there were a few hard lessons to be learned first. The surprise introduction of the medium T-34 and KV-1 heavy tanks into the fighting came as a sobering lesson to any complacent German unit.

Again, the account by Generaloberst Erhard Rauss of the fighting in Russia gives us an excellent first hand picture of the first encounters with heavy Soviet armour in the form of KV-1 tanks.

"The Russian armoured force played only a subordinate role at the beginning of the war. In the advance of 1941, our troops encountered only small units which supported the infantry in the same manner as our own self-propelled assault guns. The Russian tanks operated in a very clumsy manner and were quickly eliminated by our anti-tank weapons. The Russians carried out counter-attacks with large tank forces, either alone or in combined operations with other arms, only at individual, important sectors.

On 23rd June 1941, our 4th Panzer Group, after a thrust from East Prussia, had reached the Dubysa and had formed several bridgeheads. The defeated enemy infantry units scattered into the extensive forests and high grain fields, where they constituted a threat to our supply lines. As early as 25th June, the Russians launched a surprise counter-attack on the southern bridgehead in the direction of Raseiniai with their hastily brought-up XIV Tank Corps. They overpowered the 6th Motorcycle Battalion which was committed in the bridgehead, took the bridge, and pushed on in the direction of the city. Our 114th Armoured Infantry Regiment, reinforced by two artillery battalions and a hundred tanks, was immediately put into action and stopped the main body of enemy forces. Then, there suddenly appeared for the first time, a battalion of heavy enemy tanks of previously unknown type. The tank overran the armoured infantry regiment and broke through into the artillery position. The projectiles of all defence weapons (except the 88mm flak) bounced off the thick enemy armour. The one hundred German tanks were unable to check the twenty Russian dreadnaughts, and suffered losses. Several Czech-built tanks of the type 35(t), which had bogged down in the grain fields because of mechanical trouble, were flattened by the enemy monsters. The same fate befell a 150mm medium howitzer battery which kept on firing until the last minute. Despite the fact that it scored numerous direct hits from as close a range as two hundred yards, its heavy shells were unable to put even a single tank out of action. The situation became critical. Only the 88mm flak finally knocked out a few of the Russian KV-1s and forced the others to withdraw into the woods.

He said: 'One of the KV-1s even managed to reach the only supply route of our task force located in the northern bridgehead, and blocked it for several days. The first unsuspecting trucks to arrive with supplies were immediately shot afire by the tank.

There were practically no means of eliminating the monster. It was impossible to bypass it because of the swampy surrounding terrain. Neither supplies nor ammunition could be brought up. The severely wounded could not be removed to the hospital for the necessary operations, so they died. The attempt to put the tank out of action with the 50mm anti-tank gun battery, which had just been introduced at that time, at a range of five hundred yards, ended with heavy losses to crews and equipment of the battery. The tank remained undamaged in spite of the fact that, as was later determined, it got fourteen direct hits. These merely produced blue spots on its armour. When a camouflaged 88mm flak gun was brought up, the tank calmly permitted it to be put into position at a distance of seven hundred yards, and then smashed it and its crew before it was even ready to fire. The attempt of engineers to blow it up at night likewise proved abortive. To be sure, the engineers managed to get to the tank after midnight, and laid the prescribed demolition charge under the caterpillar tracks. The charge went off according to plan, but was insufficient for the oversized tracks. Pieces were broken off the tracks, but the tank remained mobile and continued to molest the rear of the front and to block all supplies. At first it received supplies at night from scattered Russian groups and civilians, but we later prevented this procedure by blocking off the surrounding area. However, even this isolation did not induce it to give up its favourable position. It finally became the victim of a ruse. Fifty tanks were ordered to feign an attack from three sides and to fire on it so as to draw all of its attention in those directions. Under the protection of this feint it was possible to set up and camouflage another 88mm flak gun to the rear of the tank, so that this time it actually was able to fire. Of the twelve direct hits scored by this medium gun, three pierced the tank and destroyed it."

The ground forces which tackled the mighty KV-1 were only part of a Blitzkrieg operation which repeatedly saw German advances of up to fifty miles per day during the early part of Barbarossa.

The Panzer corps were supported by the famous Junkers JU 87s, the Stuka dive bombers which were protected in turn, by Messerschmitt 109 fighters.

Although it was already obsolescent by 1941, the Stuka was to prove to be one of the most versatile machines of the war. Used as a night bomber, torpedo launcher, trainer, long range reconnaissance aircraft and a host of other specialist tasks, it was at its most fearsome as a dive bomber. Screeching out of the sky, with its morale-sapping siren at full blast like some furious bird of prey, the Stuka's airbrakes still allowed it to slow to a speed which enabled its bomb load to be delivered with almost pinpoint accuracy. With a virtually unopposed mobile flying artillery of this calibre, it was no surprise that Barbarossa was initially so successful.

After a month of victorious progress, however, even the German High Command were disconcerted by the rapidity of their own advance. Their armies were now fighting on a front one thousand miles wide. The Stukas could no longer deliver the concerted hammer blows which had punched the holes in the Russian lines which the panzers had so mercilessly exploited. Even though the Soviet airforce had by now lost approximately five thousand aircraft, the supply of replacements seemed endless.

Throughout the war Germany always lacked a four engined heavy bomber. The Russian factories in the east, which were soon churning out more effective fighter models, remained well out of Luftwaffe bombing range. The steady attrition on machines and pilots meant that German air assault began to run low on fighters.

A wounded Russian soldier is carried by his colleagues into an uncertain future as a prisoner of war.

Like the Wehrmacht, the Luftwaffe also began to encounter serious supply problems. The distance from home bases and the destruction of Russia's transport infrastructure, meant that aircraft replacement parts now had to be flown to forward airfields, using up valuable transport aircraft in the process. The lengthening supply lines were also affecting the German ground forces. Tank commanders, hundreds of miles from their Polish depots, now had to rely upon increasingly makeshift field repairs.

THE WEAPONS OF WAR

The unmistakable outline of the Stuka divebomber.

1. THE STUKA

They appear in all of the newsreels, the screaming sirens spelled terror from Poland to Moscow, but there were never more than seven hundred in service at any given time.

Despite its relative scarcity, the Stuka was to leave an impression on World War II out of all proportion to its numbers.

The men who fought against the Stuka would recognise instantly the angular gull winged shape. Those who flew in them, forever held the aircraft dear to their hearts.

First flown in 1935, the Stukas were already considered obsolete by the start of the war only four years later. But their champion, General Lieutenant Wolfram von Richthofen was confident that his warplanes would prove their worth. Originally one of the many opponents of the dive bomber concept, Richthofen had been deeply impressed by the lethal accuracy of the handful of dive bombers available to the German Condor Legion in the Spanish Civil War. So the Stukas were given a reprieve which was to last the entire six years of the war.

The overriding advantage of the Stuka was the accuracy of its bombing run. Conventional bombers of the time released their bombs at high altitude, aiming devices were rudimentary and accuracy was necessarily poor.

Dive bombers swooped down on their targets and guided their bombs towards the target allowing far greater accuracy.

With the special dive brakes applied, the Stuka could fly so low before pulling out of its dive, it could almost place its bomb on the target, and its cranked wings allowed excellent forward vision.

But there was one major disadvantage. The Stuka was very slow and cumbersome. It was almost defenceless against modern fighters such as the Spitfire or the Hurricane. Time and again, this great weakness would come back to haunt the German airforce.

Even by the exacting standards normal for aerial combat, the men who flew the Stukas had to be exceptionally fit.

Coming out of a dive, the two crewmen were subjected to a centrifugal force up to five times that exerted by gravity. Blood was drained from the retina and brain, usually leading to a temporary blindness and loss of consciousness. It was found that short, stocky, pilots in their thirties and forties were best able to withstand the high G forces involved in a dive bomb attack.

To combat the disastrous possibilities of the crew losing consciousness, the Stuka was fitted with an automatic pull-out and bomb release mechanism which prevented loss of control during this critical part of the dive bombing manoeuvre. In other respects the controls were surprisingly simple. Early versions had only two instruments, a compass and a turn and bank indicator.

Slowed down by the fixed under-carriage, top speed was less than two hundred and fifty miles an hour. The Stuka was armed with two fixed forward machine guns and a third rear-facing gun operated by the navigator, who sat with his back to the direction of travel. The Stuka carried either a single one thousand kilo bomb under the fuselage, or one five hundred kilo bomb, plus four smaller bombs under the wings.

A wing of Stukas escorted by a Messerschmitt 109.

Hans Ulrich Rudel, the most celebrated Stuka pilot of the war. Despite losing a leg he continued to fly up to four missions on almost every day of the war.

The Junkers 87 was first penned in 1933 by Hermann Pohlmann. The distinctive inverted gull wings allowed the shortest undercarriage to reduce drag. Winning a dive bomber design competition in January 1935, the first prototype had taken to the air in September 1935, powered ironically by a Rolls Royce V12 Kestrel engine. The production 87 Anton of 1937 was powered by a supercharged Jumo 680 horse er engine and with dive brakes to control its descent. By the outbreak of war, the 87B-1 boasted an 1100hp Jumo 21 engine and the cumbersome undercarriage fairings had been replaced by lightweight spats.

Stuka aces, of which the most famous was Hans Ulrich Rudel, became national heroes and both men and machines were idolised.

The Stukas were ordered in to attack the ships in Leningrad Harbour, and Hans Ulrich Rudel succeeded in scoring a direct hit on the battleship 'Marat' with a new armour-piercing bomb tearing off the bows of the 23,000ton vessel. By his great courage, diving faster and lower than anyone else in the face of ferocious anti-aircraft fire, Rudel was able to add a battleship to the fantastic tally of tanks destroyed by this fearless aviator.

The Germans had been increasingly alarmed at the quantity and quality of the new Soviet armour. Some Stukas were therefore adapted specifically for use against tanks.

One of these was flown by Hans Rudel, who now embarked on an extraordinary campaign as a tank destroyer.

The Tank Buster (Ju87 G) version was equipped with two 37mm flak 18 armour piercing cannon slung under the wings and proved highly successful. Its distinctive appearance soon earned it the nickname 'Stuka mit den Langen Stangen' or more graphically, 'Der Panzerknacker', the tank cracker. Rudel destroyed over five hundred enemy tanks in his machine.

Despite their vulnerability, the Stukas were still able to operate, being continually sent in to bolster threatened sections of the front. The Luftwaffe committed every available aircraft, however obsolete, to the fray because there was nothing else. Slowly and at stupendous cost, the war in the east was lost. The airmen were paying a heavy price for the complacency and misjudgments of Herman Goering.

Three years previously, the Luftwaffe's Stukas and bombers had dealt fearful destruction to the retreating Red Army. Now the German armies were to suffer unsparing devastation from the air in far greater measure.

With the coming of 1945 the long war drew to an end, as Germany was crushed between the might of the Western Allies and the vast and ruthless Red Army. Although Nazi Germany was in its death throws, the bitter struggle went on. Short of pilots, mechanics and planes, the Luftwaffe still flew. No more Stukas were built and production ceased in October 1944 but the surviving aircraft, in the hands of men like Rudel, flew on, still doing their duty in the face of overwhelming odds.

One of the most famous images of the war, the wounded NCO continues to urge his men forward. This determination to resist in the face of the worst possible personal circumstances was the hall mark of the Red Army from 1941 onwards.

CHAPTER 2
HITLER HESITATES

The Panzer commanders now pressed for the final thrust toward Moscow. They argued that only the continuation of the offensive would prevent the Russians from organising a fresh line of resistance. While some of Hitler's generals disagreed with the suggestion that such an attack should be launched immediately, they were almost unanimous in recommending that Moscow should become the primary objective of the next phase of the war.

Hitler, as usual, had his own ideas. His deluded brain was convinced that he alone could provide the answers. He was rightly concerned over the possibility of the gaps between the Panzer divisions and the main armies following behind, being exploited by Russian reinforcements. He also feared that the hundreds of thousands of Soviet troops left behind the German lines in the wake of the advance, might co-ordinate their actions into an effective guerrilla movement. According to the account of one Russian witness to the disarray behind the German advance in 1941 he need hardly have worried.

"Thousands of mobilised men, from various places which have already been captured, and from near the front-line zone, roam from place to place. They lack any purpose, any sense of order. They have no uniforms, a fifth are barefoot. The leaders are leaving and they are abandoning us to ruin."

Hitler had never been fully convinced of the importance of Moscow and continued to regard it as a secondary objective.

The oil fields of the south continued to exert a strong pull on him. Given Germany's strategic requirement for extra oil supplies, there was a great deal of logic in this preoccupation.

As the debate stretched out until mid August, a vital month of summer weather was wasted. The Russians had the breathing space to throw new reserve divisions into the gaps in their defences. Barely trained, poorly equipped, with some men still in the tattered remnants of their civilian clothing, their stubborn resistance nonetheless meant that the Russians were still a force to be reckoned with. Dogged defence, which bordered on the fanatical, was a feature of the Russian method of fighting, which was remarked upon by many German soldiers who served in Russia. General Rauss later recorded his own views.

"The Russians were very adept at preparing inhabited places for defence. In a short time, a village would be converted into a little fortress. Wooden houses had well-camouflaged gun ports almost flush with the floor, their interiors were reinforced with sandbags or earth, observation slots were put into roofs, and bunkers built into floors and connected with adjacent houses or outside defences by narrow trenches. Although almost all inhabited places were crammed with troops, they seemed deserted to German reconnaissance, since even water and food details were allowed to leave their shelters only after dark. The Russians blocked approach routes with well-camouflaged anti-tank guns or dug-in tanks. Wrecks of knocked-out tanks were specially favoured for use as observation posts and as emplacements for heavy infantry weapons, and bunkers for living quarters were dug under them. It was Russian practice to allow the enemy to draw near, and then to fire at him unexpectedly. In order to prevent heavy losses of personnel and tanks, the Germans had to cover the outskirts of inhabited places with artillery, tanks, or heavy weapons during the approach of their troops. Fires resulted frequently, and in many instances consumed the whole village. When the front line neared a village, the inhabitants carried their possessions into outlying woods or bunkers for safekeeping. They did not take part in the fighting of the regular troops, but served as auxiliaries, building earthworks and passing on information. The

Heavy fighting continued to be a feature of the campaign.

The ruined city of Kiev after capture by the Germans. The destruction of the city was modest by the savage standards of Stalingrad and Kharkov the following year.

Russian practice of raiding inhabited localities during mobile warfare, or converting them into strong points for defensive purposes, was the excuse given for the destruction of thousands of towns and villages during combat.

"Since the defences on the outskirts of a locality were quickly eliminated by German counter-measures, the Russians later laid their main line of resistance right through the centre of their villages, and left only a few security detachments on the outskirts facing the enemy. Permanent structures destroyed by artillery fire or aerial bombs were utilised as defence points. The ruins hid weapons and served to strengthen the underlying bunkers. Even the heaviest shelling would not drive the Russians from such positions, they had to be dislodged with hand grenades or flame throwers. The Russians, upon retreating, frequently burned or blasted buildings suitable for housing command posts or other important military installations. Quite often, however, they left castles, former country seats, and other spacious dwellings intact, after they had mined the walls in a completely conspicuous manner with delayed-action bombs, which were often set to explode several weeks later. These were meant to blow up entire German headquarters at one time. The possible presence of time-bombs in cities, railroad stations, bridges, and other important structures always had to be taken into account."

A rapid campaign to crush Russia, which should have been over by August, still had no end in sight. The German High Command had to think again. The most serious issue that they now had to deal with was logistics and supply. No great preparation had been made for a winter campaign in Russia. In addition, the German high command, German intelligence and the German military as a whole, had vastly under-estimated the ability of the Red Army to resist. The German aim was to destroy the Red Army west of the Dvina but they had failed to do so. Whatever they did to the Red Army, however mercilessly they battered at it, it seemed they could not destroy it.

One of the great sources of strength in Stalin's Red Army during the early years of the war, came from the political commissars who were attached to Red Army Units. The Russians and Germans alike detested these men but as Rauss recalled after the war, they certainly wielded a strong influence.

"The commissars found special support among the women who served within the framework of the Soviet Army. Russian women served in all-female units with the so-called partisan bands, individually as gunners in the artillery, as spies dropped by parachute, as medical corps aides with the fighting corps and in the rear in the auxiliary services. They were political fanatics, filled with hate for every opponent, cruel and incorruptible. The women were enthusiastic Communists - and dangerous.

"It was also not unusual for women to fight in the front lines. Thus, in 1941 medical corps women defended the last positions in front of Leningrad with pistols and hand grenades until they fell in the battle, and uniformed women took part in the final breakout struggle at Sevastopol in 1942. In the fighting along the middle Donets in February 1943, a Russian tank was apparently rendered immobile by a direct hit. When German tanks approached, it suddenly reopened fire and attempted to break out. A second direct hit again brought it to a standstill but in spite of its hopeless position, it defended itself while a tank-killer team advanced on it. Finally it burst into flames from a demolition charge and only then did the escape hatch open. A woman in tanker uniform climbed out. She was the wife and co-fighter of a tank company commander who, killed by the first hit, lay beside her in the tank. So far as Red soldiers were concerned, women in uniform were superiors or comrades to whom respect was paid."

The consensus among the generals was that in order to overcome fanatical resistance like this, Moscow should be the priority. Eventually, the highly-vocal objections of the generals were overruled, and not one but two major objectives were prioritised by Hitler, who demanded the simultaneous capture of Moscow and the fall of the Ukraine. In so doing he committed a major strategic blunder.

It was not just in the ranks of the German army that strategic errors were being made. In 1941, as the giant pincer movement involving Guderian's forces from Army Group Centre and the left flank of von Kleist's Army Group South, began to close its jaws on a huge pocket of Russian forces to the rear of Kiev, General Zhukov, the Soviet Chief of Staff, pleaded with Stalin for a strategic withdrawal of the troops defending the city. He was dismissed from his post. Marshal Timoshenko, the newly appointed southwest commander, arrived just in time to see the trapped Soviet divisions march into captivity.

Russian infantry on the outskirts of Kiev keep a watchful eye on the skies.

The six hundred thousand prisoners taken by the Germans, remain the highest number ever captured in a single engagement.

The battle for the Ukraine now centred on the Crimean Peninsula, where the right flank of Army Group South pressed the Soviet 51st army back towards Sevastopol. While half of the German Army Group Centre were engaged in subduing the Ukraine, Zhukov, transferred to the reserve forces behind West Front, seized the opportunity to attack the exposed flank of the German 4th army. Occupying a salient near Smolensk, the Germans were now themselves vulnerable to encirclement. Elements of the 4th Panzer army were thrown back 12kms but without sufficient tanks and aircraft, Zhukov failed to tighten the noose he had made. However, in terms of morale, Zhukov's counter thrust was highly significant. His action was the first substantial Soviet counter-attack of the war.

The men who had made this possible were the indefatigable soldiers of the Red Army, and it was now that the Germans began to give them the grudging recognition which can be traced in later accounts.

"The best weapon of the Russian infantryman was the machine pistol. It was easily handled, equal to Russian winter conditions, and one which the Germans also regarded highly. This weapon was slung around the neck and carried in front on the chest, ready for immediate action. The mortar also proved highly valuable as the ideal weapon for terrain conditions where artillery support was impossible. At the beginning of the Eastern Campaign, Russian infantry far surpassed the German in mortar equipment and its use.

"The same was true for the Russian anti-tank gun: it was of far better quality, issued in greater quantities than the German equivalent, and was readily put to use whenever captured. The anti-tank gun was an auxiliary weapon from which the Russian soldier was never separated. Wherever the Russian infantryman was, anti-tank defence could be expected by his enemy. At times it appeared to the Germans that each Russian infantryman had an anti-tank gun or anti-tank rifle, just as infantrymen of other armies had ordinary rifles. The Russian moved his anti-tank weapons to whatever tank attacks might be expected. Emplacements were set up within a few minutes. If the small gun, always excellently camouflaged, was not needed for anti-tank defence, its flat trajectory and great accuracy were put to good use in infantry combat. The Germans had a rule to cope with this. Engage Russian infantry immediately following their appearance, for shortly thereafter not only the soldier, but also his anti-tank defence will have disappeared into the ground, and every counter-measure will be twice as costly."

THE WEAPONS OF WAR

The Sturmgeschütze was to become an indispensable support for the Wehrmacht. This late 1942 variant features the long barrelled 75mm gun which gave the Stug parity with the T-34.

2. STURMGESCHÜTZE

What the German Blitzkrieg tactics demanded was an assault gun - a mobile artillery piece which could keep pace with the mechanised infantry, afford the gunners a measure of protection, and provide support on the battlefield at short notice, where it really mattered, in the very front line. The successful prototype was produced in 1936 by the Alkett company. The final vehicle was constructed from two separate elements and it mounted a heavy 75mm gun on a Panzer III tank chassis.

The 75mm was a heavier weapon than could normally be carried on a Panzer III, but the extra space for the heavier gun was achieved by dispensing with the turret and setting the gun on a fixed mount with a limited traverse. The Sturmgeschütze was born.

Throughout the long years of World War Two, the Sturmgeschütze crews never

A Sturmgeschütze of the Leibstandarte division advances in Rostov in 1941.

came to regard themselves as tank men. They wore different uniforms and still considered themselves to be artillery men, who happened to man mobile assault guns - but they were still gunners at heart.

The Sturmgeschütze had a crew of four. The commander, driver, loader and gunner. It soon became the proud boast of the Sturmgeschütze crews that their men were all volunteers, always ready to answer the infantryman's call to bring up the guns. The new assault gunners took to the role with great enthusiasm. Although the cramped interior of each Geschütze officially had room for only forty-four rounds, the crews soon found that they could carry ninety rounds of ammunition by stacking extra rounds in layers on the floor of the vehicle. This meant the guns could stay in action for longer and continue to give their support to the infantry for longer periods. In the coming years, that would be a great advantage.

Initially, Sturmgeschütze were organised into independent battalions. Each battalion composed of three troops, which originally had six guns each. The commander of the battalion also had his own vehicle. In later years, the number of vehicles in each troop was raised to ten and the battalions were re-named as Brigades, which in theory, fielded thirty-one Sturmgeschütze. In practice, these ideals were hardly ever achieved and then only highly favoured formations received the full complement.

In battle, these independent brigades were allocated to support infantry formations for a specific action and came under the command of the infantry they were ordered to support. As the war grew, the Sturmgeschütze commanders naturally gained a wealth of battle experience gained from almost constant exposure to action. So in practice, it was frequently the infantry commanders who took the lead from the more experienced assault gun leaders.

One shortcoming of the early Sturmgeschütze was the lack of a machine gun for close support against enemy infantry.

The lack of close defence capability was rectified in 1941 with the introduction of the machine gun mounted on the Model E, of which 272 were produced.

The Sturmgeschütze made a valuable contribution to the success of Operation Barbarossa, but despite the initial successes, by late 1941, it was apparent that the German armoured force as a whole was seriously under gunned.

The short 75mm gun of the Sturmgeschütze, was really designed to fire low velocity, high explosive shells in support of infantry formations, and although it used the relatively small chassis of the Panzer III, the fact that it had no turret allowed the Stug to be up gunned to incorporate the deadly long barrelled L/43 75mm gun, which could not be fitted to a Panzer III. With this gun, the Sturmgeschütze was a match for the T-34.

This much needed upgrade was first incorporated into the Sturmgeschütze Model F in 1942. The long barrelled L/43 gun, gave the armour piercing shells fired by the Geschütze, a much higher muzzle velocity and therefore a far greater tank killing capability than the 50mm gun of the Panzer III. It was now obvious that the Panzer III had evolved as far as it could and the model was phased out. From 1943, the Panzer III chassis were used exclusively for the manufacture of Sturmgeschütze, production of which continued right up to the last days of the war.

The addition of a powerful anti-tank gun made the Sturmgeschütze much more than an infantry support weapon. It was now apparent that, with its low silhouette, the Stug was a much harder target to hit than the Russian T-34. The sloped armour also helped to deflect shots away from the vehicle, and the scales gradually began to tip back in Germany's favour during the fierce tank battles of 1942.

Twenty thousand enemy tank kills were claimed by assault gun crews up to the early months of 1944.

The only major drawback of the Geschütze was the lack of a turret. This meant that instead of simply swinging the motorised turret round to face an enemy threat to the side or rear, the whole vehicle had to be moved round on its tracks.

In a mobile battle, where every second counts, the lack of a turret was a very real disadvantage, but Sturmgeschütze crews learned to adopt defensive tactics designed to lure Russian tanks into carefully constructed killing grounds.

The Sturmgeschütze manual stressed time and time again the need for the gun to be stationary when firing. In this way the highest level of accuracy was achieved. When the commanders heeded this request, the results were devastating.

The new tactics certainly worked and in early 1943, there was another increase in gun power with the introduction of the long barrelled L/48 gun which gave extra velocity, and hence extra tank killing power.

It was this new gun which equipped the definitive Sturmgeschütze, the Model G of which 7,720 were eventually manufactured. The sheer numbers produced is a reflection of just how effective and popular the Sturmgeschütze was in battle.

As the war dragged on, they became the infantry's rock in defence and his armoured fist in attack.

By 1943, the Sturmgeschütze was an indispensable part of both the Panzer Division and the ordinary infantry division. The infantry soon came to know that as long as the Geschütze were in the line, things were in control.

A Stug III with the L/43 gun which was introduced in 1942.

In those actions, a major issue for the Sturmgeschütze commanders was the limited fuel and ammunition capacity of their cramped vehicles. This produced a constant need to leave the battleline to refuel the vehicles and re-load with ammunition.

It was a standard rule of Sturmgeschütze tactical doctrine that, if possible, not all machines would be withdrawn from the line at the same time, but that they should leave the field in relays, otherwise there was a real danger that the morale of the infantry might collapse if they saw their trusted Geschütze withdrawing from the field.

Despite its undoubted success as a tank killer, there was still an infantry support role for the Sturmgeschütze. The low trajectory 7.5m gun was an excellent anti-tank gun, but to reach infantry hiding behind obstacles or other terrain features, a high trajectory howitzer was still required. A further 1100 Sturmgeschütze were therefore manufactured with the 10.5 Howitzer, which packed a deadly, high explosive punch, which could be used in support of the infantry, either in attack or (more usually) desperate defence.

By 1943, the obvious success of the Sturmgeschütze in the field, led the allies to target the Alkett factory responsible for the production of Stug III's, for priority bombing. The resultant saturation bombing severely damaged the production factories.

During the period of rebuilding, production was switched from Alkett to the Krupps tank works, but Krupps made Panzer IV's not Panzer III's.

During 1943, the 1500 Sturmgeschütze which were manufactured by Krupps, used the Panzer IV tank chassis, combined with the highly successful L/48 gun. These machines known as Sturmgeschütze III/IV's were every bit as successful as the old Stug III.

The strain of a never ending campaign can be seen on the faces of these SS men.

CHAPTER 3
OPERATION TYPHOON

Hitler's response to the errors which had diffused the energy of Barbarossa was to regroup Army Group Centre and prepare the most critical operation of the campaign. Operation Typhoon, the real drive toward Moscow, was finally under way. Seventy divisions from Army Group Centre, spearheaded by fifteen hundred tanks, would race toward the Russian capital before the rains of autumn, or the snows of winter could halt their progress.

On September 30th 1941, General Guderian's 2nd Panzer Group almost inevitably broke through the Soviet line, and had encircled the defending Bryansk Front by the 6th October. Simultaneously, the Western Front, commanded by Marshal Timoshenko, fell into a similar trap. The pockets of Vyazma and Bryansk containing nine armies of seventy-one divisions were almost completely destroyed (see page eleven). Another six hundred and sixty thousand troops faced the grim hospitality that the German army meted out to prisoners of war, and the road to Moscow lay open.

The advance to Moscow was resumed, but the delay proved to be fatal. Fuel and supplies were delivered through a system that had become stretched to breaking point, and the lines of communication were enormously over-extended. Shortages of every kind impaired the fighting ability of the front-line forces. The vague fears of the Generals who had initially harboured doubts, were beginning to take the shape of a massive logistical nightmare, which would ultimately prove insurmountable. The advance had been over areas so vast that it was impossible for comprehensive mopping-up operations to be undertaken. Behind the Germans there lay the huge expanses of territory, in which tens of thousands of Red Army troops roamed uncaptured.

And now, when Moscow was almost in sight, the mood both of commanders and troops changed. With amazement and disappointment, the Germans discovered in late October and early November, that the 'beaten' Russians showed no sign of giving in. During these weeks, enemy resistance stiffened and the fighting became more bitter with each day that passed. Zhukov had now assumed command of the troops covering Moscow. For weeks, his men had been constructing a defensive position in depth, which ran through the forests that bordered the Nara, from Serpukhov in the south, to Naro-Fominsk in the north. Skillfully camouflaged strong points, wire entanglements and thick minefields now filled the forests which covered the western approach to Moscow.

A German half track rolls through the blazing ruins of yet another Russian village.

Strong armies had been formed from the remnants of those which had been defeated farther west and from fresh formations. The Moscow workers had been called out. New army corps were arriving from Siberia. Most of the embassies and legations, as well as part of the Russian Government had been evacuated from Moscow and gone east. But Stalin, with his small personal staff, remained in the capital which he was determined never to surrender. All this came as a complete surprise to the Germans, nor could they believe that the situation would change dramatically after all of the exertions which had brought them so close.

Blitzkrieg's lifeblood was rapid movement and the spearheads were now being reduced to a perilously slow crawl. The autumn rains were heavy. In France there had been metalled roads. Here, the highways were vanishing into impassable tracts of mud in which men, vehicles and horses floundered more and more helplessly. Breakdowns increased and repairs became extremely difficult to carry out. Guderian had started Barbarossa with six hundred tanks, but by the middle of November he was left with just fifty that were operational.

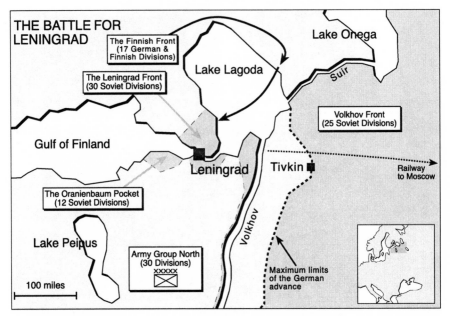

THE BATTLE FOR LENINGRAD

The Finnish Front
(17 German &
Finnish Divisions)

The Leningrad Front
(30 Soviet Divisions)

Lake Onega

Lake Lagoda

Suir

Volkhov Front
(25 Soviet Divisions)

Gulf of Finland

Leningrad   Tivkin

Railway
to Moscow

The Oranienbaum Pocket
(12 Soviet Divisions)

Volkhov

Lake Peipus

Army Group North
(30 Divisions)
XXXXX

Maximum limits
of the German
advance

100 miles

The German soldiers were overtired now and units under strength. This was particularly so among the infantry, where many companies were reduced to a mere sixty or seventy men. The horses, too, had suffered grievously, so that the artillery now had severe difficulty in moving its guns. The number of serviceable tanks in the panzer divisions was far below establishment. Incredibly, since Hitler had believed that the campaign was effectively over, he had actually ordered that industry at home cut down on its production of munitions, so only a trickle of replacements now reached the fighting units. Winter was about to begin but there was no sign of any winter clothing to be seen anywhere.

On the Baltic front, von Leeb's Army Group North had captured the city of Novgorod, a vital target in the approach to Leningrad. The beleaguered defenders of Novoguch had fought to the death but this resistance had been rendered futile following the German discovery of the city's defensive plans on the corpse of a Soviet officer. General Hoepner's 4th Panzer Group resumed its drive toward Leningrad but without supporting infantry its progress was limited.

Leningrad was a vital centre of the wartime production industry, and reserves and equipment were poured into the defence of the city. The citizens themselves formed into militia, divisions which were flung against the Germans more in despair than hope. Following a basic training period averaging sixteen hours, the first militia divisions were sent to the front only six days after being formed. The second division marched to the front only two days after its establishment, and the third, the same day it was established.

Despite all of the adversity, there certainly was a surge of patriotism, but there was also, as the war went on, a deepening feeling of revenge which led to extraordinary sacrifices on the part of ordinary people. Nonetheless, some Russian civilians obviously felt caught between two fires, but one senior Soviet officer summed up the terms of the choice when he said, "we were faced with a choice between two dictators. Hitler on the one hand and Stalin on the other, but we preferred to pick the one who spoke Russian."

With the arrival of the 18th Army to reinforce the Panzers on the 8th, the German stranglehold on the city of Leningrad tightened further. The capture of Schlusselburg to the east signalled the end of rail transport. Despite the best efforts of the population, the first shells began to rain down on Leningrad early in September. It marked the beginning of a crucial episode in the war; the epic siege of the city which would last for nine hundred days.

The German invaders now controlled all of western Russia on a line from Leningrad in the north, to Rostov on the Black Sea, and the Red Army was still retreating before them. The 'Scorched Earth' policies of the Russian armies had served them well against Napoleon, and once again the old tactics were adapted. The first few months of the war, had robbed the nation of nearly fifty per cent of her grain producing lands. Where the armies had fallen back, vast tracts of crops lay ruined in the fields. The rotting carcasses of livestock, slaughtered to deprive the Germans of food, mingled their stench with the corpses of soldiers and civilians. Villages tumbled into ruins and became the silent memorials of their former inhabitants. The mangled wreckage of sabotaged industries smouldered beneath the skies. Amidst the ruin, thousands of starving, orphaned children searched vainly for their parents.

But the fighting spirit of the Russians was far from crushed. It had been inflamed by accounts of the slaughter of prisoners of war, and the murder and torture committed by the German invaders. Even the constant series of military reverses failed to dampen the ardour of defenders whose country had been ravaged.

During the early advances, lines of supply were desperately over extended. The tanks were soon worn out by the thousands of miles they had travelled, and the climactic conditions were taking their toll on engines which were never given adequate time for repair and maintenance.

As early as October, crucial shortages of spare parts had developed; for example, the lack of air filters to extract the summer dust from the air. Dust was sucked into engines, and led to worn out pistons and massive extra oil consumption, which in turn placed a strain on fuel supplies.

It was against this background - the familiar pattern of trading space for time - that

The tenacious resistance of the Red Army grew stronger as the Germans approached Moscow.

the autumn campaign was waged. The Germans soon learned to have respect for their adversary, as Rauss recalled.

"The innate aptitudes of the Russian soldier asserted themselves to an even greater degree in defensive actions fought in forests. The Russian command was very adept at choosing and fortifying forest positions in such a way that they became impregnable. On the edge of woods toward the enemy, the Russians left only outposts for guarding and screening the main line of resistance, which was withdrawn deep into the forest itself. That security line also formed the spring board, and the support for reconnaissance, scouting, and other operations. The main line of resistance frequently ran parallel to the opposite edge of the woods and a few hundred yards inside the woods. Very extensive woods often concealed groups of bunkers in the central part. These bunkers, an intermediate position, were to delay the advance of the Germans, deceive him as to the location of the main position, and serve as support for the outposts. The Russians also protected the exposed flanks of a forest position by groups of bunkers. Important approach routes were blocked by individual machine-gun or anti-tank gun bunkers, echeloned in depth. The immediate vicinity of the bunkers was protected by mined entanglements of branches and abatis, as well as by snipers in trees. Furthermore, the Russians used to mine all bypasses and clearings in numerous places. These measures greatly delayed German progress through a forest, because the bunkers could be taken only after costly fighting, and because engineers had to be called upon for time-consuming mine-clearing operations. Important forward strong points in forests had facilities for all-around defence. A forester's house or a hamlet would often form the central point of the fortified position. A defence trench surrounded by obstacles and mine-fields completely encircled the position. The few sally ports were guarded by sentries and moveable barriers. A ring of bunkers, connected with each other and with the fortress, enclosed the central point. The intermediate position was blocked by barbed wire, entanglements of branches, and mines. The individual bunkers were placed along the approach routes.

An extensive system of bunker groups formed the battle position and made possible an unbroken defence of the front. In the battle position, all the defence expedients were found in even greater numbers. Entanglements of branches interwoven with barbed wire, and mined abatis to a depth of several hundred yards, were no rarity. These obstacles prevented sudden thrusts along the roads. Wherever there might have been a possibility of bypassing these obstructions, one could be sure that mines or tank traps had been installed. In such cases the German troops would often end up in a swamp or an ambush. All bunkers and defence installations were so well camouflaged that they could never be discovered by aerial reconnaissance, and only at very close range by ground reconnaissance. Because of the system of advanced strong points and security positions, it was in many cases impossible for German scouting parties even to get close to the main defensive position. While reconnaissance in force, by at least a reinforced battalion, might succeed in breaking through the outer protective screen, it frequently would bog down at the supporting position of the Russian outposts. However, if the Russians gave way without offering much resistance, the utmost caution was indicated, since a further advance was sure to end in a prepared ambush. In such cases, entire German companies were repeatedly wiped out, the prisoners being massacred.

In the latter half of August 1941, the German 6th Panzer Division was to begin a thrust toward Leningrad from the Porechye bridgehead on the Luga River. The bridgehead was completely surrounded by woods, and the sector to be attacked lay in medium-growth, partly marshy woods with thick underbrush. The sector was occupied by the 2nd and 3rd Russian Proletarian Divisions. The most advanced Russian position was located about three to four hundred yards ahead of the German front. The Russian trenches were narrow and deep, and had no parapets. The excavated earth had been scattered in the surrounding rank marsh grass, and the trenches were so well camouflaged with branches, that neither reconnaissance patrols nor aerial photography had been able to spot them during the preceding four weeks of fighting. The wire entanglements were no higher than the dense growth of grass hiding them. Single roads from the southwestern and northeastern ends of the bridgehead cut through the woods to a village beyond. The two roads were blocked by heavily wired abatis and mine fields. On the far edge of the woods, a second position was located atop a sand dune, a third ran through the village, and a fourth lay behind the village. The second position was particularly well constructed. It consisted of a deep anti-tank ditch, in the front wall of which, the Russian riflemen had entrenched themselves, and bunkers for heavy weapons had been installed.

The German attack was to be launched along the two roads mentioned above. A reinforced armoured infantry regiment, supported by strong artillery elements and a rocket launcher (Werfer) battalion, advanced along each of these roads. Individual tanks were to support the engineers in the removal of the road blocks. In spite of very heavy fire concentrations on the projected points of penetration, the Russians could not be budged from the narrow, invisible zigzag trenches. To be sure, the German tanks were able to reach the barriers, but the dismounted engineers were unable to remove the blocks in the defensive fire, which continued unabated. The infantry following up sought fruitlessly to find other weak spots in order to effect a break-through. Repulsed everywhere by the murderous defensive fire of an invisible enemy, it finally stopped, knee-deep in swamp-land, before the wire entanglements in front of the still

Despite the best efforts of the besiegers, KV-1 tanks continued to roll off the assembly line in Leningrad. Many were driven straight into battle, others were diverted to Moscow.

unknown Russian position. Not until the following night did one German company succeed in crawling forward, man by man, through the deep-cut bed of a brook which was overgrown with grass and bushes, and infiltrated through the entanglement. That particular point had not been attacked therefore. Strong German reserves were immediately brought up. They widened the point of penetration, and cleared the trenches and strong points of the westerly sector after hours of hand grenade fighting. The Soviets continued to maintain their position in the eastern sector. German forces could be directed against the rear of the enemy, only after a thrust into the depth of the western sector had reached and rolled up the second position. After bitter hand-to-hand fighting, the German forces were finally able to scatter the Russians, also at that point, and to clear the road. Only then, after a two day battle, which exacted a heavy toll of losses from both sides, could this invisible defensive system in the woods be surmounted."

Entirely new to the Germans was the Russian use of forest fires as a hot weather weapon. In midsummer, when the trees were tinder-dry, the Russians attempted to delay German forces by putting forests to the torch. Not only the physical, but the psychological impact of such fires was severe. The crackling of the burning trees, the acrid grey-black smoke, the increasingly unbearable heat and the feeling of uncertainty put troops under a severe strain.

THE KEY BATTLES

1. THE SIEGE OF LENINGRAD

The siege of Leningrad was the stage for a bitter struggle that would, in later years, be recognised as a key event in that conflict of inhuman savagery. The 900 days of siege has become a byword for suffering and dogged resistance. When General Zhukov arrived to take over the defence of the city on the 10th September 1941, he found the defenders in an advanced state of disorganisation and the inhabitants close to panic. Undaunted, he briskly set about bolstering its defences. A shortage of anti-tank guns was dealt with by converting anti-aircraft artillery to the task of attempting to halt the panzers. Six brigades of naval infantry and students were formed and reinforcements drafted in from the Karelian isthmus. Zhukov began to take the fight to the Germans, through raids and counter-attacks but by now, the German troops had pierced the inner circle of defences and were rampaging through the suburbs.

After a furious exchange of advances and retreats, by the end of the month the defenders were hanging on to their city by their fingernails. It seemed inevitable that Leningrad would capitulate. But as Zhukov awaited a renewed assault, the 4th Panzer Group suddenly departed to join the battle for Moscow and the remaining German forces began to build defences. Hitler had decreed that Leningrad would not be taken by force, it would instead be starved into submission.

At Leningrad, food supplies to the besieged city had been worsening throughout the autumn. By late November they were at their lowest ebb of the whole siege. Manual workers were receiving only 250 grammes of bread per day, one third of their normal requirement. Without water for sanitation and basic medical supplies, disease became inevitable. As temperatures fell to the minus twenties, thousands began to die each day. Total starvation threatened constantly.

To the Germans, collapse seemed imminent. Back in Berlin, a reception with Adolf Hitler as guest of honour was organised to celebrate the fall of the stricken city. The invitations were printed but never posted.

The resistance remained stubborn and defiant. Even women soldiers in the Red Army were in combat units. The ferocity and inhumanity of the conflict beggars the imagination.

An early view of some of the defenders of Leningrad. These fresh faces would soon be care-worn by months of battle.

Russian troops hug each other in delight after the siege is lifted.

The Russians marked a road across the frozen south west corner of Lake Ladoga, and by the 22nd November convoys of lorries were barely staving off famine in the city. It was a hazardous passage through the biting north eastern gales which swept across the lake.

Yet for all its horror, the Russians knew that defending this lifeline to the city was the only possibility of keeping the inhabitants alive.

But the food coming across the ice was too little too late for some. Victims of starvation, suffering from falling blood pressure and the wasting of the heart and internal organs, would never regain their health. Many would die months after food and medical supplies finally arrived. The children who survived would emerge totally traumatised by the siege, as an eyewitness recalled:

"It was reflected in the way many of the children played all by themselves. In the way that even in their collective games, they played in silence with grave faces. I saw faces of children which reflected such thoughtfulness and sorrow, that those eyes and faces told one more than could be gathered from all the stories of the horrors of famine."

Red Army tanks parade through Moscow on their way to the front.

CHAPTER 4
GENERAL WINTER TAKES CONTROL

By the 14th October 1941, the forces of Operation Typhoon, Hitler's drive to capture Moscow, had struggled through a week of torrential rain and tenacious Russian resistance. The roads had disintegrated into canals of bottomless mud, along which wheeled vehicles could drive only at a snail's pace and only if they were towed by tanks.

This was the Rasputitsa, the season of mud, which came as a debilitating surprise to the Germans in 1941. General Rauss went to great lengths after the war to explain the great significance of the muddy season.

"German losses of tanks and motorised equipment of all types were extra-ordinarily high during the autumn muddy period of 1941, the first time that the mud of Russia was encountered. For example, Second Panzer Group, operating in the Orel area at that time, lost sixty per cent of its tanks in mud. A division of Fourth Panzer Group, operating in the area north of Gzharsk during the same period, lost fifty tanks without a shot being fired, thirty five of them within three days. These losses were most serious since no replacements were received. Germany at that time was producing only eighty five tanks and forty assault guns monthly.

Large-scale operations are impossible during the muddy season. In the autumn of 1941, an entire German army was completely stopped by mud. The muddy season lasted a month.

Pursuit of the enemy who had been beaten at Bryansk was impossible. Only divisions which had reached the Bryansk-Orel-Tula road could move. Units became separated and intermingled, with only scattered elements in contact with the enemy. The bulk of the force stuck fast or moved fitfully forward in short marches. Motor vehicles broke down with clutch or motor trouble. Horses became exhausted and collapsed. Roads were littered with dead draft animals. Few tanks were serviceable. Trucks and horse-drawn wagons bogged down and railroad supply was not equal to the situation."

The Germans had no conception of mud as it exists in European Russia. In the autumn of 1941, when front-line troops were already stuck fast, the German High Command still believed that mud could be conquered by brute force, an idea that led to serious losses of vehicles and equipment. At the height of the muddy season, tractors and recovery vehicles normally capable of traversing difficult terrain are helpless, and attempts to plough through the muddy mass makes roads even more impassable. Tanks, heavy recovery vehicles, and even vehicles with good ground clearance simply pushed an ever-growing wall of mud before them until they finally stopped, half buried by their own motion. A sudden frost in the autumn of 1941 cemented a crippled buried column into a state of complete uselessness, and it never moved again. Because it could not be reached in any other way, gasoline, tow-ropes, and food supplies were airdropped along the line of stranded armour, but all attempts to move were futile. Often, when drivers found themselves bogged down far from any habitation, they abandoned their vehicles and set out on foot to contact friendly troops in the nearest village, or sought food and shelter from local civilians in order to remain alive until the worst of the muddy season passed.

For the muddy seasons, vehicles with high ground clearance, light weight, and low unit ground pressure were necessary. German trucks had low ground clearance, and could not get traction in deep mud. Since German supply cars had wheels too narrow for muddy terrain, they sank deep into soft ground. Even the German Maultier and Ostschlepper of the later years were bogged down in mud, as their tracks were too narrow. Rauss noted that the awkward-looking and slow Russian tractor of pre-war vintage, salvaged the heaviest most deeply mired loads after German equipment failed

Well-equipped Red Army troops supported by light tanks go over on the offensive in the winter of 1941.

The Rasputitsa was particularly difficult for motorcyclists to negotiate. Their use declined dramatically after October 1941.

to budge them. Russian trucks, too, were much better for muddy terrain, and the Germans promptly put captured Russian vehicles into service.

Despite the conditions, the Germans had advanced to within 300kms of the Russian capital.

The Russians had passionately defended every inch of their motherland with little regard for their own lives. Their suffering had been intense but there was still more and worse to come.

In Moscow, the nerve centre of the Soviet Union, the proximity of the German armies threw the inhabitants into total disarray. Mass evacuations were organised, while some citizens simply fled of their own accord. Even Stalin and his government were rumoured to be preparing to abandon their capital.

The remaining citizens of Moscow were scoured for recruits to form a civil defence force which was hastily mobilised and sent to the front.

On the 20th November, the thermometer suddenly dropped to thirty degrees of frost, accompanied by heavy falls of snow. With steadily decreasing momentum and increasing difficulty, the two panzer groups continued to battle their way towards Moscow. By throwing in their last ounce of strength they managed to push through Klin, and the armoured vanguard reached the Moscow-Volga canal. At this point their northern flank was suddenly attacked by fresh Russian formations which had shipped across from the frozen canal.

In the direct advance on Moscow the leading German units reached Oseretkoye during the last days of November, and armoured reconnaissance troops even penetrated the capital's outermost western suburbs. It was a forlorn attempt. Forward units glimpsed the domes of the Kremlin in the distance. It may just as well have been a thousand miles away.

Hitler had insisted that his armies should divide and approach Moscow from the north and south simultaneously. Now they were only 15kms from their target. The spires of the Kremlin were tantalisingly within their gaze but Hitler's arrogance in failing to provide winter supplies was now disastrously limiting progress.

Without anti-freeze, motor vehicles would not start and planes could not fly. In the final assault which had begun on the 1st December, the Germans came as close as 12kms to the Kremlin. In fact, the very tip of the German offensive reached the terminus of the Moscow tram system. The spires of the Kremlin could be seen in the distance.

At the end of December, the Germans were pushing their very last battalion down to the front line and the Red Army on the other side was desperately trying to deploy the final and important reserves into position. The two armies were desperately stretched, but in terms of responsiveness, the Red Army just had the vital and important edge which came from the arrival of the fresh Siberian divisions. With that, the last offensive powers of the two panzer groups ground to a final halt in ice and snow.

Field-Marshal von Kluge now decided to call off the attack, which had become hopeless and which could only result in unnecessary casualties.

His decision was the correct one in the circumstances. Within the next few days Zhukov was to launch the great Russian counter-offensive which began on December 6th. It was initially directed against the two panzer groups north-west of Moscow. The turning-point in the East had been reached: the German hopes of knocking Russia out of the war in 1941 had been dashed, at the very last minute.

With the first snows came a cruelly bitter winter. The temperature continued to fall and the German soldiers now paid dearly for the arrogance of the High Command that had refused to admit the possibility of anything other than a quick, decisive campaign.

At this crucial juncture, the Russians got the break they so desperately needed. Stalin now learned from Sorge, his spy in Japan, that the Japanese government did not intend to attack in the east. Freed of the nightmare of war on a second front, he ordered the transport of 22 fresh divisions of well-equipped Siberian forces to Moscow. They were to prove decisive.

The November frosts came late but sharp. General Guderian had earlier requested winter supplies but had been rebuked for negative thinking. At least the German troops began to find a concrete use for the propaganda leaflets they had been issued with, stuffing them into their uniforms to keep the cold at bay.

In Moscow, Stalin struggled to kindle the flame of civilian morale by staging the traditional Revolution day parade despite the dangers of aerial bombardment. In his speech at Lenin's tomb, he again appealed to the ancient Russian tradition of heroism in the face of adversity. "The war you are waging is a war of liberation, a just war. May you be inspired in this war by the heroic figures of our great ancestors."

In November, the Chief of the General Staff summoned the chiefs of staff of the three German army groups on the Eastern Front, to attend a conference at Orsha on the Dnieper. The crucial question on the agenda was whether the German armies in the east should now dig in along the line of the present front and there await the renewal of better campaigning weather in the spring, or whether the three army groups should continue to attack during the winter months.

The representative of Rundstedt's Army Group South was against further offensive operations and in favour of going over to the defensive. Army Group North was so weak that there could be no question of fresh attacks being mounted in their sector. Army Group Centre, alone voted in favour of making one last attempt to capture Moscow. The reason given was that, once the capital was in German hands, it should be possible for individual panzer divisions, operating east of the city, to cut the main rail communications with Siberia, thus starving the Russian forces of supplies and reinforcement.

After this conference immediate and detailed discussions took place with the actual commanders in the field. Field-Marshal von Kluge repeatedly visited his front-line units and even asked the German privates and N.C.O.s for their opinion.

For long hours on end the commanders-in-chief discussed the situation. The final decision was that one last attempt would be made by Army Group Centre, one final attack launched, with Moscow as the objective. The Supreme Command was well aware that this could not begin before the end of the muddy period, they had to wait until the soil was frozen solid and the tanks could once again roll forward, but the Russian winter was to prove a harsh mistress.

Few men had more than summer clothing and frostbite took an agonising toll.

German machinery and guns had never been designed to function in such extremes. Engines seized up, metal tank tracks split asunder, ammunition would not fire. The fierceness of the cold was far beyond the experience of most Germans, but with incredible exertions they kept up a semblance of defence.

"The obliteration of landmarks in snow-covered terrain makes orientation difficult. Russian villages are hard to identify from a distance, and then a church built on high ground or a church tower is the only visible sign of an inhabited place. If neither is present, woods filled with screeching birds usually indicate that a village is nearby. The Russian peasant stores his winter supplies in advance and digs in to spend the winter completely cut off from the outside world.

Cold reduces the efficiency of men and weapons. At the beginning of December 1941, 6th Panzer Division was but nine miles from Moscow and fifteen miles from the Kremlin, when a sudden drop in temperature to -30? F, coupled with a surprise attack by Siberian troops, smashed its drive on the capital. Paralysed by cold, our troops could not aim their rifle fire, and bolt mechanisms jammed or strikers shattered in the bitter winter weather. Machine guns became encrusted with ice, recoil liquid froze in guns, ammunition supply failed. Mortar shells detonated in deep snow with a hollow, harmless thud and mines were no longer reliable. Only one German tank in ten had survived the autumn muddy season and those still available could not move through the snow because of their narrow tracks. At first the Russian attack was slowed with

An early version of the T-34 passes a column of re-inforcements marching up to the front.

hand grenades but after a few days the German prepared positions in villages and farmhouses were surrounded or penetrated.

We held out to the northwest of Moscow until 5 December, and on the next day the first retreat order of the war was given. In the months of the offensive, our battalions and companies had dwindled to a handful of men. The Russian mud and winter had wrought havoc upon their weapons and equipment. Leadership and bravery could not compensate for the lowered fire power of our divisions. The numerical superiority of the Russians, aided by climatic conditions, saved Moscow and turned the tide of battle. Hitler neither expected nor planned for a winter war."

Fighting for the possession of villages played a still greater role in the winter. The villages straddled the few roads which had been cleared of snow, and offered warm quarters. Cleared roads and warm quarters were the two basic prerequisites for winter warfare in Russia. Therefore, inhabited localities retained their outstanding tactical importance, even though they could easily be bypassed by ski troops even in deep snow. Experience had shown that ski and sleigh forces might seriously harass the enemy, but they would never be able to bring about major decisions.

The tactics of winter warfare therefore centred around contests for the possession of roads and inhabited places. In Russia, villages and roads were infinitely more important than they were on the rest of the Continent. In other German theatres of war any one particular road never became a crucial factor, since the well-developed road net always offered a choice of alternate routes. In the East, the possession of a single road often was a life or death matter for an entire army. Of course, inhabited places were also tactically important in France and along the Mediterranean, and offered welcome shelter. Properly clothed, however, the troops were able to remain in the open for a long time without freezing, or even endangering their health - an impossibility in the East. The extreme tactical importance of inhabited places during the six months of winter, explains the fact that the Russians frequently would much rather destroy them than surrender them to the enemy.

Unless forced by circumstances to do so, the Germans did not launch offensives in midwinter. During local attacks communication reaches or tunnels for infantry could be dug through snow with considerable speed. While such trenches offered effective concealment if skillfully sited and camouflaged, they were practically useless for protection. Whenever artillery support was needed, snow had to be cleared from firing positions and ammunition storage areas.

With the onset of the Russian winter adequate shelter is a necessity in tactical operations. His entrenching tools useless in frozen ground, the German soldier could only find cover in a snow hole and wait until a dugout or similar shelter was blasted out

A German armoured car in the final stages of Operation Typhoon. At this stage of the war the capture of the Russian capital was still a distinct possibility.

of the frost-bound soil. Blasted shelters were usually pitch dark, and the small open fires used for heating, filled every crevice with smudge and smoke. For above-ground shelter, the Finnish use eskimo type igloos, but this type of shelter never became popular. Native log houses in the forests of the northern and central regions of European Russia are excellent heat retainers and are highly resistant to impact.

When German troops were attacking Tikhvin in the winter of 1941, cold set in suddenly. Lacking winter clothing and adequate shelter, the Germans suffered more casualties from cold than from enemy fire, and the attack had to be halted as the more warmly dressed and better-equipped Russians gained the initiative. The German troops were withdrawn to avoid further weather casualties as Rauss noted.

"The defender has a definite advantage in winter because, as a rule, his positions cannot be seen in snow except at very close range. He is able to keep his forces under cover and wait until the moment that fire can be used most effectively. The attacker on the other hand, is impeded in his movements and is easily detected, even in camouflage clothing. The principal weapon of the defender is the machine gun. Its performance is not diminished by snow, in which mortars and light artillery lose most of their effectiveness.

When defensive positions were not occupied until winter, we found it impossible to build shelters and emplacements in hard frozen ground. Machine guns and rifles had to be placed on a snow parapet that had been built up and packed hard. If well constructed, and water poured over it to form an ice coating, the parapet offered some protection against enemy fire.

When organised positions are established before snowfall, parapets must be increased in height as the snow level rises, and care taken to keep trenches and approaches free of snow at all times. Trenches and dugouts, provide better cover in winter than in other seasons. Snow-covered obstacles remain effective and covered by a snow crust that will bear a man's weight. Barriers against ski troops are effective only as long as they project above the snow. Obstacles must be removed when snow begins to melt, or they will obstruct visibility and fields of fire.

When swamps freeze over, the defender is suddenly faced with a situation changed to his disadvantage. Our divisions that fought defensive actions when swamps were impassable barriers were at a great disadvantage against the same enemy, in the same location, when swamps froze over. The increased frontage created by the frozen swamp could be defended only by employing additional artillery and much greater quantities of all types of ammunition. Similarly, the winter freeze-up is disadvantageous to a weak defender behind a water barrier. The freeze turns rivers into routes of approach toward defensive positions.

Since the Russians often penetrated artillery firing positions, we had to train artillerymen in infantry close-combat tactics. Because snow sometimes makes it impossible to evacuate guns, artillery crews were trained in demolition of field pieces.

The Russian winter covers roads, countryside, and vehicles with a crippling coat of ice, and when sand is not available, entire columns are forced to halt. Icy roads can rob an offensive of surprise or be fatal to a withdrawal. Ice conditions prevail every winter in all parts of Russia. During the German withdrawal from the Moscow area in the winter of 1941-42, ice hindered the entire operation. A few days before the order to retreat from the suburbs of Moscow, 6th Panzer Division, by building a defence around its last five tanks, held off an attack by Siberian troops who presented prime targets in their brown uniforms as they trudged forward in deep snow. This local success facilitated the disengagement of the division and provided time for the destruction of its last 88mm anti-aircraft guns, necessary because no prime movers were available. Twenty-five prime movers were lost in the autumn mud of 1941, and seven had fallen victim to winter cold and snow. The withdrawal proceeded, according to plan on the first day but the next day, moving over hilly terrain, vehicles skidded on icy roads, and trucks which had been abandoned during the preceding muddy season blocked the roads, adding to the difficulties.

Fearful that the pursuing Russians would overtake and destroy the rear guard if time were spent in extricating each vehicle, the German practice was to load as much material as possible on trucks still serviceable and put the remaining equipment to the torch. The rear guard was reinforced, and the withdrawal continued with brief delaying actions based on villages. Inhabited places were vital as we lacked proper winter clothing, but they were attractive too, to the Russians who preferred permanent type shelter. The retreat became a race from village to village.

In a few days our forces reached Klin, northwest of Moscow, which could not be used to house the division overnight, as the city was on the main route of other divisions steaming west. However, a large quantity of explosives were found in Klin and were used to blast temporary shelter in the ground outside the city. Attempts to obtain dirt from the blasted shelters for sanding roads were useless because the explosions loosed great chunks of solidly frozen earth which could not be pulverised. The division held before Klin for one day and then completed its withdrawal across the front-line Smolensk-Moscow highway."

Hitler took a close interest in the actions of units that were surrounded. The early successes such as the 1st Panzer Division's ability to extricate itself from a difficult situation had a profound impact on Hitler's thinkng.

When the German offensive against Moscow came to a halt on 6 December 1941, the 1st Panzer Division was located at a point fifteen miles north of the Russian capital. It was immediately ordered back to Klin (see Map 1 p.75) with the mission of keeping that town open for the withdrawal of other German armored forces. Deep snow obstructed every movement, and the highway running through Klin was the only route over which the withdrawal of mechanized and motorized columns could be effected.

The division reached Klin, after fighting the elements as well as the enemy, and succeeded in holding that important junction against persistent Russian attacks until the retrograde movements of other German units through the town were completed. At that point, however, as the division was ready to break contact and withdraw in the direction of Nekrasino, it found itself completely surrounded by strong enemy forces. The division was ordered by higher headquarters to abandon its vehicles if necessary, and to break through to Nekrasino where it would be able to link up with other German forces.

During the days of heavy fighting that preceded the entry of the division into Klin, the road to Nekrasino had been cut by the enemy on several occasions. In these engagements other German units lost numerous vehicles by enemy action and collisions. Wrecks had piled up all along the road and left no more than a narrow lane between them.

By reconnaissance in force, the encircled division discovered that enemy resistance was weakest southeast of Klin, and that a breakout in this direction would be most likely to succeed. The terrain, however, was such that practically all vehicles would have to be left behind. There were from 800 to 1,000 wounded in Klin who could not be evacuated without transportation. Furthermore, despite considerable loss of equipment, the encircled force was still well provided with vehicles and not inclined to give them up, if that could possibly be avoided.

After short deliberation it was agreed that the division, in order to retain its mobility, would have to break out along the road to Nekrasino, although that road itself was held by enemy forces in considerable strength. Chiefly responsible for this decision was the large number of casualties that were to be evacuated at any cost.

In preparing for the breakout, the division made use of its experiences during a previous encirclement at Kalinin. There, after executing a feint in a different direction which diverted some of the hostile forces, the division had succeeded in making a surprise breakout, losing no equipment and suffering few casualties. The great flexibility of the artillery had been of decisive importance. Shifting their fire rapidly from one target to the other, all pieces were able to support the diversionary attack as well as the actual breakout. Equally important had been the possibility of throwing all the tanks that survived the diversionary maneuver into the main effort.

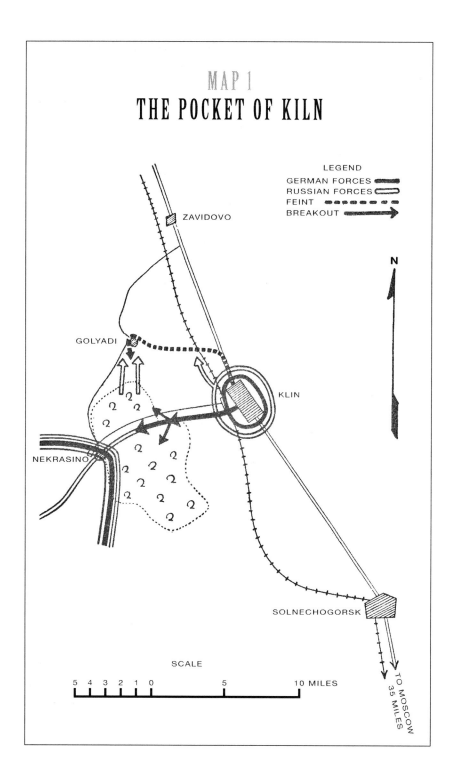

MAP 1
THE POCKET OF KILN

LEGEND
GERMAN FORCES
RUSSIAN FORCES
FEINT
BREAKOUT

N

ZAVIDOVO

GOLYADI

KLIN

NEKRASINO

SOLNECHOGORSK

TO MOSCOW
35 MILES

SCALE

5 4 3 2 1 0   5   10 MILES

The deteriorating conflicts highlighted just how unprepared the Wehrmacht actually was for the harsh reality of the Russian winter.

After a careful survey of the situation around Klin, a plan was adopted. All available tanks, one company of armored infantry, and one rifle battalion were to conduct a diversionary break-through north of Klin, and then to proceed in a westerly direction toward the town of Golyadi. Turning sharply south after reaching Golyadi, these forces were to initiate an attack in the direction of the main road. The artillery was to remain in position around the railroad station of Klin. The main breakout toward Nekrasino was to take place as soon as the Russians reacted to the threat near Golyadi and began to divert their forces from the main road. The Germans calculated that the turning movement at Golyadi would force the enemy to shift his front toward the north in order to avoid envelopment from that direction. Initially, the entire German artillery and all available antiaircraft weapons were to support the forces carrying out the feint.

While all remained quiet in the area designated for the main effort, the German units were assembled in proper order inside the encycled city. H Hour for the diversionary maneuver - actually an attack with limited objective - was set for dawn. The time of the main break-through depended on the development of the situation.

The intended deception of the enemy was accomplished with full success. A well-organized German task force fell upon the Russians at Golyadi and caught them by surprise. At the appearance of German tanks the Russians immediately shifted their reserves to meet the diversionary attack which they assumed to be the main German breakout. The attacking German troops, incidentally, had not been informed that their effort at Golyadi was no more than a feint. It was felt that they would not fight with quite the same zeal if they knew that they were merely trying to deceive the enemy. Only the division artillery commander was entrusted with the full details of the plan, including the code word for shifting fire to his new targets on either side of the Klin-Nekrasino road. The German task force took Golyadi and pivoted south. As expected, the enemy began to pull out from the area of the main road and to move north across the railroad line, determined to counter the threat of envelopment.

This was the appropriate time - about noon of the same day - to launch the main breakout along the road to Nekrasino. Upon pre-arranged signal, artillery and antiaircraft weapons shifted their fire. Only one artillery battalion continued to fire on the old target so as to cover the withdrawal of the diversionary force from Golyadi. Simultaneously, on the road leading out of Klin toward the west, the main attack got under way. The division's armored infantry battalion drove the first gap into the lines of an enemy taken completely by surprise. Dismounted armored infantry and motorcycle troops followed and widened the penetration. Some of the tanks initially engaged in the diversionary maneuver had made their way back to Klin and were now committed on both sides of the road. Under their protection, the wounded on trucks and sleds and accompanied by armored personnel carriers were moved out of the town. By now the artillery was covering the flanks of the break-through column. In the eastern part of the city combat engineers held off the enemy while the evacuation took its course. With the rate of progress determined by the movement of numerous vehicles, and by the need for gradual displacement of the artillery which was in turn covered by tanks and armored cars operating north and south of the road, the entire force fought its way through to Nekrasino, where it was received by other German units.

Undoubtedly the division owed much of its success to the proper employment of its combat elements, but it was primarily the maintenance of strict traffic control that permitted the evacuation of an unusually large number of vehicles and thus determined the outcome of the entire operation. All vehicles that broke down were immediately pushed off the road to keep the column moving without interruption. A large number of officers and noncommissioned officers with minor combat injuries had been added to the military police to assist in the strict enforcement of traffic discipline. The division staff, at first located at the western edge of Klin and later with the main body of the division, directed the initial break-through and the subsequent movements of individual elements with the use of radio and messengers, but without telephone communications.

Substantially intact, the division emerged from the pocket of Klin, taking along its casualties and nearly all of its equipment. Twenty-four hours later, on a different sector of the front, it was again in action against the Soviets.

With the situation stabilised, Zhukov's western front began to drive back the northern arm of the German encirclement and southern front halted Guderian's forces around Tula to the south. Mobile groups of Russians destroyed fuel dumps and artillery deep behind the German lines. The troops of the Third Reich, now faced fully-equipped Russian infantry, snugly clad in their felt boots and greatcoat. Harried by ski battalions they watched the Russian T-34 tanks crash through snow and woodland, while their own panzers sluggishly negotiated the roadways. German morale wilted. The hard pressed soldiers, most of them still clad in their summer uniforms and tight leather boots, fell back rapidly, often abandoning huge caches of equipment in their haste.

Encouraged by their breakthrough, the Russian high command attempted to adapt the German strategy themselves and attempt to encircle the entire Army Group Centre.

Every German soldier outside Moscow knew that this was a battle for life or death. If the Russians succeeded in defeating them here, there could be no hope. In 1812 Napoleon had returned with the shattered remnants of his Grand Army. In 1941 the choice for the Germans was only to hold fast or to be annihilated.

Four battalions of French volunteers assigned to Fourth Army proved less hardy than their German counterparts. Field-Marshal von Kluge addressed them on the field of Borodino and spoke of how, in Napoleon's Grand Army, Frenchmen and Germans had once before fought shoulder to shoulder against the common enemy. Unfortunately, though they fought bravely when sent into action on the following day, the Frenchmen could not stand up to the fierceness of the enemy's attack, nor to the cold and blizzards so unlike anything they had ever known at home. The French Legion was overrun and suffered heavily both from the enemy and from the cold. Within a few days it had to be withdrawn from the front and sent back to the west.

Now it was suddenly realised even at Hitler's headquarters that the war in the East was in fact only beginning; and, horrifying though it was, that the German troops would have to fight the ferocious battles to come, without proper winter clothing. Hitler now issued desperate orders for the despatch of winter clothing to the East. In Germany, collections of furs were made on a huge scale and in fact a great deal was accomplished along these lines with remarkable speed. However, it was too late, with the trains on overstretched rail networks already earmarked for essential supplies. Months passed before the clothing thus collected could actually reach the troops. The soldiers had to spend their first winter in Russia, fighting heavily, and equipped only with their summer uniform, greatcoat and blanket. What was available in Russia itself

German infantry in Schusselburg, the gateway to Leningrad, autumn 1941.

in the way of felt boots, fur caps and woollen underclothes was commandeered, but this was only a drop in the ocean and scarcely affected the condition of the mass of the German soldiers.

Supplies were usually short. Only a few railways ran into the area behind the front. These were frequently cut by the partisans. The water froze inside the boilers of the German engines, which were not built to withstand the Russian climate. Each engine could draw only half the normal number of wagons. Many of them became stuck for days on end in the snow and ice. Urgent requests for artillery shells could not be met. In this desperate hour, in order to encourage the soldiers on the Eastern Front, train-loads of red wine were shipped from France and Germany. The frustration of a unit which received a train-load of wine instead of the shells it urgently needed to defend itself, can only be imagined. Worse still, even the wine was useless. At forty degrees Centigrade below zero, not an unusual temperature, it had often frozen in transit, burst its bottles, and all that remained were chunks of red ice.

In the opening moves of the Russian counter-offensive, Russian forces attacked north of Moscow, crossing the Moscow-Volga canal from the east in the direction of Klin and striking the left flank of General Reinhardt's Third Panzer Group in the area south of the Volga lakes. At the same time they attacked the front of Fourth Panzer Group, farther to the south, a particularly powerful thrust being directed westwards

The soil of Mother Russia was to be the last resting place for more than two million German war dead.

from Moscow along the line of the Moscow-Smolensk highway: this thrust hit the junction of Fourth Panzer Group with Fourth Army. The German panzer forces could not, in their weakened condition, withstand such tremendous pressure and were forced to withdraw slowly, fighting hard in snow and ice, with the purpose of recreating a unified front farther to the west. This new withdrawal necessitated the abandonment of more heavy equipment. The occasional roads and tracks were deep in drifting snow and many guns and tanks became immobilised. German casualties due to enemy action were heavy, but heavier yet were those caused by frostbite. This affected in particular the men's feet, for the unsuitable boots with which they were issued were too tight to permit the wearing of more than one pair of socks. Eventually even Hitler had to agree to the withdrawal of the two panzer groups. In mid-December the Russian offensive was extended southwards and new attacks were launched against Fourth Army between Serpukhov and Djutkovo. Here the enemy succeeded for the time being only in achieving local penetrations and Fourth Army managed in general to maintain its front intact.

The real danger spot was south of Fourth Army. There Guderian's Second Panzer Army (formerly Second Panzer Group), with only very weak armoured forces still at its disposal, was being attacked by the enemy in overwhelming strength. The Russians began a powerful advance on Tula, which Second Panzer Army was in no state to resist. Having obtained this first objective, one part of the Russian force engaged here continued to attack westwards, while the remainder turned north-west towards Kaluga. Another attack was launched on the Oka sector in the Tarusa-Aleksin area: here again, part of the Russian force drove on westwards, while part turned north-west, in this case towards Maloyaroslavets and Medin.

Despite Hitler's orders to stand firm, by the end of the year, the Germans had withdrawn up to 150kms from Moscow. Generals Guderian and Hoepner were dismissed for retreating without permission.

The Russian counter-attack was further strengthened by the reinstatement of officers condemned to the prison camps during Stalin's great purges. They were ferocious warriors.

As the wounded commander of the 222nd Rifles told his German interrogators: "If a man has a penal camp behind him, death holds no terror for him." Less distinguished prisoners were released into penal battalions which performed the most dangerous tasks, such as clearing minefields and storming strongpoints. The casualty rate in these battalions was the highest in the Red Army but prisoners still volunteered for military service. The death rate in the camps had increased sevenfold since 1940.

This was when Stalin sounded the most alarming warning note. This was when he issued the order, "Not one step backwards." And he meant not one step backwards. He imposed penal battalions on the Red Army. Anybody moving out of line, perhaps some 400,000 Russian soldiers were placed in penal battalions during the war. At this stage of the war, the influence of the Communist party and of its representatives in the Army - the commissars - was tremendous. The commissar was probably the most controversial man in the Russian Army. Even in the Soviet Union opinions varied concerning his usefulness, his position, and his duties. According to Erlhard Rauss he was the driving force of the Army, ruling with cunning and cold-bloodedness.

"Among the troops themselves, the relationship of the soldier to the commissar apparently was endurable in spite of the commissar's uncompromising strictness and severity. The higher headquarters on the other hand appear to have regarded him with mistrust. Testimony to that conclusion is found in many remarks of General Petrov, the commander of the Fiftieth Army, to Commissar Shabalin, which the latter recorded verbatim in his diary. General Petrov once ironically asked Shabalin, who was sitting next to him, in the tank: "Well how many have you shot today?" Shabalin added the note 'Such sarcasm.' The commissar was thus often considered as alien element by headquarters.

In the fighting east of Roslavl in August 1941, a Russian tank company that had been sent into action suddenly stopped on the battlefield. The leader of the tank company had received an order before going into action to refuel at a fuel depot somewhat to the rear of his bivouac area. He did not, however, want to take the trouble to go back, as he thought that it would be possible to refuel further forward at the divisional command post nearer the front. But there was no opportunity to refuel at that point. The tank company just reached the battlefield and then ground to a halt because of lack of fuel. Thereupon, the company commissar drew his pistol and shot the commanding officer on the spot.

The example set by the commissars is largely responsible for the tenacious resistance of the Russian soldier, even in hopeless situations. It is not wholly true that the German commissar order, directing that upon capture, commissars be turned over to the SD (Security Service) for 'special treatment', that is execution, was solely responsible for inciting the commissars to buttress last-ditch resistance; the impetus was much rather fanaticism together with soldierly qualities, and probably also the feeling of responsibility for the victory of the Soviet Union. The previously mentioned occupation of the bunkers on the Bug and the continued resistance in the citadel of Brest Litovsk can be traced to the influence of the commissars.

In innumerable other cases, dogged perseverance even under hopeless conditions was to be credited to the soldierly conduct of the commissars. For instance, in

A commissar party meeting at the front conducted by the commissar.

September 1941, long after the castle of Posyolok Taytsy (south of Leningrad) had been taken, and strong German troop units had been drawn up in the castle park. German tanks passing near the park wall with open hatches drew single rounds of rifle fire from close range. The shots were aimed at the unprotected tank commanders who were looking out of the turrets. Not until three Germans had been killed by bullets through the head, did the passing tank unit realise that the shots were coming from a narrow trench close under the park wall ten yards away. The tanks then returned the fire, whereupon all thirteen occupants of the trench met death. They were the officers of a Russian regimental headquarters, grouped about their commissar who fell with his rifle cocked and aimed.

After the German divisions broke out of the Luga bridgeheads in August 1941, the commander of a tank force inspected several Russian tanks which had been knocked out two hours earlier near a church. A large number of men were looking on. Suddenly, the turret of one of the knocked-out tanks began to revolve and fire. The tank had to be blown up. It turned out that among the crew, which had been assumed dead, there was a commissar who had merely been unconscious. When he revived and saw the many German soldiers around him, he opened fire.

In April 1942, when the Germans took a strong position along the Osuga (southwest of Rzhev), they continued to receive rifle fire from one lone barricaded bunker. All demands for surrender were in vain. When an attempt was made to shoot through the embrasure with a rifle, the Red soldier grabbed it and fired the last three shots. Two of the bullets wounded German soldiers. The commissar, who was defending the bunker alone in the midst of his dead comrades, then shot himself with the third.

It might appear that much of the fighting spirit and concern for the welfare of the troops which the commissars displayed, should have been the responsibility of the commanding officers and not that of the commissars. However, it was always a question of situations in which something had to be done. The commanding officers generally did little, while the commissars acted. The passive character of the Russian officers was responsible for the fact that it was not the commander but the commissar who discovered the road to action. Therefore, the commissar was really a necessary part in the structure of this Red Army. He was a sort of 'front-line conscience.'

If the commissar was viewed by the Germans as a larger than life figure, there was also a danger that the dogged resistance of the Russians might be attributed to some superior quality not possessed by the enemy. This view certainly prevailed in some parts of the high command echoed by Rauss.

"Disregard for human beings and contempt of death are other characteristics of the Russian soldier. He will climb with complete indifference and cold-bloodedness over the bodies of hundreds of fallen comrades, in order to take up the attack on the same spot. With the same apathy he will work all day burying his dead comrades after a battle. He looks toward his own death with the same resignation. Even severe wounds impress him comparatively little, for instance, a Russian sitting upright at the side of

Russian Cossack cavalry were used by both sides in the campaign.

their street, in spite of the fact that both lower legs were shot away, asked with a friendly smile for a cigarette. He endures cold and heat, hunger and thirst, dampness and mud, sickness and vermin, with equanimity. Because of his simple and primitive nature, all sorts of hardships bring him but few emotional reactions.

His emotions run the gamut from animal ferocity to the utmost kindliness; odious and cruel in a group, he can be friendly and ready to help as an individual.

In an attack the Russian fought until death. Despite more thorough German defensive measures he would continue to go forward, completely disregarding losses. He was generally not subject to panic. For example in the break-through of the fortifications before Bryansk in October 1941, Russian bunkers, which had long since been bypassed and which for days lay far behind the front, continued to be held when every hope of relief had vanished. Following the German crossing of the Bug in July 1941, the fortifications which had originally been cleared of the enemy by the 167th Infantry Division, were re-occupied a few days later by groups of Russian stragglers, and subsequently had to be painstakingly retaken by a division which followed in the rear. An underground room in the heart of the citadel of Brest Litovsk held out for many days against a German division, in spite of the employment of the heaviest fire power."

A number of more questionable conclusions were drawn from the observations of German officers. Chief among them was the belief that they were facing men who were so different from their German enemies that they were almost another species.

"In addition to the simplicity which is revealed in his limited household needs and his primitive mode of living, the Russian soldier has close kinship with nature. It is no exaggeration to say that the Russian soldier is unaffected by season and terrain. This immunity gave him a decisive advantage over the German, especially in Russian territory where season, temperature, and terrain play a decisive role.

The problem of providing for the individual soldier in the Russian Army is of secondary importance, because the Russian soldier requires only very few provisions for his own use. The field kitchen, a sacred institution to other troops, is to the Russian soldier a pleasant surprise when it is available but can be dispensed with for days and weeks without undue hardship.

During the winter campaign of 1941 a Russian regiment was surrounded in the woods along the Volkhov, and because of German weakness, had to be starved out. After one week reconnaissance patrols met with the same resistance as on the first day; after another week only a few prisoners were taken, the majority having fought their way through to their own troops in spite of close encirclement. According to the prisoners, the Russians subsisted during those weeks on a few pieces of frozen bread, leaves and pine needles which they chewed, and some cigarettes. It had never occurred to anyone to throw in the sponge because of hunger, and the cold (-10?F) had not affected them.

The Russian soldier is able to adapt himself to terrain features, and actually to merge with them. He is a master of camouflage, entrenchment and defence construction. With great speed he disappears into the earth, digging in with unfailing instinct so as to utilise the terrain to make his fortifications very difficult to discover. When the Russian has dug himself into his native soil and has moulded himself into the landscape, he is a doubly dangerous opponent.

The utmost caution is required when passing through unknown terrain. Even long and searching observation often does not reveal the excellently camouflaged Russian. Frequently, German reconnaissance patrols passed through the immediate vicinity of Russian positions or individual riflemen without noticing them, and were then taken under fire from behind. Caution must be doubled in wooded areas. In such areas the Russians often disappear without a trace, and must be driven out individually, Indian fashion. Here sniping from trees was particularly favoured by the Russians as a fighting method.

Despite this unbridled admiration for the fighting qualities of the Red Army soldier, even General Rauss was able to pinpoint, what he considered to be, a number of serious deficiencies.

"The unpredictability of the mood of the Russian soldier and his pronounced herd instinct at times brought on sudden panic in individual units. As inexplicable as the fanatic resistance of some units, was the mystery of their mass flights, or sudden wholesale surrender. The reason may have been an imperceptible fluctuation in morale. Its effect could not be counteracted by any commissar.

A word about the craftiness of the Russian. He seldom employed large scale ruses. The usual tricks, such as feigning the existence of troops by increased fire and other means, were just as common with the Russians as with all armies. They seldom carried out feint attacks. The Germans found, however, that they had to be on guard against dishonesty and attempts at deception by individual Russian soldiers and small units. One trick, a particular favourite, was to feign surrender, or come over to the enemy with raised hands, white flags, and all the rest. Anyone approaching in good faith would often be met by sudden surprise fire at close range. The Russian soldier, who can lie motionless for hours on end, often feigned death. An unguarded approach often cost a German his life."

With men like these at his disposal, as the new year approached, there was every reason for Stalin to feel optimistic about the outcome of the war.

Many civilians paid the penalty for alleged partisan activity, and summary executions like these were very common. Note the Wehrmacht officers and spectators. Clearly war crimes like these were not the sole reserve of the SS.

Advancing Soviet troops pass abandoned German vehicles in the winter of 1941.

Hitler believed that he personally could ward off the catastrophe which was impending before Moscow. His resolute order that the troops must hold fast regardless in every position and in the most impossible circumstances was probably the correct one. Hitler realised that any retreat across the snow and ice must, within a few days, lead to the dissolution of the front and that if this happened the Wehrmacht would suffer the same fate that had befallen the Grande Armée. In the circumstances then prevailing the divisions could not have been withdrawn more than three to six miles a night. More could not be asked of the troops or of the horses in their present exhausted condition. The withdrawal could only be carried out across the open country, since the roads and tracks were blocked with snow. After a few nights this would prove too much for the troops, who would simply lie down and die wherever they found themselves. There were no prepared positions in the rear into which they could be withdrawn, nor any sort of a line to which they could hold on.

So during the weeks which followed the battle moved slowly westwards. The German armies, fighting fiercely, were forced back step by step. The Russians repeatedly broke through the front, but it was always just possible for the hard pressed Germans to throw them out again. The combat strength of the companies was now frequently reduced to forty men. Losses in weapons and equipment were heavy. Until the end of December the principal danger remained the threat to Fourth Army's southern flank.

Despite this great superiority in strength, the Russians had not succeeded in destroying the German front west of Moscow by the end of 1941. However, the acute crisis had by no means been passed.

In January the thermometer sank to its lowest point, 42 degrees of frost Centigrade. Hitler later ordered that a medal be struck, the Eastern Medal, for distribution to all those who had taken part in the heavy fighting on the Eastern Front during the winter of 1941-42. To possess this medal was, and is, regarded as a very special distinction. To the troops, it became nicknamed the order of "the frozen meat".

The German Blitzkrieg had slowed to a crawl, halted and was now grinding into reverse. It also seemed that the great exodus of industry to the east had been successfully accomplished.

While the next three months would prove critical, the economic war had been put on a sound footing. Before November, the Soviet Union had lost between one half and two thirds of its productive capacity in coal, pig iron, steel and aluminium, along with one quarter of it's engineering capacity. The industrial output of the country had been halved.

The Russians had nonetheless managed to move out considerable elements of tank factories and aircraft factories. For example, the Kharkov tractor works which produced tanks, was taken to the East. The workers in that factory walked along the railway line under German gun fire to get in the trains to be moved out. The first priority was to get the equipment out, then the workers.

In 1942, as the Wehrmacht bit deeper into Russia, there had to be a second wave of evacuations, the largest industrial migration in the history of the world. Well over one thousand-nine hundred plants were moved eastwards, and an aircraft factory within seventeen days of being relocated, was producing its first aircraft.

The eastern industrial enclaves rapidly became the cornerstone of the Russian war effort. The instant expansion of the Ural, Siberian and Kazakstan centres of production in the first year of the war, was nothing short of miraculous.

The conditions of work were horrendous. Many of the evacuated workers were labouring in sub-zero temperatures, while the factories were still being constructed around them. They slept on the floors beside their machines or in crude dug-outs next to the factories. Food was scarce and medical resources virtually non-existent. In the first phase of the re-location, output per head was poor and the mortality rate among the workers was high. By the summer of 1942, output had begun to climb. As conditions improved, the production levels rose, until the contribution of these areas reached two and a half times the production of the entire pre-war Soviet economy.

On land, the T-34 tank was now becoming standard, to the dismay of the German panzer groups. When the first of these medium tanks were met by the 17th Panzer Division, they found that their shells simply bounced off it's heavy, sloped armour, while its high velocity 76mm turret gun proved devastating.

The first T-34 encountered by the Germans ploughed through the advancing Germans for nine miles, before being halted by a field artillery howitzer at short range. Its powerful diesel engine enabled it to sail over terrain that the panzers could not even consider possible.

But despite Soviet optimism, the war was far from nearing its end. The Russian defenders had paid a terrible price for their resistance and the toll in human terms would continue for the next three years.

The Russians still say that 1942 was a worse year than 1941. Two crucial things occurred. Stalin appears to have had a rush of blood to the brain and decided on premature offensive operations in the late winter, early spring of 1942, and a direct result of that was perhaps the greatest disaster which befell the Red Army. In the summer of 1942, with the German drive to the south and further east, the Red Army was nearly destroyed. But what happened there mystified Hitler, because instead of the great encirclement operations of 1941, the Red Army was not there. It had actually begun to retreat in good order.

The Soviet casualties in the first six months of the invasion had been staggering. It was only fifty years later that it would be admitted, that one and a half million troops had perished in the defence of Moscow alone. Many of those who were taken prisoner by the Germans faced a terrible fate.

The German High Command alleged that the Russians had failed to abide by the Geneva Convention on the treatment of prisoners of war and encouraged German troops to seek revenge on such 'barbarous sub-humans'. The Soviet Union had in fact undertaken to observe the Geneva Protocols and through neutral Sweden, had requested that Germany do the same. The Germans' response was to shoot prisoners out of hand, to gas them, starve them and deprive them of the medical supplies necessary for their survival. Many were crammed into railcars and left in sidings to perish; others were force marched until they died from exhaustion. More were simply exposed to the deadly cruelties of the Russian winter.

Hundreds of thousands of Soviet prisoners had been murdered by 1942, and this was to set an horrendous trend which would continue throughout the course of the war.

The total number of Russian prisoners killed would eventually be reckoned at three and a half million.

Herman Goering told Ciano, Mussolini's envoy, that Russian prisoners, having been forced to eat the soles of their own boots, had then resorted to cannibalism and had also eaten a German sentry. "Some nations" he continued, " must be decimated

The SS officer, "Panzer" Meyer was typical of the men who sought to destroy the power of the commissars. Standing orders called for the immediate execution of all who fell into German hands.

...there is nothing to be done about it."

The paltry figure of three and a half million slaughtered POWs was a drop in the ocean for Reichsführer SS Heinrich Himmler. Himmler's plans for the new order in Europe, envisaged the reduction of the Slav population by at least thirty million. It was Himmler, and his deputy Heydrich, who were the real masters of occupied Russia. During his subsequent trial at Nuremburg, Field Marshal Keitel, after the war, when asked why the supposedly civilised commanders of the German army allowed the barbarities of the Russian invasion to occur, protested that, "Even the Commander in Chief of the army did not have the executive power or authority to issue and enforce laws in the occupied east. This prerogative belonged strictly to Heydrich and Himmler who had, de facto, discretionary powers over the life and death of population and prisoners, including prisoners of war."

Himmler's sinister executioners, the Schutzstaffeln or SS, became the supreme rulers of western Russia. Even before Barbarossa, the SS had discussed with the army officers how the campaign of terror they were to unleash in the wake of the invasion could be facilitated. In May 1941, four Einsatzgruppen were formed, with the primary aim of eliminating the ideological opponents of the Reich. Soviet officials, Commissars and Jews were to be rounded up and shot to death. In the event, those who were dispatched swiftly by a bullet were the fortunate ones.

Local Jewish leaders in Russia were forced to assemble their people in designated areas. From these collection points they were transported to killing fields, where they

Infantrymen in the closing stages of Operation Typhoon advance under cover of a Panzer III.

were stripped of their clothing and riddled with machine-gun fire. The sheer numbers involved often meant that the wounded were also tipped into the burial pits and covered up to suffocate.

At Kiev in September 1941, over 33,000 Jews were murdered in a single operation which lasted only days. In Pinsk, the carnage was accomplished with the use of grenades, dogs, axes and the cavalry of the SS. It was nightmarish work, even for the SS. They were rewarded with treble pay and long holidays. Erich Ohlendorf, one of the Einsatzgruppen commanders, boasted that he had personally disposed of 90,000 victims, mainly Jews, in the first year of the war.

But it was not only Jews who suffered. Anyone could be accused of being an official or a commissar and summarily executed. German troops were actively encouraged to commit outrages on an occupied population which was to be subjugated by terror. People were brutalised for real or imagined offences, despite regulations, and there are authenticated cases of women raped in the streets in full view of horrified onlookers.

As well as carrying out this policy of repression and "ethnic cleansing", officials in Russia were also obliged to provide forced labour for the German war economy. This allowed male civilians in the Reich to be freed for military service.

The German officials in Russia went about the selection task with an eerie mixture of barbarity and incompetence. Potential recruits were gathered without any discrimination as to their suitability. They were often left unfed for long periods and conditions on the westbound freight trains which carried them, were insanitary and inhuman. Babies born on the journey were ripped out of their mother's arms and flung onto passing embankments to perish. Not surprisingly, by the end of 1941, 100,000 of those transported from the Ukraine were sent back as unfit to work. Many did not survive the return journey. Those waiting to travel westwards saw dead comrades being unloaded from trains they themselves would have to occupy.

This treatment of occupied peoples, some of which had welcomed the Nazis as saviours from the tyranny of Stalin, eventually gave rise to resistance movements determined to exact revenge for the brutalities which had been inflicted on them. The atrocities were etched deep into the psyches of those who witnessed them and inspired an implacable hatred for the perpetrators.

Hitler was rapidly losing faith in the commanders who had failed to bring Barbarossa to a successful conclusion. He had already dismissed both the cautious von Rundstedt and the audacious Guderian. The friction between Hitler and his generals became vocal and more rancorous as the winter wore on. Despite this, as the January initiative became bogged down in the spring thaw, Stalin had little to show for an ill advised offensive, which was so ruthlessly driven, that it produced more Russian than

German casualties.

The Volkhov Front managed to penetrate von Leeb's Army Group North, but its Second Shock Army was isolated at the spearhead of the penetration and the attack was repulsed.

Further south, North West Front encircled ninety-thousand men of von Leeb's army in an eight hundred square mile area near Demyansk. However, in an impressive operation which won the personal praise of the Führer, the Luftwaffe managed to stave off a withdrawal, by providing the Demyansk pocket with two hundred and seventy tons of supplies each day, until eventually a corridor was pushed through to relieve the defenders.

The 29th army of the Kalinin Front, which had almost completed an encirclement of a large portion of army Group Centre, was itself surrounded and destroyed. Army Group South managed to contain the bulge that was developing under attack from the Russian South and South West Fronts. In the Crimea, Russian gains were restricted to the Kerch Peninsula.

It had been the most brutal winter in living memory and both sides emerged exhausted, although the German armies should have been well prepared for the terrible conditions. Army General Meretskov wrote:

"I will never forget the endless forests, the bogs, the water logged peat-fields, the pot-holed roads. The punishing battle with the forces of the enemy that went on side by side with the equally punishing battle with the forces of nature."

The clothing and equipment of the Russian infantryman suited his summer as well as winter requirements. The Germans were amazed at how well the Siberian infantry was clothed in the winter of 1941-2. As might be expected, the fighters in the Arctic were likewise suitably clothed. The Russian infantryman was inferior to the German and to the Finn only in skiing. Of course, attempts were made to correct this deficiency through intensified training but all efforts were doomed to failure, since there was never more than one pair of skiis available for several men."

Equipment carried by all Germans was often discarded by the Russian infantryman as non-essential. Gas masks were commonly stored in division depots; steel helmets were rarely worn in the arctic wilderness.

The German armies emerged from the winter fighting in a state described by General Franz Halder, Hitler's Chief of Staff, as "disastrous".

Of the one hundred and sixty two divisions facing the Red Army, only eleven were fully capable of offensive operations. For the sixteen panzer divisions in the east, only one hundred and forty serviceable tanks were available and most divisions were only twenty per cent mobile. Nevertheless, Hitler was determined that a full-scale attack

Partisans set explosive charges on a railway line.

should be resumed. He saw it as a simple question of advance or retreat.

If the German armies stepped back, then Russia could regroup her forces, recover her raw materials and rebuild her western industries. Halder even considered recommending a withdrawal to the pre-war border in Poland. Quite wisely he never mentioned this to Hitler.

Hitler had been convinced by the economic lobby in Germany, that without fresh oil reserves it could not sustain the war effort. The oil fields of the Caucasus beckoned temptingly. All thoughts of withdrawal were pushed aside.

The losses of manpower, vehicles and tanks which had been suffered since the outbreak of hostilities, could not fully be made good for the new offensive, so infantry divisions were now to total seven battalions instead of nine. The battle strength of a company was reduced from one hundred and eighty troops to eighty.

Between November 1941 and March 1942, only seven thousand five hundred vehicles were supplied to replace the seventy five thousand which had been lost, and fuel oil was in short supply. Mobility had been seriously affected. The panzer divisions which would take part in the summer offensive in the south, contained barely one hundred and thirty five tanks each. Even this had only been achieved by seriously weakening the Northern and Central sectors.

The one weapon that Hitler did have on his side was surprise. Stalin had assumed

The huge exodus of Russian manufacturing capacity from West to East was one of the most astonishing achievements of the war.

that Hitler would resume his attack on Moscow and heavily reinforced its defensive reserves. But when the Germans struck on the 8th May, it was the Crimean Front which was torn apart by von Manstein's 11th Army.

The German strategy was to clear the flanks for a concerted drive towards the oil fields of the Caucasus. While von Manstein subdued the Crimea, Timoschenko's South West Front which lay on the northern flank of the advance, was to be destroyed by the 9th and 17th armies.

When the German encirclement was completed, almost the total reserve of T-34 and KV-1 tanks, painstakingly built up over the winter months, was in German hands along with over two thousand guns and almost two hundred and fifty thousand prisoners.

In the south, von Manstein had by now entered the final phase of his Crimean campaign and only the fortress of Sevastopol, besieged since the previous year, was still under Soviet control. After 250 days of dogged resistance, Sevastopol finally capitulated on the 4th July. The victorious troops were ordered north to Leningrad despite pleas to cross the Kerch strait and bolster the main offensive.

The German forces were now organised into two groups. Army Group B struck eastwards from Kursk to the north and Kharkov to the south but failed to encircle the retreating Soviet forces. Hitler, convinced that the main body of the Red Army had retreated to the area north of Rostov, ordered a huge encirclement of the city. In doing so, he pulled the 4th Panzer Army away from its advance down the Donetz Corridor towards Stalingrad. It was a fatal mistake. Von Kleist was to write later:

" The 4th Panzer Army was advancing on my left. It could have taken Stalingrad without a fight at the end of July, but was diverted south to help me in crossing the Don.

I did not need its aid. It merely congested the roads I was using. When it turned north again a fortnight later, the Russians had gathered just sufficient forces at Stalingrad to check it."

After taking Rostov, Army Group A continued along the Black Sea coast towards the foothills of the Caucasus.

Hitler had planned to take Stalingrad and then proceed southwards. He was now committed to achieving both objectives simultaneously. By late August, Army Group A was running into stiff resistance from the newly formed Trans Caucasus Front, defending the span of the huge mountain chain from the Black Sea to the Caspian. A Russian South East Front was also established to protect the plains to the north-east of the mountains.

The Caucasus Front contained Georgians, Armenians and Azerians who were well aware of what a German invasion would mean for themselves and their families. Their resistance was desperate and determined. Approximately half the adult males of Georgia would eventually sacrifice themselves in the bitter struggle for their homeland.

Not only was resistance hardening in front of Army Group A, but its strength was constantly being eroded to bolster the battle for Stalingrad to the north. The Caucasian oil wells had been the primary target of the German summer offensive. The taking of Stalingrad was at first simply an obvious target to protect the left flank of Army Group A. Had Stalingrad not been named in honour of the Russian leader, it might have remained a subsidiary target.

THE KEY BATTLES

2. THE DEMYANSK POCKET

The fierce battles which raged around the trapped German forces in the pocket at Demyansk during the early months of 1942, are not in themselves examples of the extreme violence of that campaign, or particularly representative of the scale of the fighting.

The events at Demyansk are of crucial importance for the strategic legacy which they left behind.

With the armies of the world focused around the events of Operation Typhoon during the latter part of 1941, equally dramatic events were beginning to unfold in the sector of the German Army Group North, where the 16th army was attacked by the Russian armies of the north west front, which fell unexpectedly on the lines of the 16th Army, on 7th January 1942.

The German General von Leeb was refused permission to withdraw and sensing the imminent destruction of the entire 16th Army, asked to be relieved of his position. His wish was granted by Hitler and von Leeb was relieved of his command and replaced by General Kurt Holden.

Although the situation did deteriorate to the extent that von Leeb had predicted, the German forces fighting around Demyansk were surrounded in the pocket which was formed on the 8th February 1942.

At this desperate juncture, the Luftwaffe was called upon to keep the pocket supplied. With their assistance the defenders were able to hold out until the 21st March. When they were relieved by the German forces, which had been launched against the pocket in operation Fallreep, the defenders had endured 73 days of intense fighting.

The enduring legacy of the Demyansk pocket was to be much more sinister. It proved to Hitler that it was possible for encircled forces to hold out until they were relieved, and in so doing, it sowed the seeds of a policy which was to have disastrous consequences for hundreds of thousands of German soldiers. Another direct consequence of the successful supply of the troops by air, was the fact that it bolstered Herman Goring's arrogant belief that the troops encircled at Stalingrad

could also have been kept supplied from the
air. The terrible fate of the men of the 6th
Army bears witness to the hollowness of that
boast.

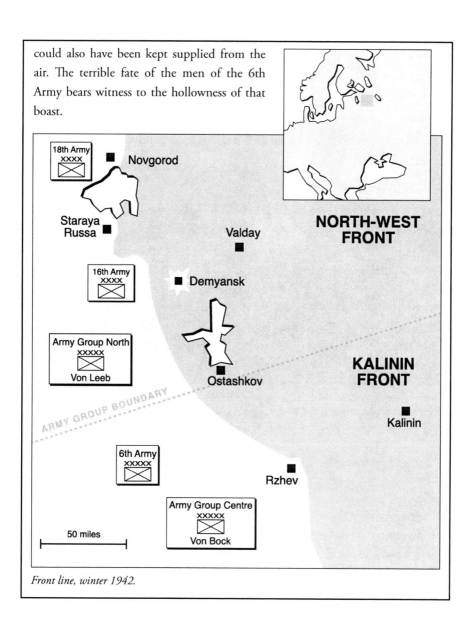

Front line, winter 1942.

THE WEAPONS OF WAR

The early war version of the T-34 had a small two man turret which gave problems in aiming and firing the gun. It was one of the many qualities of this vehicle that it could upgrade to take a larger turret with room for an extra crew member and a larger calibre 85mm high velocity gun.

3. RUSSIAN ARMOUR

In the entire course of military history , there can be few cases of a more profound or disturbing shock, than that which awaited the German Wehrmacht in the early months of the Russian campaign. The first encounters with the T-34 and KV-1 produced a nasty and unpleasant wake-up call for the men of the armoured divisions, who had begun to consider themselves invincible, and their machines to be world beaters.

It was certainly not the quality or even the quantity of the German armour which gave Hitler his surprise victories in Poland, France and the Balkans. The new tactical doctrine of Blitzkrieg, combined with the extreme disarray in the ranks of some of his enemies, the surprise quality of the German attack and the excellence of the German communications and training, were the key factors in those successful campaigns. What the Germans had not yet encountered was superior armour in determined hands.

During 1940 and 1941, the numbers of Panzer III and Panzer IV tanks had risen steadily, but there were still large numbers of Panzer I, Panzer II, Panzer 35(t) and Panzer 38(t) in the forces which were fielded during operation Barbarossa. As if to compound matters, the Panzer III was equipped with an anti-tank gun of insufficient calibre for the task which they were about to face. The Panzer IV was really designed in an infantry support role, although it had a larger gun than the Panzer III in the form of a short barrelled 75mm gun, it was a low velocity weapon designed to fire high explosive shells in an infantry support role, a less than perfect weapon for the coming encounter with the T-34.

In the first few weeks of the campaign the unsuspecting German forces encountered the first T-34 which began to appear in real numbers during the latter stages of Operation Typhoon. The T-34 with its wide tracks, sloping armour, and high velocity 76mm main gun, was to become the real nemesis of the German army. More than any other single vehicle which was produced during the entire course of the war, the T-34 can lay claim to being the most important weapon of the war. Ultimately more than forty-thousand were produced, and although the Germans would produce better vehicles in the form of the Panther and the Tiger, they could never hope to compete with the sheer numbers rolling off the Soviet production lines.

Everything about the T-34 was designed for mass production, the welding was crude but adequate and the machines were simple but robust in design, and equipped with an anti-tank gun of sufficient calibre for the task which they were about to face.

The T-34 was certainly a rough and ready vehicle, it lacked any form of refinement, but the armour was good, the cross-country performance was excellent and it packed a deadly punch in battle. Once it had proved itself in the early stages of the war, it was quickly put into production as Russia's main battle tank. Not only was the T-34 adequate for the battlefield, as the war progressed, it also proved to be capable of being upgraded to carry larger guns and a bigger crew. Unlike many of the machines which entered service in 1941, the T-34 was still being produced at the end of the war.

The first T-34 to see action was driven by a four man crew. The original vehicles lacked a radio which placed them at a severe disadvantage against the German tanks in battle. In 1941 the Russians were still attempting to communicate between tanks using a system of flags. Had the communication between Russian tanks been better and the training methods improved, it is almost inconceivable that the Wehrmacht could have produced the successes of 1942. Inside the vehicle the lack of even a rudimentary internal communications system, such as that found in German tanks, produced some very real communications difficulties inside the noisy cramped interiors of the tank.

In tandem with the T-34, during 1942 the Russians also introduced a new heavy tank in the form of the KV-1. The KV was produced in two main variants, the anti-tank KV-1 was by

the standards of the day, very heavily armoured for the time. The infantry support variant, the KV-2, was equipped with a huge howitzer, which was carried in a massive slab sided turret. The shock of meeting these massive tanks for the first time, has been covered in greater length in pages 31 and 32 of the main text, but it is sufficient to stress that these two vehicles were the cause of the string of urgent demands for both an upgrade in main armaments and also in armour which came from the German field commanders during 1941 and early 1942.

It was not until the introduction of the Tiger in late 1942 that the Germans could really match the T-34 for battlefield ability.

Desperately needed tanks continue to roll off the assembly lines during the siege of Leningrad. Despite the seriousness of the situation, many of the machines were diverted south to the defence of Moscow.

THE KEY BATTLES

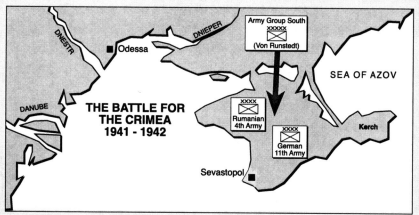

Sevastopol (besieged October 30th 1941 - July 2nd 1942).

3. SEVASTOPOL

With the commencement of the German offensive in 1942 Hitler, for once, completely out foxed Stalin. While Stalin expected a further assault on Moscow, Hitler's gaze had already turned southwards and the oil fields of the Caucasus would form the focus for the German offensive which would come where the Russians least expected it, in the South. The capture of Sevastopol was a major step on the road towards this strategic goal and was the major achievement for the German forces in their highly successful summer campaign of 1942. Sevastopol was a true fortress in every sense of the word, it was ringed with a series of huge forts arranged around its perimeter, which were linked by extensive tunnels buried deep beneath the ground.

This tough defensive network had already seen off a determined German assault in late 1941 but with the Wehrmacht again in the ascendancy, the situation in mid-1942 looked bleak for the defenders. The forces fighting in the Crimea were under the capable direction of Field Marshal von Manstein and in his determination to capture Sevastopol, von Manstein brought up the very heaviest artillery in the arsenal. Perhaps the most famous of these are the massive Karl series of mortars, six enormous self-propelled weapons which fired a shell of over two tonnes a piece. The first four of these infernal weapons were named after the Norse gods Thor, Odin, Zui, and Loki, with two more, rather bizarrely, named after the biblical figures Adam and Eve. In addition to their Karl mortars, von Manstein also brought up a massive artillery piece carried on a series of railway carriages and known as "Big Dora" it was one of the largest artillery pieces to be deployed in the whole course of the war, its ninety foot long barrel had a range of just under thirty miles. In addition to these Super weapons there was a huge assemblage of conventional artillery of all types.

The battle itself opened with a seventeen day bombardment, followed by a five day taste of what von Manstein described as "annihilation fire". Despite the benefits of the solidly constructed concrete defences, the opening barrage was able to crack the defensive positions like a nut. However there was still a great deal of intense fighting for Manstein's 11th army and the supporting Rumanian troops to deal with. In addition to the concrete defences of the fortress, there were miles of trenches defended by deep barbed wire concentrations. There were also enormous minefields which had to be negotiated. These were defended by concealed pillboxes, automatic flame throwers, mortar positions and machine gun nests. The final assault on the Sevastopol Fortress which opened at dawn on June 7th, was therefore preceded by twenty seven days of unremitting bombardment, nonetheless almost every single one of the vast array of Soviet defensive positions, from concrete bunkers, to slit trenches and pillboxes, had to be taken in hotly contested individual actions. The enormous Soviet fortress named Fort Stalin proved to be a particularly difficult point to take and the extensive emplacements

A Russian battleship at anchor in the harbour of Sevastopol lends its heavy guns to the defence of the port.

The largest calibre guns in the German armoury were called upon to reduce the defences of Sevastopol.

known as Maxim Gorkii had to be beaten into submission by the concentrated fire of the Karl mortars. Even then the survivors fought on and could only be cleared from the labyrinth of tunnels and a series of vicious hand to hand fights carried out below ground in choking smoke by men wearing gas masks.

Finally, the resistance of the Soviet garrison was brought to its knees as the Black Sea fleet found it more and more difficult to bring in reinforcements and supplies of ammunition began to run low and the garrison was slowly pounded into surrender. It was not until June 30th 1942 that the defenders finally gave up the struggle and Sevastopol fell into German hands. It can be argued that the capture of Sevastopol was to prove the last major victory for the German army on the Eastern front. The terrible events which were to take place at Stalingrad were now only a matter of weeks away, after that, a pattern of almost unremitting failure lay ahead.

CHAPTER 5
THE BATTLE FOR STALINGRAD

Stalingrad became a symbol of Russian endurance, of German capability. It also had an important strategic significance. If the Germans had cut across the Volga, they would have sliced right through the Russian lines of communication, for oil and for transport. Stalingrad was not an altogether facile quest on Hitler's part but it became invested with enormous psychological significance. Both sides in this ghastly chest to chest struggle could not be unlocked. One side, it seemed had to be destroyed and the other become victor. It had the quality of a titanic struggle, the political importance which was attached to Stalingrad by both Hitler and Stalin was immensely significant.

It was Hitler who first began to find the symbolism of its name difficult to resist. On the 23rd July the capture of the city was placed on a par with the southern advance. By September, defeat of the city named after his arch-rival was unthinkable. Stalin too was aware of the symbolic significance involved. As early as the 1st July, with the German 6th Army approaching the big bend of the Don, and threatening the road to the city, Stalin told Timoshenko, "I order the formation of an Army Group Stalingrad. The city itself will be defended by the 62nd Army to the last man".

German grenadiers in the ruins of Stalingrad, September 1942.

At the time of Stalin's order, the 62nd Army were desperately preparing a defensive position at the Kalach bridge-head, west of the Don, supported to the south by the 64th Army and 1st Tank Army.

On the 30th July, the German 6th Army struck north and south of this formation and by the 8th August it was encircled. The remnants of the 62nd and 64th Army pulled back to form a defensive perimeter around Stalingrad, leaving the approach road virtually undefended. On the 23rd August, the 6th Army, under General Friedrich Paulus, and the 4th Panzer Army crossed the Don and sped towards the city.

Despite the resolute defence of the outnumbered Soviet forces, the Germans crashed through the suburbs. Only a rapid withdrawal to the inner city on the 30th August prevented a complete encirclement of the forward defences.

The depleted Russian ranks were bolstered by the addition of one hundred and twenty five thousand adult citizens and seven thousand male youths, between the ages of thirteen and seventeen. Workers in the munitions factories handed over weapons and equipment to their soldiers as soon as they came off the production lines. As the battle grew in intensity, they were forced to use them themselves.

In their eagerness for a rapid victory, the Germans made a severe tactical error. The area bombing by the Luftwaffe, which was ordered as a prelude to the final assault, created a natural fortress, and it also constricted the mobility of the attackers. It turned the struggle for occupation into 'Rattenkrieg' (rat's war), through the rubble choked thoroughfares of the city.

German tank superiority and aerial dominance counted for very little. The German army's whole tactical training had been concerned with how to avoid such a war of vicious attrition. The defenders on the other hand, proved adept at this hide and seek struggle through the labyrinth of ruined buildings and blocked alleyways to which Stalingrad was reduced.

The battle zones contracted to minuscule proportions. In the larger buildings, floors and even stairways were transformed into centres of conflict. Any overview became almost impossible, as the individual buildings changed hands several times in a single day. Back in Germany, the slow progress of its army gave rise to jokes parodying the official reports from the front:

"Today our troops captured a two roomed flat with kitchen, toilet and bathroom. They managed to retain two thirds of it, despite hard-fought counter-attacks from the enemy."

Nevertheless, the sheer weight of the German attack began to tell. By mid September, the defence of the city seemed on the point of being overwhelmed.

The answer to the question, how close were the Germans to winning the battle of

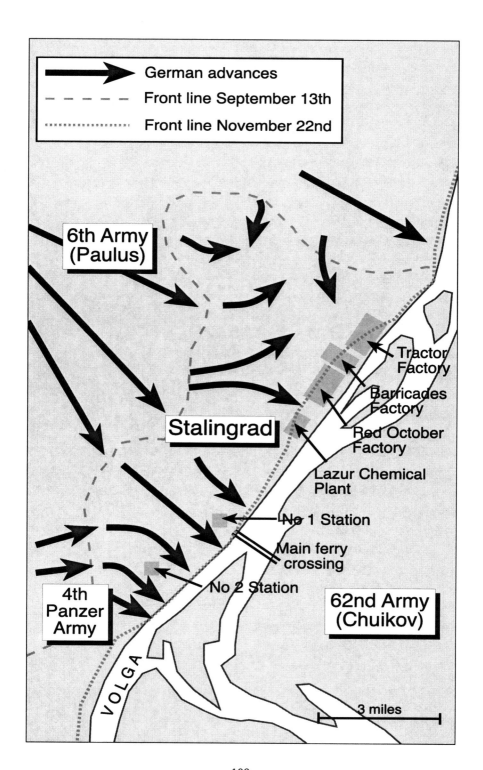

German advances

Front line September 13th

Front line November 22nd

6th Army (Paulus)

Tractor Factory

Barricades Factory

Stalingrad

Red October Factory

Lazur Chemical Plant

No 1 Station

Main ferry crossing

No 2 Station

62nd Army (Chuikov)

4th Panzer Army

VOLGA

3 miles

Stalingrad, is a sobering one.

They actually came about four hundred yards from victory. The final stages of the German attack in October, had driven the Russians right down to the waters edge. They were never pushed off, but they got to the stage where the battle was grinding down Russian battalion after Russian battalion. It was a case of who could hang on the longest. But in the period from 24th October, running into the first few days of November, it appeared to be touch and go.

The result of the war in the east hung once again in the balance. Hitler was disregarding the tactics of the *vernichtungsgedanke*, the idea of annihilation by swift blows to the flanks and rear, which had been the basis of all German successes to date. He was disregarding the needs of the campaign in the Caucasus by diverting crucial amounts of manpower to Stalingrad. And totally out of character, he was ignoring the weaknesses of the German flanks along the sixty mile salient which the attack on Stalingrad had created. Hitler was risking everything in his growing obsession with this one city.

The Red Army, pressed back against the Volga with the smoking ruins of Stalingrad in front of them, was once again on the rack. The optimism of the early spring had turned sour in a soul-destroying series of defeats, which saw further huge tracts of their homeland fall into enemy hands. Should Stalingrad now capitulate, the blow to their morale would be immense. More ominously, the fall of Stalingrad would seal the fate of the Caucasus and pave the way for the final breech of the Volga - the only barrier to stand between Nazi Germany and absolute control of the European continent.

For all the excesses and brutalities of Stalin's Russia, it's collapse would unleash an era of cold blooded slaughter and mayhem such as the world had never before witnessed. In the words of Josef Goebbels, "A time of brutality approaches, of which we ourselves have absolutely no conception, in fact we are in the middle of it. We shall only reach our goal if we have enough courage to destroy, laughingly to shatter, what we once held holy, such as tradition, upbringing, friendship and human love."

The battle for Stalingrad had continued unabated for four agonising months, during which time the Germans had captured ninety per cent of the city. But with a display of heroic courage in the face of defeat, the Russians finally threw out their tormentors and with them, Hitler's demented vision of Russian enslavement and world domination.

As early as August, the German High Command had warned Hitler of the dangers of advancing Army Group A into the Caucasus, while simultaneously using Army Group B to attempt the capture of Stalingrad. (See map p.113)

German military resources were totally inadequate to safeguard the flanks of this double spearhead. A gap soon developed between Groups A and B which was two hundred miles wide and guarded by just a single division. Not only did Hitler ignore the warnings of his generals, which grew more urgent as the campaign developed, but he continuously weakened the flanks of the two Groups, by siphoning off forces to feed his ongoing obsession with capturing Stalingrad.

As von Manstein wrote later, "To leave the main body of the army group at Stalingrad for weeks on end, was a cardinal error. It amounted to nothing less than presenting the enemy with the initiative and it was a clear invitation for him to surround the 6th Army." That encirclement happened in November 22nd 1942.

On November 26th, Hitler delivered a personal message to the beleaguered troops of Stalingrad, ordering them to stand fast and promising to do all in his power to support them. The problem of supplies was turned over to the Luftwaffe which had so valiantly supplied the pocket of Demyansk the previous spring. Goering, its commander, was summoned before Hitler and agreed to guarantee five hundred and fifty tons of supplies per day. Despite the scepticism of the army Chiefs of Staff, the airlift began on 25th November. The results of the first days of the operation were ominous for the troops still fighting the 'Rats War' among the cellars and ruins of the city.

Only sixty five tons were delivered on day one, the same quantities arrived on day two, on the third day no supplies whatsoever reached the desperate German forces.

The Luftwaffe had no safe landing grounds in the vicinity of the 6th Army. As the German perimeter of control around the city shrank under Russian pressure, this

Russian civilians attempt to escape the horrors of Stalingrad.

situation consistently deteriorated. Thick fogs made flying hazardous, if not impossible. Freezing temperatures meant that aircraft servicing became a tortuous task for the German mechanics. Added to this, the Red Air Force was increasing its sorties and the tactics of its pilots were sharpening as the conflict wore on. The airlift proved a fiasco and the German troops began to starve.

The airlift was only part of Hitler's strategy to relieve the situation in Stalingrad. Von Manstein was ordered to form a relief force, to be known as Army Group Don. Its immediate objective was to "Bring the enemy attacks to a standstill and recapture the positions previously occupied".

Von Manstein's strategy involved an attack by Army Group Don towards Stalingrad and a breakout westwards by part of the 6th Army. When both assault forces met, they would provide a corridor through which the remnants of the 6th Army still engaged in Stalingrad could be withdrawn. Von Manstein's problems began even before his forces could attack the Russians. The reinforcements which would give Army Group Don its only hope against vastly superior Russian numbers, failed to arrive.

Worse, the Russian strength in the area was increasing. The 4th Panzer Army was forced to launch the offensive alone. The bulk of the fighting would fall upon the shoulders of the 6th Panzer Division at the head of the German forces.

The cause of the attempt by Army Group Don to relieve the encircled 6th Army was later described in detail, after the war, by Rauss who wrote a long account of how. Army Group Don was to come agonisingly close to achieving its objective but ultimately, the superior weight of Russian forces would take its toll.

"Here, there existed only temporary field positions, and the defence had to be conducted in a mobile manner. At first, the Russians pushed a cavalry corps, strengthened by armour and camel troops, forward along the Don, to the Kurmoyarskiy Aksay River for reconnaissance and for screening the movements of their infantry and tank forces assembling in the rear.

The German 6th Panzer Division was ten to twenty per cent overstrength and had to conduct the main thrust. When its leading elements arrived, the vanguard of the Red calvary corps was just moving into Kotelnikovo (about 26th November 1942). It was driven back, and the assembly of German forces continued. The attempt to take Kotelnikovo in an assault by the entire cavalry corps on 5th and 6th December 1942, ended in a smashing defeat of the Russian corps at Pokhlebin. Meanwhile, the enemy cautiously advanced two rather weak infantry divisions along both sides of the railroad, onto the elevations north of the city and pushed back several outposts. After the bitter experience of Pokhlebin, however, he did not dare attack Kotelnikovo again. He assembled his main force, the Third Tank Army and additional infantry forces, between the Aksay River and the Mishkova River sector. His entire defence forces were drawn up in three echelons, one behind the other, twenty miles in width and forty five miles in depth. The impression was gained by the Germans that the enemy would move up under the protection of his advance infantry and cavalry division, and then, with his entire tank army, attack the 6th Panzer Division which was marching up along, in order to destroy it in the wide forefield of Stalingrad before it reached the city. The move, however, did not materialise. On that occasion the Russians either missed a chance, or else did not feel strong enough to attack the division, which was equipped with two hundred tanks and self-propelled assault guns, as well as a large number of anti-tank weapons. Neither did the Russians act to save their reinforced cavalry corps from destruction on 5th and 6th December, and also looked on idly on 12th December, while the beginning of the relief thrust of the German 6th Panzer Division rolled over his advance infantry divisions and scattered them. The northernmost of the two divisions here lost its entire artillery. The weak remnants of the Russian cavalry corps were also caught on the fringes of the mighty assault and were so badly mauled that they played no further part in the course of the offensive. Thus, the 6th Panzer Division, without protection on its northern flank, was able to cross the Aksay River as early as the third day.

Its southern wing was protected by the 23rd Panzer Division (in regimental strength with fifteen to twenty tanks) which followed in echelons.

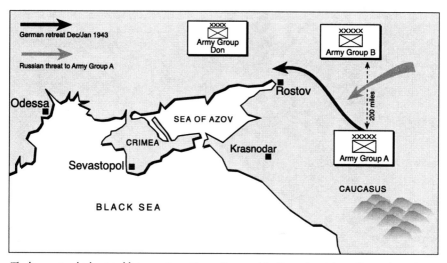

The large gap which existed between Army Group B around Stalingrad and Army Group A opening in the Causasus was always a concern for the High Command. Once Stalingrad was surrounded and the real possibility of a Russian advance on Rostov appeared, Army Group A was in real danger of being cut off. Hitler allowed the retreat just in time to save Army Group A.

The crossing of the Aksay River met only weak resistance from advance elements of a Russian mechanised corps, which was soon overcome. In an immediate follow-up thrust by all German armoured units, Verkhniy-Kumskiy, the key point of the assembly area of the Russian Third Tank Army, was taken. Not till then were the enemy tanks stirred into action, but now they displayed very spirited activity. Speed was imperative. Therefore, the Russian commander was compelled to radio all his orders and reports in

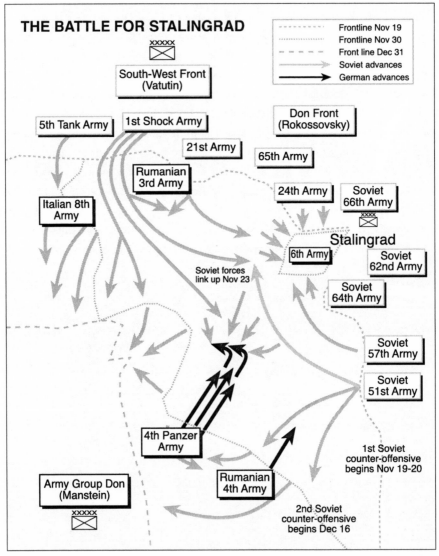

The thinly held German front was a major concern in 1942. The Rumanian 3rd and 4th Armies bore the brunt of the assault on November 19th.

the clear. Because the Russians were forced to put their cards on the table, the German forces, although numerically far inferior, were able during the ensuing several days of bitter tank fighting, to attack Russian elements in lightening moves and beat them decisively before they could receive help. In the melee that followed, the Russians occasionally succeeded in concentrating greatly superior forces which threatened to become dangerous to the division. The German armoured forces then immediately withdrew, only to attack the Reds from the rear again the moment an opportunity presented itself.

Both sides made large-scale shifts under cover of darkness. By lightning-like feints and changes of direction, it was repeatedly possible for the Germans to attack strong Red tank concentrations, simultaneously from all sides, in the large hollows of the hilly terrain, and to destroy them to the last tank. In this manner a number of so-called tank cemeteries originated where from fifty to eighty knocked-out tanks, mostly T-34s, stood in clusters within a small area. The German bomber wing, repeatedly bombed them by mistake. Neither German nor Russian aircraft could take any part in the seesaw tank battles, since the opposing tanks were frequently so intermingled that they could not be differentiated. Although air activity on both sides was very lively, it was forced to limit itself to attacking motor pools and supply lines. The air arm was of no decisive importance.

While the tank battle north of the Aksay River was still in progress, Russian tank and motorised brigades crossed the river in a southerly direction and attempted to cut off the bridge crossing, which was strongly held on both sides of the river. This had to be avoided under all circumstances but without depleting the German armoured forces, then engaged in crucial battles. Soon the bridgehead was surrounded. Although more than a dozen Russian tanks were knocked out, just as many surviving tanks overran the entrenched German infantry and penetrated to a rather large village located in the centre of the bridgehead and defended by the German 57th Armoured Engineer Battalion. Not a single engineer or rifleman deserted his post. Each man became a tank buster. Just as fast as Russian tanks entered the village, they burst into flames. Not one escaped. Three times the Russian repeated this assault, and three times he was repulsed. Then a reinforced infantry regiment attacked him from the rear, scattered the entire force, and knocked out 14 tanks. That opened the route of advance again and assured the free flow of supplies across the bridge.

When strong Russian motorised infantry with numerous anti-tank weapons entered the battle at Verkhniy-Kumskiy, the German armoured infantry forces were tied down supporting their neighbour and other forces engaged at the Aksay River, leaving the German armoured units so severely restricted in their freedom of movement that they had to be withdrawn to the Aksay River. The Russian, however, had suffered such heavy tank losses, that he did not dare risk the rest of his tanks in a pursuit. He contented himself with defending a long ridge south of Verkhniy-Kumskiy. The premature attempt, ordered by a higher command, to roll up this ridge position from the flank with the combined armoured elements of the 6th and 23rd Panzer Divisions failed. Its failure was caused by lack of sufficient infantry to silence the numerous anti-tank guns and rifles which were entrenched in deep anti-tank pits and well camouflaged by high steppe grass. Although it was perfectly possible to roll from one end of the ridge to the other, the Russian motorised riflemen popped up again afterwards like jack-in-the-boxes and, with their numerous anti-tank rifles, knocked out many an armoured vehicle. The combined German armoured force suffered considerable losses and had to be recalled in the evening without having accomplished its mission.

Not until two days later did a planned attack of the entire 6th Panzer Division succeed in taking the position and cleaning it out. In the subsequent night attack, the German armoured infantry recaptured the stubbornly defended village of Verkhniy-Kumskiy, destroyed a number of emplaced tanks, numerous anti-tank guns, and over one hundred anti-tank rifles. At dawn of the following day, the elevated position north of the village was taken in co-operation with the newly arrived 17th Panzer Division, which had only the combat strength of a reinforced battalion. The 11th Panzer Regiment, which up to this time had been held in reserve, was employed in the pursuit and inflicted heavy losses upon the Russians who were retreating through a single defile.

In the midst of the pursuit, however, the entire 6th Panzer Division had to turn to the east, to support the neighbouring 23rd Panzer Division on the right, since it was being pushed back beyond the Aksay River by a newly arrived Russian rifle corps. The further pursuit toward the north had to be left to the weak 17th Panzer Division, which lacked sufficient driving force to destroy the beaten Russian forces.

The turning of the 6th Panzer Division against the rear of the new enemy had decisively changed the situation in the 23rd Panzer Division. The Russian corps immediately broke off its attack and hastily retreated eastward in order to escape the deadly blow that would have been dealt it very soon, had it remained. The Red tanks and anti-tank gun fronts thrown against the German 6th Panzer Division had been scattered before, and German armour was about to cut off the Russian escape route. At this critical moment too, the Russian corps commander radioed his urgent orders in the clear.

But the objective of the German panzer division was Stalingrad, not the pursuit of a corps in a different direction. As soon as the 23rd Panzer Division, relieved of enemy pressure, could again advance, pursuit of the corps was halted. The 6th Panzer

Street fighting in Stalingrad.

German troops supported by a Panzer IV draw breath before the launch of another attack on Stalingrad. By September the huge casualty toll had begun to seriously undermine the combat strength of many formations. Company strength was frequently no more tha fifty or sixty effectives from a nominal role of three hundred.

Division then turned north and after hard fighting reached the Mishkova River sector at Bolshaya Vasilyevka. At that point the Stalingrad garrison was supposed to make contact with the division. Two bridgehead's were quickly formed, the village taken, and the entire division concentrated in a small area for mobile defence. It had already covered two-thirds of the distance, and stood thirty miles from Stalingrad: the flash of signal rockets from the city could be observed at night. It remains a puzzle why the German 6th Army (Field Marshal Paulus) did not break out at that time (20th December).

In forced marches the Russian brought up additional strong forces from the Stalingrad front and the Volga, in order to support the beaten Third Tank Army and throw back the German forces. Since the Russians no longer had sufficient tank forces available for this purpose, they hoped to overwhelm and destroy the German forces with the newly forced infantry main-attack army. The Red riflemen surged forward in multitudes never before encountered. Attack wave followed attack wave without regard for losses. Each was annihilated by a terrific hail of fire, without gaining so much as a foot of ground. Therefore, the Russians went around the two flanks of the German division in order to encircle it. In the course of this manoeuvre they came between the German artillery positions and the panzer regiment. Firing from all barrels, one hundred and fifty tanks and self-propelled assault guns attacked the Russian masses from the rear when they tried to escape the fire from the artillery. In their desperate situation many Russians threw down their weapons and surrendered. Succeeding elements flowed back. Red forces which had penetrated into the village were driven out again by a counter-thrust of the German infantry, and Russian tanks which had broken through were knocked out. The Russian mass assault had collapsed.

On 22nd December the German 6th Panzer Division had regained its freedom of movement. By a further forward thrust of eighteen miles on 24th December, the division was to help the encircled 6th Army in breaking out of Stalingrad. That operation, however, never materialised, because the division suddenly had to be withdrawn on 23rd December and transferred to the area north of the lower Don (Morosovskaya) to bolster the collapsed Chir front. This move definitely sealed the doom of the German forces at Stalingrad. The remaining two weak panzer divisions, the 17th and 23rd were not even sufficient to make a stand against the Russian forces, let alone repulse them. But also the enemy was so weakened by his losses, which included more than four hundred tanks, that he was unable to make a quick thrust against Rostov, an action which would have cut off the entire Caucasus front."

Against all the odds, by 17th December, von Manstein had reached a position only thirty five miles short of Stalingrad, forcing sections of the Red Army surrounding the city to break away from the siege to block the advance. By the 20th the relief had gained another five miles and was just thirty miles from making contact with 6th Army.

Von Manstein urgently requested Hitler to allow the 6th Army to retreat towards him and bring the Russians under fire from east and west. Once the German forces met, then the three thousand tons of supplies assembled behind the 4th Panzer Army, could be pushed through to those retreating from the city. Faced with silence from Führer Headquarters, von Manstein himself gave the order for the breakout to begin.

It would have been a desperate gamble for the 6th Army. Only one hundred of its tanks remained operational and these held sufficient fuel for a journey of twenty miles or less. The physical ability of Paulus' half starved troops to mount any sort of mobile campaign was also questionable. Faced with these risks, and in possession of previous orders from Hitler to stand firm, Paulus disobeyed the direct order of von Manstein, his superior officer, and did not attempt to break out. In doing so he doomed the majority of the quarter of a million soldiers under his command to slow and painful death.

With the fate of the 6th Army sealed, events to the north and the south of the city now began to draw attention away from the plight of the army marooned in Stalingrad, far more than the struggle for one city was now at stake. The issue was no longer the fate of a single army but the entire southern wing of the front and, ultimately, of all the German armies in the east.

The debate over the contribution made by the men trapped at Stalingrad still rages today. If the resilient Stalingrad garrison had caved in and the Red Army, as it planned to do, moved westwards at high speed, it would have been able to seal off the German Army Group A in the Caucasus. That would have trapped an enormous number of men. The argument has been advanced that by holding on in Stalingrad until 3rd February, and constraining a large element of Russian forces, it enabled German troops who had penetrated deep in the Caucasus, to get out and pull back. They then managed to build up an improvised defence line and this more or less stabilised the situation.

At one stage, the whole of the German southern wing appeared to be in great jeopardy. By Christmas Eve the Red Army was within striking distance of Rostov. Only two days earlier Army Group A had begun its withdrawal from the Caucasus. Should the Russians have reached Rostov before them, their retreat would have been cut off.

The ordinary German soldiers only gradually became aware of the magnitude of the disaster which was upon them

By the New Year the 4th Panzer Army, having abandoned the 6th Army to its fate, had withdrawn as far as Rostov. It provided the only effective barrier between the advance of Soviet forces and the capture of the city. By January 7th the Red Army was only thirty miles from Rostov but remained slow to exploit its superiority. Hitler

The last defenders of Stalingrad are taken into Russian captivity.

also remained slow to order a complete evacuation of the south. He waited until 27th January when Army Group A seemed doomed, to finally allow its retreat through Rostov.

In Stalingrad the situation of the 6th Army had deteriorated rapidly throughout January. On the 8th, Paulus was offered terms for a surrender by the Russians. Hitler refused to allow him to capitulate.

By now German troops were collapsing from starvation and exhaustion. They were dying of exposure and some were committing suicide. Even when Army Group A was withdrawn beyond Rostov and the 6th Army's continued resistance served little strategic purpose, Hitler still refused to allow them to surrender. On January 31st he made Paulus a Field Marshal. On the following day, with all his options exhausted, Paulus finally surrendered. He became the first Field Marshal since the unification of the State to fall into enemy hands.

Announcing the disaster at Stalingrad to the rest of the forces in the East, the German High Command requested that officers in the field read out the last message received by short wave radio from the ruins of the tractor factory - Red October. "We are the last survivors in this place. Four of us are wounded. We have been entrenched in the wreckage of the tractor factory for four days. We have not had food for four days. I have just opened the last magazine for my automatic. In ten minutes the Bolsheviks will overrun us. Tell my father that I have done my duty and that I shall know how to die. Long live Germany! Hail Hitler!".

The spectacular victory won by the Red Army at Stalingrad led almost immediately to a search for the cause of the debacle. After the war, one of those who was quick to appear in print was General Kurt Zeitzler. Zeitzler was Chief of the Army General Staff during 1942. Like many others, he was happy to provide a comprehensive explanation of his wartime service in Russia. A full examination of his account is particularly useful here, as it highlights what appears to have been widely expressed concerns over the impending Russian attack at Stalingrad, in the months leading up to the battle. Zeitzler's account is also interesting because it paints a very thorough and convincing picture of a man in day to day contact with the Fuhrer.

Zeitzler's memoirs of the events surrounding the Stalingrad battle formed a chapter in the book "Fatal Decisions" first published in the 1950s. That particular volume collected together the thoughts of many of the German High Command who had been involved in some of the most decisive actions of World War Two. As with all works of this type, Zeitzler's account needs to be handled with some caution, the reader has understandable grounds for suspecting the motives of the writer. After all, who would set out to deliberately undermine themselves with a ready made scapegoat in the form of Adolf Hitler who, of course, could not answer back. If Zeitzler's account is to be accepted without question, he appears to have been almost psychic in some of his predictions with regard to the events which were about to befall the 6th army, and there is, at least, some documentary evidence which appears to contradict some of his own testimony. Most notably his own elaboration on Hitler's order, "The Ergansung Zum Operationsbefehl NVI" (23rd October) in which Zeitzler emphasises that the Russians "were in no position to mount a major offensive with any far reaching objective."

On the other hand, it can be argued that the course of subsequent events was so clearly obvious that it did not take a military genius to predict how events would unfold. In his account of the build up to the disaster at Stalingrad and the subsequent refusal by Hitler to allow the 6th Army to break out, one does suspect the presence of some hindsight. However, the consensus generally, is with Zeitzler, and most serious historians accept his account as being a genuine, if slightly self serving portrait of the events at the most senior level.

Zeitzler began his account with a very telling insight into the world of Adolf Hitler. He recalled of his own surprise appointment as Chief of the Army General Staff. He was formerly Chief of Staff with Army Group D.

"I took an aeroplane and as soon as I arrived, Hitler treated me, as was his custom, to a monologue of several hours duration. It was not possible for me to interrupt this harangue, in which Hitler expressed his deep dissatisfaction with the course of events on the Eastern front and particularly the break down of the offensive. As usual Hitler did not look for the true causes of this, that is to say, the erroneous choice of objectives and the fact that the means available were inadequate to achieve the desired ends. Instead, Hitler chose the course which was far more convenient to himself, of blaming the troops and their commanders. He referred with particular bitterness to what he described as the incompetence of Field Marshal and Colonel-General Halder. Suddenly he broke off and ended his monologue with the words "and so enough, I have decided to appoint you Chief of the General Staff of the Army". As was his usual method, whenever he made a mistake he placed the blame upon someone else, who was then dismissed and a new man appointed in his place. He never drew the right conclusions from the miscarriage of his plans, had he done so, though he could not, of course, have put right the past, he could have least have diminished the future effects of his errors".

In outlining Hitler's strategy for the year 1942, Zeitzler was aware that the resources at his disposal were just about sufficient to capture Stalingrad, but from the outset he claims to have stated to Hitler that those resources were insufficient to hold the prize once it had been won. Zeitzler moved on to paint a gloomy picture of the conditions of the German front line armies, which were in, what he described as, " a very bad way". Once again, the responsibility for this situation was largely placed on the convenient shoulders of Adolf Hitler. It was Hitler who had been determined to capture the city which was named after his bitter rival. As the offensive ground to a halt at all points, it was again Hitler who decided that the city should be captured by a series of small-scale attacks.

In Stalingrad itself, Hitler ordered a series of assaults by specialist shock troops,

The forlorn column of German prisoners are marched into captivity after Stalingrad. The survivors were treated with callous inhumanity by their captors, but in their weakened state it is debatable just how many of the 90,000 would still have died. In any event only 5000 ever saw Germany again.

with the intention of capturing a city block by block and even building by building, a course of action which was typical of the Führer's highly intrusive management of the campaign at a micro level. This hallmark of Hitler's still clearly gave rise to great concern among the generals. With this in mind Zeitzler recalled the presentation he made to Adolf Hitler in the weeks before the massive Russian counter-offensive which broke upon Stalingrad in 19th November 1942.

Zeitzler claims to have listed five main concerns in his presentation which were as follows:

i) The amount of territory now occupied in Russia was too large for the German army to control.

ii) The weakest sector on the whole of the Eastern front, was without question the northern flank of a army group South, which stretched from Stalingrad towards Army Group Centre. In addition, Zeitzler also pointed out that this sector was held by the weakest and least reliable of the forces at the disposal of the Wehrmacht, namely the Rumanians, Italians and the Hungarians. This, he said represented "an enormous danger" which had to be eliminated immediately.

iii) The supply of men, equipment, weapons and ammunition to the Russian front was completely inadequate. Zeitzler pointed out to Hitler that each month losses far exceeded the irregular flow of replacements and that "disastrous consequences" would surely follow.

iv) The Russian army was now both better trained and better led than it had been in 1941, and greater caution should now be exercised by the German army.

v) Greater consideration needed to be given to providing the troops with supply and a detailed study needed to be undertaken of the utilisation of the railways, which represented a severe supply bottleneck.

Zeitzler must have been apprehensive in presenting such a gloomy report to a man who was infamous for his violent and childlike reaction to things which displeased him. But on this occasion Hitler was remarkably conciliatory and even appeared to accept some of the concerns raised by Zeitzler as being genuine. However the Führer finally dismissed Zeitzler and his report with a patronising little speech, in which he assumed the role of the veteran Eastern front warrior talking down to the new recruit:

"You are too pessimistic. Here on the Eastern front we have been through worse periods than this before you joined us, and we survived. We will get over our present difficulties too. Of course at some points along the front the German soldiers are outnumbered. But they are far superior in quality to the enemy. Our weapons are better too. And in the near future we shall have new weapons which will be better still."

Undaunted by the immovable attitude of Hitler, which Zeitzler would have at least anticipated, he continued to attempt to persuade Hitler of the dangers posed by the approaching Russian offensive now accepted as a fact among the German High Command. Zeitzler's next move was to attempt to persuade the Führer of the wisdom of his alternative option to Hitler's strategy, of simply staying put and defending.

In Zeitzler's opinion, the most obvious and most effective answer was to simply withdraw from Stalingrad in order to shorten the front and close the wide gap which existed between Army Group B and Army Group Centre. This would also have had the welcome effect of creating a strong German reserve force, to provide some relief and reassurance for the hard-pressed front line, as currently there were no real strategic reserves worthy of the name. Zeitzler must have known by now that even the suggestion of such a plan was like a red rag to a bull. Hitler clung obstinately to his policy of standing fast at all times and he flew into a rage at the first suggestion that the topic was even likely to be raised.

One small compromise which Zeitzler was able to extract from Hitler, was the creation of a new Panzer Corps (the 48th) under the command of Lieutenant General Heim. In this case the term Panzer Corps was probably a rather flattering description for a force which boasted only two armoured divisions.

Although the German 22nd Panzer Division was a first class unit, the Rumanian Panzer Division, which was the second armoured formation in the corps, left a great deal to be desired. It was equipped with a mixture of captured Russian tanks and the outdated Panzer 38(t) from Czechoslovakia. This rather makeshift formation was the only significant reserve behind the Northern flank of Army Group B. According to Zeitzler he had already identified this as the most likely place for the Russian offensive. To further compound matters, Hitler insisted that the new Corps could only be released on his expressed authority.

Despite the fierce arguments which raged between Hitler and Zeitzler, the last rumblings of the formerly mighty German offensive continued to doggedly grind their way through the city of Stalingrad. Battalion after battalion had been decimated by the appaling demands of the street fighting, and despite the fact that they were now poised to finally seize the remaining portion of Stalingrad, the agenda changed, the real issue was now the imminent Russian counter-offensive.

It came on the morning of 19th November 1942, when the urgent messages started to stream in from the Rumanian front, north west of Stalingrad. The first reports gave details of a very heavy artillery bombardment along the whole length of the front. At first it looked as if Hitler would behave in a more rational fashion. Without undue prevarication he released Panzer Corps Heim to the command of Army Group B. Of course, no one yet suspected the impending scale of disaster, but already Zeitzler was requesting Hitler to allow him to order the withdrawal of the 6th Army from Stalingrad. Hitler refused permission as he fully expected the commitment of Heim's 48th Panzer Corps to stabilise the situation. In fact the situation continued to deteriorate. Panzer Corps Heim was itself attacked during its own preparations to go over to the offensive.

In desperation, Zeitzler flew to Hitler's headquarters in order to reason with the Führer personally. He was astonished to find that Hitler, supported by Jodl and Keitel, felt that the transfer of a single Division from Army Group A, currently fighting in the Caucasus, would be sufficient and to retrieve the situation where Heim had failed with his Corps. Zeitzler vigorously argued against such a simple solution. In any event, he knew that it would take at least 14 days to bring a division all the way from the Caucasus. By that time the situation might well have deteriorated further. In a rare attempt to reach a compromise, Hitler, who clearly had not been listening to Zeitzler's argument, now offered to bring not one but two divisions from the Caucasus to the aid of Army Group B. This was further evidence of Hitler's rapidly declining powers of comprehension, a second division travelling by the same route as the first would have to wait until that division had been transported and unloaded after its torturous journey on the overcrowded Russian rail network. Feeding divisions piecemeal into a battle

Field Marshall Paulus, accompanied by General Arthur Schmidt and Colonel Wilhelm Adam, surrenders to the Russians on February 1st 1943. A defining moment in the history of World War Two.

of this nature was clearly suicidal and this should have been obvious to the Supreme Commander. In response to Zeitzler's repeated demands for a withdrawal, Hitler once again lost his self control:

"I won't leave the Volga! I will not withdraw from the Volga!"

The deterioration of the northern flank had proceeded far more quickly than even the high command could have envisaged. The grave situation developed into a major crisis when, on November 20th, the Russians launched the second wing of their grand encircling attack. This time the blow was struck to the south of Stalingrad and, once again, the Russian offensive was aimed at the weaker Rumanian divisions who crumbled under the ferocious Russian assault. With the continued progress made by the northern arm of the assault, it was now a certainty that Stalingrad would become encircled.

When the news reached Hitler that Heim had failed to retrieve the situation with his Panzer Corps, he was reduced to an infantile fit of rage. In an apoplexy of fury he demanded that Heim be immediately relieved of his command, reduced to the rank of private and thrown into jail. Such was the bizarre manner in which Adolf Hitler conducted the largest conflict in the history of humanity.

By the evening of 22nd November, Zeitzler received the news he had dreaded. Over the radio, Paulus, commander of the 6th Army, informed his superiors that his army was now encircled, he asked for permission to break out, but Hitler personally replied that the 6th Army was to form a defensive hedgehog and await relief. Turning to Zeitzler, Hitler proudly proclaimed that Stalingrad would now be designated as a"fortress". By this stage relations between the two men had deteriorated to the point where Zeitzler was no longer concerned over the consequences of frankly speaking his mind. He dismissed Hitler's fanciful ideas and pointed out that simply designating a position as a "fortress" might possibly create the illusion of strength and preparedness in the mind of the civilian population but that it meant nothing to the soldiers on the ground, and even less to the enemy. A fortress could not be called into being simply by a change in terminology, it required careful planning, a long period for the preparation of defences, and the stockpiling of arms, ammunition and food. This was the exact opposite of the situation at Stalingrad, where the 6th Army was already low in every category of supplies.

It was not just at Stalingrad where the Wehrmacht faced potential disaster. By mid-November 1942 the northernmost corps sector of Army Group Center extended seventy miles, from the town of Velizh north to the army group boundary. Inadequately covered by LIX Corps, the line contained two large gaps, each about ten miles wide and partly swampy but not entirely impassable. There, only reconnaissance and combat patrols provided a minimum of security. Despite persistent requests by the army group commander, no reinforcements arrived to strengthen the precarious German defenses on that sector.

Late in November the Russians attacked north and south of Velikiye Luki (Map 2 p.130) and succeeded in encircling the city which was held by a strong regimental combat team of the 83rd Division. A few miles farther south two additional German combat teams suffered the same fate. Thus three separate German pockets completely cut off from the main force were created in the same general area.

By that time all available reserves of Army Group Center had been thrown into the fierce battle at Rzhev and could not be extricated for the relief of the encircled units in the Velikiye Luki area The army group commander therefore requested authority from Army High Command to order breakouts of the encircled forces toward the west. If carried out at once, these could have been accomplished without great difficulty or excessive casualties, but it would have meant pulling the German line back about ten to fifteen miles. The new defense positions, as proposed by army group, would still assure the undisturbed operation of the Nevel-Novosokolniki-Nasva railroad, and the resulting Russian salient was then to be reduced, as soon as possible, by a German flank attack from the south.

Hitler, who in December 1941 had assumed direct control of all military operations in Russia, flatly rejected this proposal. Instead, he ordered that the pockets be held at all costs, that other German forces, by attacking from the west, re-establish contact with the encircled units, and that the front be pushed even farther to the east. He referred to a recent German success in a similar situation at Kholm by the same officer who now commanded the 83rd Division in the area of Velikiye Luki. Army group tried in vain to call Hitler's attention to the lack of reserves and the extreme hardships imposed by winter weather and difficult terrain. All such representations were impatiently brushed aside.

The two German combat teams surrounded in the area south of Velikiye Luki meanwhile conducted a fighting withdrawal toward the west. With the assistance of other German forces, they broke out of encirclement and succeeded in establishing a new front.

At Velikiye Luki the Germans had previously constructed a perimeter of hasty field fortifications around the town. Advance positions, located several hundred yards from the edge of the city, proved of considerable value during the initial stages of the siege. The encircled garrison consisted of a strong infantry regiment of the 83rd Division, two artillery battalions, one observation battalion, one engineer company, two construction battalions, and strong service and supply units. The pocket commander, a lieutenant colonel, had assumed command of his regiment only a few days earlier, and accordingly

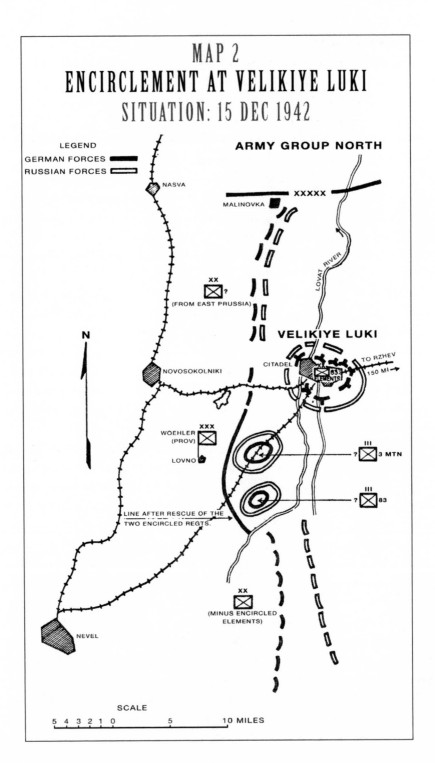

MAP 2
ENCIRCLEMENT AT VELIKIYE LUKI
SITUATION: 15 DEC 1942

LEGEND
GERMAN FORCES
RUSSIAN FORCES

ARMY GROUP NORTH

NASVA

MALINOVKA

XXXXX

LOVAT RIVER

XX
?
(FROM EAST PRUSSIA)

VELIKIYE LUKI

N

CITADEL

83
(ELEMENTS)

TO RZHEV
150 MI

NOVOSOKOLNIKI

WOEHLER
(PROV)
XXX

III
? 3 MTN

LOVNO

III
? 83

LINE AFTER RESCUE OF THE
TWO ENCIRCLED REGTS.

NEVEL

XX
(MINUS ENCIRCLED
ELEMENTS)

SCALE
5 4 3 2 1 0   5   10 MILES

did not know his troops.

The enemy had so disposed his forces that at the beginning of December only two Russian brigades were deployed in a wide arc west of Velikiye Luki. As late as two weeks after the pocket was closed, a breakout in that direction would still have been possible, but despite the personal intervention of the army group commander, Hitler did not change his mind. The pocket was to be held, and should only be relieved by a push from the west.

With no reinforcements in sight, the troops required for this relief thrust could only be taken from other sectors of Army Group Center, all of which had been severely drained in an attempt at strengthening Ninth Army at Rzhev. The direction for the attack was to be from southwest to northeast with the so-called citadel - a part of Velikiye Luki west of the Lovat River - designated as the primary objective. (Map 3 p.133)

It was obvious that LIX Corps, already responsible for an excesssively wide sector of the front, could not be expected to take on the additional task of conducting this attack. The situation not only called for the use of fresh combat units but also for the establishment of a new tactical headquarters to direct the proposed relief operation. Unable to pull out a corps headquarters from any other sector, army group had to resort to an improvisation. A provisional corps headquarters, Corps Woehler, was formed under the command of the army group chief of staff assisted by the army group training officer, the chief artillery officer, and another young staff officer. Subordinate to LIX Corps which remained responsible for supply and administraion, the newly formed command group was ready to take charge of the front sector opposite Velikiye Luki by mid-December. Its command post, established on 15 December at Lovno, was no less improvised than the staff by which it was occupied. A one-room peasant hut had to serve as living and working quarters for six officers, three clerks, three drivers, and two orderlies.

The terrain designated for the attack was desolate, rolling country, virtually without forests. Here Stalin's scorched earth policy had been fully effective in the Russian retreat of 1941. Subsequent partisan operations completed the work of destruction. Most of the formerly inhabited places had vanished and even their last traces were now blanketed by heavy layers of snow. No roads or recognizable terrain features broke the monotony. Orientation was extremely difficult and at night a matter of pure chance. The entire area gave the impression of a landscape on the moon.

The German units initially available for the attack were a division from East Prussia, the 83rd Division minus elements inside Velikiye Luki, the mountain regiment that had escaped encirclement south of the city, and two construction battalions. They had been weakened by considerable losses in men and materiel and were suffering from the effects of heavy frosts alternating with sudden thaws. Although their morale appeared unbroken, their combat value was definitely limited. Fortunately, their new commander, because of his experience as army group chief of staff, had no difficulty in finding out at what depots in the army group area ammunition and equipment could still be obtained. With railroads and transport planes doing their part, it took only a few days for the troops to be resupplied and re-equipped with new winter clothing. This brought about a rapid decline in the number of cold weather casualties.

Reinforced by a motorized division, a battalion of light infantry, two batteries of 105-mm. guns, and a rocket projector brigade, the improvised corps continued its preparations for the attack. They had to be cut short, however, since Hitler advanced the attack date by several days despite all objections by army group. The attack was launched shortly before Christmas but, after making good progress at first, bogged down at the half-way mark.

By now it had become clear that additional forces of considerable strength would have to be brought up in order to achieve success. The reinforcements finally made available consisted of two divisions and one tank battalion. At least one of these divisions, however, proved wholly inadequate for the type of operation in which it was to participate. Originally used as an occupation unit in western Europe, it had recently been transferred east and employed as a security force on a quiet sector of the Russian front. Two of its regimental commanders were considerably over-age and incapable of leading their units in combat. The third regimental commander, who was still in good physical condition, actually had to command each of the three regiments in turn as they were successively committed in the attack.

Army group had requested the approval of the Air Force for the employment of a parachute division which was then in a quiet position southeast of Velizh. In the German system of organization, parachute units were part of the Luftwaffe and Goering refused, insisting that the division remain intact in its present position. Undoubtedly this refusal was one of the chief reasons why the liberation of Velikiye Luki failed.

The second German relief thrust was launched early in January 1943. Leading elements advanced to less than five miles from the northwestern outskirts of the beleaguered city. (Map 3 p.133) At that stage, however, enemy pressure against the long flanks of the penetration forced the Germans to assume the defensive.

Inside the pocket, the citadel on the left bank of the Lovat River had meanwhile become the refuge for some 500 wounded from all parts of the city. On 5 January the Russians attacked from the north and succeeded in cutting through the town and severing the citadel from the main part of Velikiye Luki. Thus two separate pockets came

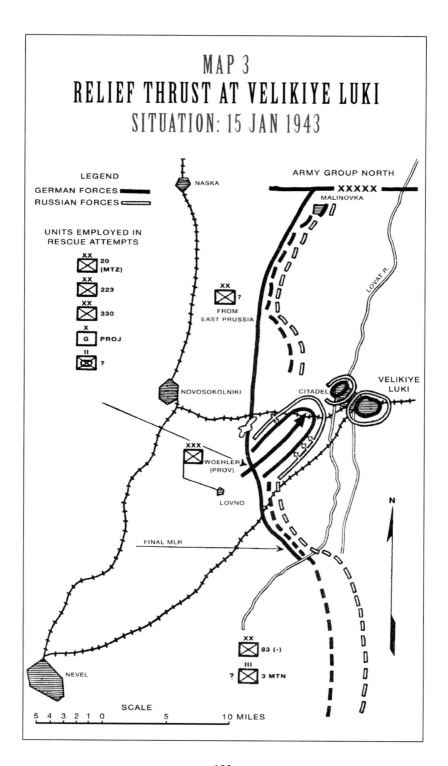

MAP 3
RELIEF THRUST AT VELIKIYE LUKI
SITUATION: 15 JAN 1943

LEGEND

GERMAN FORCES

RUSSIAN FORCES

UNITS EMPLOYED IN
RESCUE ATTEMPTS

20 (MTZ)

223

330

G PROJ

?

NASKA

ARMY GROUP NORTH

XXXXX

MALINOVKA

LOVAT R.

FROM
EAST PRUSSIA

NOVOSOKOLNIKI

CITADEL

VELIKIYE
LUKI

WOEHLER
(PROV)

LOVNO

FINAL MLR

N

NEVEL

83 (-)

? 3 MTN

SCALE

5 4 3 2 1 0   5   10 MILES

into existence, each one precariously defended after the loss of all positions beyond the edge of the town, and particularly threatened by enemy attempts at infiltrating from block to block.

Liberating the main German force encircled in the eastern part of Velikiye Luki had become even more difficult. In any event, the immediate objective was to cut through the ring of encirclement that surrounded the smaller pocket west of the river. A general advance of the corps front, however, as demanded by Hitler, was by now definitely out of the question.

After lengthy negotiations the Air Force finally released one battalion of its parachute division for commitment at Velikiye Luki. It was too little and too late, but a last attempt had to be made to open a rescue corridor to the citadel. In order to bolster the fighting strength of the encircled garrison, a reinforced company of light infantry riding on trucks and tank destroyers was to ram its way through the enemy into the surrounded citadel. On 10 January, in a daring daylight attack, this force took the Russians by surprise and succeeded in joining the German defenders inside the pocket.

During the night of 14-15 January, the parachute battalion was to advance in a surprise attack to the southwest side of the citadel. There, by 01:00, the fresh troops recently arrived in the pocket were to attempt a breakout, taking with them all wounded who were still able to march. Although initially led by a regimental commander familiar with the area, the parachute battalion lost its way in the featureless terrain and failed to reach its objective. The citadel force broke out nevertheless, and in the early morning hours, reduced by casualties to about 150 men, appeared at the corps' advance command post on the Novosokolniki-Velikiye Luki railroad line.

By now, irreplaceable losses in the ranks of the German relief force made it impossible to repeat the rescue attempt. Also, no more radio signals were coming from the eastern part of Velikiye Luki - a clear indication that in six weeks of relentless fighting, despite the most determined resistance, the German force in the eastern pocket had been wiped out to the last man. The pocket commander's final radio message, received on 14 January, was, "With last strength and ammunition still holding two bunkers in center of city. Enemy outside my command post."

The struggle for Velikiye Luki was over. While it had the effect of tying down a greatly superior and constantly growing enemy force for six weeks, it also resulted in the annihilation of the German garrison, exorbitant casualties among the relief forces, and a loss of terrain along the entire corps sector. (Map 3) The important Nevel-Novosokolniki-Nasva railroad line still remained in German hands, free from enemy interference. However, the plan proposed by army group would have assured the same result without necessitating the futile struggle for Velikiye Luki. At the end of this ill-fated operation German casualties amounted to 17,000 officers and men, 5,000 of whom perished in the beleaguered city, while 12,000 were lost in rescue attempts from outside. Even if the relief thrust had eventually succeeded, the cost was far too high.

A tense situation as German grenadiers move into early morning sun light during the advances of 1942.

THE WEAPONS OF WAR

The Nashorn or Rhino - one of the new breeds of self-propelled tank hunters.

4. PANZERJAEGER

The Sturmgeschütze experience had shown that by dispensing with a tank turret, it was possible to mount a much heavier gun on the existing tank chassis.

Unfortunately, the first attempts to produce a specialist tank hunter ignored the benefits of the Sturmgeschütze experience and favoured the simple expedient of mounting a 4.7cm anti-tank gun on the chassis of the tiny Panzer I. It was a failure. Although the 4.7 was more effective than the puny 3.7, which originally equipped the Panzer III, it was still feeble compared to the 75mm gun of a Russian T-34. In addition, the open fighting compartment gave only limited protection to the crew. Another problem was the instability of the top heavy assembly. Frequently these tank hunters simply toppled over.

During 1942, frustrating attempts were made to improve upon the Panzer I in the form of the Marder II and III tank destroyers. These strange hybrids used the Panzer II chassis, the Czech 38t chassis and sometimes even mounted a captured Russian 76mm anti-tank gun. They proved to be little more than an improvised stop gap in a steadily worsening situation on the Eastern Front, but they did go some way towards holding the advancing tide of Russian armour while real tank killers could be developed.

The first two specialised tank hunting machines proved to be almost as disappointing as the Marders. The massive Elefant looked good on paper. It was based on the eighty Porsche chassis which had been built for a proposed rival to the Tiger. This gave the five man crew the same all round protection as the Sturmgeschütze. In addition, the Elefant was massively armoured, and sported the deadly 88mm gun. It made a much heralded debut at the Battle of Kursk.

Despite all the portents, the Elefant proved to be an unmitigated disaster. The designers had not heeded the lessons from the early experiences with the Sturmgeschütze and unforgivably the Elefant was not equipped with a machine gun for close defence. Once they got to close range, Soviet tank hunting teams had a field day. The hapless crews inside the Elefant had no means of effective resistance against infantry and forty of the eighty Elefants deployed at Kursk were destroyed in the first two days of fighting.

The remaining machines were ignominiously withdrawn to be refitted with machine guns before being sent to Italy where the survivors were destroyed in the battles following the Anzio landings.

More effective in battle than the Elefant was the Nashorn or Rhinoceros. It also featured the fearsome 88mm gun, but inexplicably left the crew unprotected in an open fighting compartment. The high silhouette of the Nashorn made it an easy target, but nonetheless, nearly five hundred were issued during 1943 and 1944.

The Nashorn was phased out with the introduction of the first really successful purpose designed German tank hunter, the Jagdpanzer IV.

Manufactured by Vomag, this sleek machine boasted low silhouette, an 88mm gun, a machine gun for close defence, and gave its crew the all round protection of thick, well sloped armour. The first really effective purpose designed tank killer had arrived, but in 1944, it had arrived too late to tip the balance.

The allied bombing campaigns, now paralysing Germany's industry, limited the numbers produced to just under 1800. By this stage of the war, that was never going to be enough to stem the tide of armour flooding in against Germany from every side.

To complement the Panzerjaeger IV in these last ditch battles, the Czech manufacturers, Praga, finally managed to produce a first class tank destroyer. This was the Hetzer. Much smaller than the Panzerjaeger IV, it nonetheless packed a highly effective 76mm gun. Coupled with very good sloping armour, excellent mobility and a very low silhouette, this small vehicle, which resembled a miniature Panzerjaeger, was deceptively powerful and was much loved by its crews.

Fortunately for the Germans, Praga were an efficient manufacturer and two thousand five hundred machines reached the hard pressed front lines.

Supplied in even more limited numbers was the next machine to emerge from the German armament industry - the Jagdpanther. Based on the successful chassis tank design for the Panther tank, by following the principle of dispensing with the turret, the Jagdpanther could carry a high velocity 88mm gun (as opposed to the 76mm gun of the ordinary Panther). Its superb sloped armour gave the Jagdpanther enormous defensive advantages, a relatively low silhouette and a fearsome attacking power. However, production difficulties meant only three hundred and fifty of this type, the best tank destroyer of the war, ever reached the front.

In even shorter supply than the Jagdpanther was the cumbersome Jagdtiger, a veritable fortress on tracks. In keeping with the German practice of mounting larger guns into turretless tanks, the Jagdtiger mounted a massive high velocity 128mm gun which was so powerful it could destroy any allied tank on the battlefield at almost any range. Fortunately for the allies, only forty eight were produced and these so late in the war that even their massive firepower could not hope to thwart the inevitable tide of defeat. Most were destroyed by their own crews when they ran out of fuel, broke down or had fired the last of their ammunition.

The first tank hunters proved barely adequate for the job. As the war progressed, they became increasingly efficient culminating in the highly effective Jagdpanther. There were simply never enough machines to hold back the tide.

THE WEAPONS OF WAR

The Wespe or Wasp 10.5cm on the Panzer II chassis.

5. STURMARTILLERIE

As the war wore on, and Germany's situation grew increasingly desperate, her hard pressed armies found themselves facing superior firepower from increasingly heavy enemy artillery. To combat this, the Wehrmacht needed a variety of mobile gun platforms, capable of moving heavy artillery to hard pressed sections over the vast battlefields of Russia.

A successful adaptation of the Panzer I chassis, was the re-design which allowed it to carry a heavy 15cm gun, to produce heavy self propelled artillery support which could be moved right up to the front line - this was the sig 33.

These self propelled guns were first deployed in the campaign for France during 1940 and proved highly successful. There was one major drawback, in the arrangement of such a big gun on such a small chassis. It was so top heavy that the gun was very liable to topple over. This undignified trait led to the search for a better alternative. Naturally, the first step was to examine the larger Panzer II chassis.

Like the Panzer I, the Panzer II chassis was also developed as a self propelled gun carriage. In this respect, the Panzer II worked only a little better than the Panzer I. Although it gave a slightly lower profile, and hence better stability and a greater

The Hummel or Bumble Bee - one of the new breed of self-propelled artillery.

measure of protection to the crew, it was only manufactured in tiny quantities. Only twelve were made and all appear to have been dispatched to Africa to equip the Afrika Korps.

Neither the Panzer I or the Panzer II chassis could really deal with the requirement of the heavy 15cm gun. The lateral solution to the problem was found by reducing the weight of the gun from 15cm to 10.5cm. This produced the Wespe, which was a 10.5cm gun on a Panzer II chassis, an excellent design which was light enough to keep up with the troops, but heavy enough to produce an effective barrage. Six hundred and eighty two of these were produced from 1942 and 1944.

With the introduction of the Wespe, the possibilities for the Panzer II appear to have been exhausted. German engineers moved on to examine the possibilities inherent in the Panzer III, Germany's main battle tank in the early years of the war. This proved to be a much more fertile hunting ground.

For artillery support, the Panzer III chassis yielded the Hummel or Bumble Bee, which used the Panzer III chassis to carry a heavy 15cm gun for mobile artillery bombardment. This vehicle overcame all of the drawbacks of the previous self propelled gun and 666 machines entered service - there was a huge demand for the front line units and there were enough to go round.

These excellent machines could give mobile artillery support to the hard pressed panzer divisions, then quickly move location before they could be targeted by the superior numbers of allied artillery.

In total, some thirteen hundred of these two types of self propelled guns were made from 1942 to 1945, giving essential artillery support to the great advances of 1942 and covering fire for the desperate Wehrmacht divisions during their headlong retreat into Germany, during 1944 and 1945.Although the 4.7 was more effective than the puny 3.7, which originally equipped the Panzer III, it was still feeble compared to the 75mm gun of a Russian T-34. In addition, the open fighting compartment gave only limited protection to the crew.

CHAPTER 6
VON MANSTEIN'S MIRACLE

After Stalingrad the full fury of the Russian counter-offensive was unleashed against the retreating Germans. The jubilant Russian forces now surged westwards to bring the fight to the enemy. To the north of Voronezh the Soviet attack had taken Kursk by 7th February. Kharkov fell on the 16th despite the orders of Hitler that it be held to the last man. A major push southwards towards the Sea of Azov and westwards towards the River Dnieper, threatened to completely encircle the remaining forces of Army Group Don and the section of Army Group A which had escaped from the Caucasus.

The numbers with which the Russians attacked and the speed of their advance now proved their downfall. Crippled by lack of transport bogged down in the early thaw and short of supplies, the Soviet thrust suddenly ran out of steam only thirty miles from the Dnieper crossing. Von Manstein immediately seized his opportunity and launched a series of brilliant counter-attacks. Von Manstein set about methodically chopping off

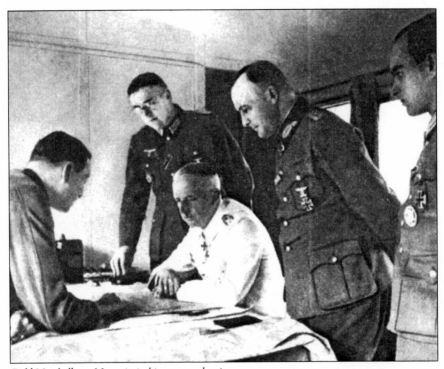

Field Marshall von Manstein in his command train.

the spearheads of the Russian attack, and, by doing so was able to stabilise the German front.

Only a month after being re-taken by the Russians, Kharkov was once again in German hands. By 19th March, Belgorod, more than fifty miles north east of Kharkov, was also retaken. The thaw was now in full flood and the annual spring lull descended on the whole of the Eastern Front. For the German army it marked the close of a disastrous winter campaign. The Caucasus had been lost as well as a large section of the Donets Basin and the strategic Don Bend. 6th Army had been destroyed, four other Axis armies had been gutted and Stalingrad now lay 500 miles to the west of the German lines.

Yet, in the end, the German generals counted themselves lucky that the situation was not far worse. Once again during the winter of 1943 the Germans had found themselves retreating, having come tantalising close to reaching their ambitious objectives.

The twin failures of Stalingrad and the Caucasus were enormous psychological bombshells for German morale. The German army's belief in its own invincibility, dented by the retreat from Moscow, had now completely disintegrated. As supreme war-lord, most of the blame for this lay squarely on the shoulders of Adolf Hitler.

However, while the military tactics of Hitler were proving increasingly impossible for his generals to stomach, the political blunderings of the brutal and debauched administrators of occupied Russia were presenting them with a problem no less indigestible. For long stretches of the previous year, as many as twenty four divisions of the German Army had been diverted to attempting to suppress the growing menace of partisan sabotage. The rapid massacre of Soviet Jews, the indiscriminate torture and slaying of simple resistance, had totally backfired against the Reichskommisars of the conquered territories. Far from inducing a paralysing terror it produced the best recruiting programme the partisans could wish for.

In May of 1942 the first attempt was made to co-ordinate the disparate bands of partisans which had formed in response to the savage "Untermensch" policies of the German occupation. Republican and regional partisan headquarters were set up and an official liaison between the movement and the Red Army was established for the first time. This meant that the activities of the partisans could now be directed against objectives of crucial importance to the overall military strategy.

By 1943 the conditions of the Russian troops at the front had improved tremendously. The spring lull meant that soldiers who had gone for months without washing could now visit the steam baths, which had been erected behind the lines. The break in the fighting gave the field tailors' shops the chance to repair damaged uniforms, sped up the delivery of the precious letters from home and allowed the exhausted troops a much needed period of rest and relaxation. While the conditions of the Russian soldiers continued to improve as the war wore on, the lot of their German counterparts, began to deteriorate. In fact by the spring of 1943, the German army in the East was almost on the point of collapse.

In March, the Eastern Front, still extending from Finland in the North, to the Black Sea in the South, was almost half a million men short of establishment. Divisional strength had been reduced from nine to six battalions, while the casualty rate among experienced officers and NCOs had been particularly high.

Equipment levels were low, by February only five hundred German tanks remained serviceable and most of these were still inferior to the Russian T34s.

The situation in the panzer brigades became so desperate that Hitler was forced to recall General Heinz Guderian to active service. Guderian, one of the most able and audacious of the panzer leaders had been dismissed from his command in the winter of

The sudden Russian advances hard on the heels of the Stalingrad battle had to be stemmed quickly.

The medium mortar provided the mobile artillery support which the Red Army relied upon for even the most minor attack. A skilled operator could keep three bombs in the air at a time.

1941, ironically for withdrawing forces without permission. He was now charged with responsibility for "the future development of the armoured troops along lines that will make that arm of the service into a decisive weapon for winning the war".

Guderian was encouraged by the continued upswing in the production of the Panzer VI "Tiger" tanks, fifty six tons of well armoured mobile artillery armed with a modification of the devastation 8.8cm anti-aircraft gun. The tiger boasted a top speed of 23mph on the road. In addition to the Tiger, the appearance of the Panzer V 'Panther' gave the Germans qualitative parity with the Russians for the first time since the beginning of the war. The Panther, weighing forty five tons, was lighter and more mobile than the Tiger with a top speed of 34mph but its high velocity 7.5cm gun possessed considerable penetrative ability. Improved assault guns and tank destroyers were also appearing. Also taking into account the upgunning of the Panzer Marks III and IV, Guderian felt that his forces had a chance of winning the battle for Kursk. Although Germany could not supply these weapons in the same quantities as the Russians, it was hoped that their possession by experienced crews would offset Soviet numerical superiority.

Guderian's need for time to reorganise and re-equip the panzer divisions mirrored the requirements of the German army as a whole. The idea of any immediate victory in Russia was now simply the stuff of rhetoric.

Given the inability of the German army to defend its complete front, such a draw could not be achieved by defensive tactics. The reverses to be imposed on the Red Army would have to be forced by a series of limited assaults. Von Manstein's counter-attacks which had prevented complete disaster during the previous winter had impressed

Hitler. He was invited to put forward a plan for the crucial summer campaign.

Von Manstein presented Hitler with two offensive alternatives.

The first was to prepare for a Soviet assault which would almost certainly be launched in the Ukraine and withdraw before it. Wheeling to the left, German forces would them mount a decisive attack on its exposed Northern flank, encircling the leading spearhead of the Russian advance.

The second alternative was to cut off the enormous Soviet salient which had emerged to the North of Kharkov and to the South of Orel - a bulge extending 70 miles westwards from Kursk and measuring approximately one hundred miles in width.

Hitler chose the second alternative despite the dilemma which it posed for the attacking forces. It was vital to attack before the Soviet generals got wind of the plan and could prepare defences. It was also crucial to von Manstein that the offensive be launched before the Russians recovered from the losses incurred the previous winter. On the other hand, if the attack were to take place in mid-May, as von Manstein insisted, German manpower and equipment might not be sufficient to ensure victory.

Guderian was against the operation from the start, arguing that the new Panther and Tiger tanks must be held back until they were available in sufficient quantities "to ensure a decisive success". Hitler postponed the date of the attack until July, in the hope that by then the number of new tanks would tip the balance of firepower in Germany's favour.

By now Russian Air Force reconnaissance had improved to the point where Stalin's awareness of German dispositions was comprehensive and generally accurate. Stalin's agents had also managed to infiltrate German headquarters and he was supplied with additional intelligence by his spy ring in Switzerland, code named 'Lucy', which had many high levels contacts inside Germany. Stalin's knowledge of German preparations was so precise he even knew the date chosen by Hitler for the launch of Operation 'Citadel'.

Stalin, advised by Zhukov, prepared patiently and thoroughly for the German advance. The Soviet lines consisted of six belts of defenders composed of anti-tank posts, thick minefields and 3,000 miles of trenches supported by 3,000 tanks and 20,000 guns.

The German assessment of the quality of the Russian guns and tanks were later described from bitter personal experience from Rauss.

"The efficiency of the Russian artillery varied greatly during the various stages of the war. In the beginning it was unable to achieve an effective concentration of fire, and furthermore was unenthusiastic about firing on targets in the depth of the battle position even when there was excellent observation. The Rogachev water tower, for

As the war progressed, the T-34 was up-gunned with a fearsome 85mm weapon.

example, and the railroad control towers, as well as the high embankment at Zhlobin, all of which were in Russian hands during the battle in the Dnepr-Berezina triangle, commanded a view over the entire area for many miles, nevertheless, they were not used for directing fire on the very important targets behind the German lines. On the Kandalaksha front, continuous German supply transport, operations at the Karhu railroad station took place within sight of Russian observation posts. These operations were never taken under fire by Russian artillery. On the other hand, the Russian artillery liked to distribute its fire over the front lines, and occasionally shelled a road intersection located not too far from the front.

During the course of the war the artillery also developed to a high degree the use of mass as a particularly characteristic procedure. Infantry attacks without artillery preparation were rare. Short preparatory concentrations lasting only a few minutes, frequently employed by the Germans to preserve the elements of surprise, seemed insufficient to the Russians. Thus, counting on the destructive effect of massed fire, they consciously accepted the fact that the Germans would recognise their intentions of attacking. Russian artillery fire often had no primary targets but covered the entire area with the same intensity. The Russian artillery was most vulnerable to counter-battery fire. It ceased firing or changed position after only a few rounds from the German guns.

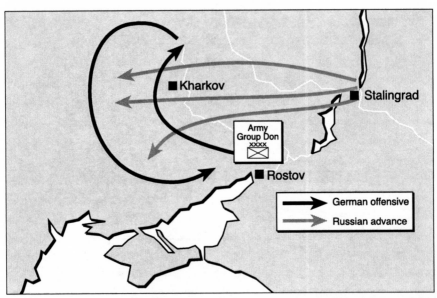

Von Manstein was able to stabilise the situation at the front in a masterpiece of tactical manoeuvring, which left the lead elements of the advancing Red Army forces isolated from their supply lines. The weakened Russian forces were then defeated in detail and a new front line ranging rest of Kharkov was established.

The rigidity of the fire plan, and a certain immobility of the Soviet artillery - at least during the first years of the war - was pronounced. Only in rare cases was the artillery successful in promptly following the infantry. Most of the time the artillery was unable to follow up; it remained stuck in the old positions, leaving the infantry without fire support. This practice frequently took the momentum out of the Russian attacks.

Attack tactics of Russian artillery improved constantly during the war. Eventually, however, their tactics resolved into an ever-repeated, set scheme. Heavy preparatory fire, laid down broad and deep and lasting from one to two hours, was the initial phrase; it rapidly mounted to murderous intensity. Once an attack was about to get under way, the Russians would suddenly lift their fire from very narrow lanes (about eighty to one hundred yards wide) along which the infantry was to advance. At all other points the fire continued with undiminished fury. Only the most careful German observation allowed recognition of those lanes. This method gave the impression that artillery preparation was still continuing in full force, though in reality the infantry attack had already begun. Here again, one notes the same concept, human lives meant nothing at all. If defensive fire forced the Russian infantry out of their narrow lanes, or if their own artillery was unable to maintain the lanes accurately - Nichevo! - those were operating expenses.

However, despite many shortcomings, the Russian artillery was a very good and extremely dangerous arm. Its fire was effective, rapid and accurate. Particularly during the large-scale attacks in the summer of 1944 it became apparent that the Russians had learned well how to mass and employ large artillery units. Establishment of a definite point at which to concentrate their efforts and the use of superior masses of artillery, crushed the thin lines of German opposition in many places at the Eastern Front before the actual attack had begun. This successful procedure of establishing definite points of main effort will be used by the Russians in the future, whenever they have the masses of artillery and ammunition required.

The heart of the Russian armoured force was the well-known T34 tank. Because of its wide tracks, its powerful engine, and its low silhouette, the performance of the T34 in Russian terrain was frequently superior to that of the German tanks, particularly with respect to cross-country mobility. To the surprise of all the German experts, the T34 easily negotiated terrain theoretically secure against mechanised attack. The calibre of its guns was too small however, and forced the Russians to produce several new types of tanks (KVI and Stalin) which, like the German models, became successively heavier. Despite all improvements the new tanks remained on the whole, inferior to the T34. The Russians recognised this fact, and continued to mass produce the T34 until the end of the war.

Not until late did the Russians decide to launch concentrated attacks by large tank forces. During the first years of the war, Russian tanks generally were used for local infantry support. Soviet tank attacks as such took place only after a sufficient number of the vehicles had become available. Here too, the Russians adhered to their usual habit of employing great masses of men and machines.

Tank attacks generally were not conducted at a fast enough pace. Frequently they were not well enough adapted to the nature of the terrain. These facts the Germans noted time and again through the entire war.

The training of the individual tank driver was inadequate; the training period apparently was too short, and losses in experienced drivers were too high. The Russian avoided driving his tank through hollows or along reverse slopes, preferring to choose a route along the crests which would give fewer driving difficulties. This practice remained unchanged even in the face of unusually high tank losses. Thus the Germans were in most cases able to bring the Russian tanks under fire at long range, and to inflict losses even before the battle had begun. Slow and uncertain driving and numerous firing halts made the Russian tanks good targets. Premature firing on the Russian tanks, though wrong in principle, was always the German solution in those instances. If the German defence was ready and adequate, the swarms of Russian tanks began to thin out very quickly in most cases. This fault in Russian tank tactics can be corrected only by peacetime training, but it can hardly be totally eliminated.

On the whole, the Russian armoured force was not as good as the Russian artillery. Limited flexibility, and the inability of the subordinate commanders to exploit favourable situations rapidly and adroitly, were evident and frequently prevented the Russians from achieving successes almost within their grasp. Toward the end of the war, however, the inadequate facilities of the Germans were no longer able to stand up against the masses of equipment of the Reds."

With every passing moment, the successful outcome of the Kursk offensive grew more necessary for Hitler. German morale, depleted by the failures at Stalingrad and in the Caucasus, was now further undermined by the field defeat in North Africa. Hitler's inability to adequately supply Rommel with men and materials led to disaster at Medenine in March, and the eventual collapse of the Axis African forces in May. Southern Europe now lay totally exposed to the threat of Allied attack. In Britain, the RAF and the American Air Force prepared to launch massive bombing raids against German industrial and civilian targets, as a prelude to invasion from the West. Hitler not only needed a victory at Kursk, he needed victory on a scale which would allow him the breathing space to fend off the enemies which were beginning to close around him. Anything less would prove a catastrophe.

On the Russian side, for the first time, the Red Army would be prepared for a major German offensive. It was determined to make the most of its advantage.

On July 5th 1943, as von Manstein and von Kluge approached the Kursk salient in a classic pincer movement involving one million men and two thousand seven hundred tanks, the "death-ride" of the panzers was about to commence.

Adolf Hitler was fully aware of the absolute necessity of success at Kursk but when the roaring waves of German armour crashed into the salient in July 1943, the attack which the German army was about to unleash was already doomed to failure. The essence of von Manstein's strategy for the battle had been to exploit the mobility and tactical superiority of the German panzer units. Instead, the German tanks drove confidently toward a grinding war attrition where the advantage lay squarely with the defenders.

The effectiveness of a Russian defence which limited the progress of von Kluge's 9th Army to an advance of some six miles. It was then ground to a halt by Rokossovsky's Central Front to the north of the Kursk salient. In the south von Manstein's 4th Panzer Army advanced 25 miles by the 10th of July and threatened to penetrate the Voronezh Front under Vatutin. Reserves from the Steppe Front to the north had to be pumped

The first Tiger tanks to reach the front appeared in the winter of 1942/3. Their numbers were very small.

into the battle to bolster the salient's defenders and prevent the 4th Panzer from breaking through into open country.

After the war Rauss was able to bring together a number of sources to present a comprehensive picture of the Kursk battle for the operational level.

"Equally instructive was the Russian conduct of battle in the defence against the German pincers attack on Kursk in July 1943. The exhaustion on both sides after the preceding long winter battles led at this sector of the front to a pause of three months, which both opponents used to replenish their forces and to prepare for Operation Zitadelle. The Russians expected the attack precisely at the location and in the manner in which it was undertaken, and prepared their defence accordingly.

Behind the most endangered sectors, opposite Byelgorod and Orel, they constructed defence systems of hitherto unknown depth, and strengthened them with all kinds of obstacles. To be prepared against surprise armoured thrusts, all points susceptible to penetration were safeguarded up to a depth of 30 miles by fully manned anti-tank gun fronts, anti-tank ditches, mine fields, and tanks in emplacement's, in such numbers and strength that to overcome them could have called for great sacrifices and much time. Behind the pressure points north of Byelgorod and south of Kursk, sufficient local forces stood ready everywhere. Noteworthy were the numerous alternative firing positions and the fact that the bulk of the numerous Russian artillery pieces were kept as far to the rear as their maximum range allowed, so as to escape counter-battery fire from German heavy howitzer batteries and to be able, in case of reverses, to support the infantry as long as possible. The Russian batteries preferred firing positions in forests, or in orchards adjacent to inhabited localities. For mobile operations, the Russians very adroitly employed multi-barrelled rocket projectors. Strong strategic reserves were assembled farthest east, in the region of the Oskol River, in such a manner that after the attacked German divisions had exhausted themselves in the above-mentioned defence system, the reserves could launch a counter-attack, or, at worst, contain an enemy break-through. In the bulge extending far to the west, however, the enemy had stationed only weak and inferior forces, which were not backed by any deep defence system. During the long waiting period each side learned about the other's situation, and intentions down to the last details. The Russians, for instance, broadcast to the German lines by loud-speaker the secret day and hour of attack well in advance, and in the sane manner announced two postponements of the offensive. Nevertheless, the German attack was carried out at the precise point at which the Russians expected it. As anticipated, it did not develop into a dynamic offensive but became a slow wrestling match with an enemy firmly clinging to a maze of trenches and bunkers - an enemy who, unshaken by preparatory fire, offered dogged resistance. Many positions could

Cossack cavalry units were useful to infiltrate German lines and caused mayhem in the logistics and back-up services.

only be taken after prolonged hand grenade duels. The Russians employed stronger tank forces only against what they guessed to be the weakest point in the German attack wedge - the flank of XI Infantry Corps which attacked on the right wing. Every one of these counter-attacks was repulsed.

On the very first day of the attack, 5 July 1943, several German divisions each sustained losses up to 1,000 dead and wounded. The german armour too, suffered substantial losses each day from the strong anti-tank defenses and mine fields. This, as well as the divergent directions of thrust of the various corps, visibly diminished the momentum of the German attack. When, after about 2 weeks of bloody fighting, there was no longer any hope of reaching the desired objectives, and when German forces even began to meet reverses in the Orel area, the attack was called off, and previous territorial gains were relinquished. By excellent organisation of defences, and adroit conduct of battle, the Russians had brought about the collapse of the German offensive. Shortly thereafter they launched a counter-offensive with fresh reserves and effected a major break-through. The Germans had fallen into Zhukov's cunningly prepared trap. As Guderian acknowledged "By the failure of Citadel we had suffered a decisive defeat. The armoured formations, reformed and re-equipped with much effort had lost heavily in both manpower and equipment and would now be unemployable for a long time to come. There was the real prospect that they would never be rehabilitated in time to

Russian troops advance past the billowing clouds of smoke from a knocked out German tank destroyer.

defend the Eastern Front. From now on the Russians were in undisputed possession of the initiative".

The biggest gamble of Hitler's career was destined for failure. In the north the effective Russian defence limited the progress of von Kluge's 9th Army to an advance of just six miles, before it ground to a halt. In the south von Manstein's 4th Panzer Army advanced twenty-five miles and by the 10th of July threatened to penetrate the Voronezh Front under General Vatutin. Reserves from the Steppe Front to the north had to be pumped into the battle to bolster the defenders and prevent the 4th Panzer from breaking through into open country, but it was not enough.

THE KEY BATTLES
4. THE CITADEL OFFENSIVE

Once von Manstein had managed to stabilise the situation on the southern flank of the German army, a short period of relative calm prevailed from April 1943 through to the end of June. During this much needed respite, the battered German divisions were able to regroup and draw breath for the coming summer campaign which had all the hallmarks of a campaign which would produce the deciding moment in the war.

This was certainly how Hitler viewed the great offensive which was to be given the code name operation Citadel "It makes my stomach churn to think of it" was how Hitler summed up the coming offensive to his generals but he, like them, saw no option to a further offensive in the East. The Germans knew that an Allied landing on the Italian mainland was imminent and a quick decision in the East had now become imperative. The Germans also knew that the Red Army had several tank armies concentrated into the Kursk salient which pointed straight to the heart of the German front lines. If these forces were not attacked soon, they would themselves be capable of a huge offensive which the overstretched German army would be lucky to escape. The intelligence certainly proved correct in this instance, as some 40 per cent of the Red Army's battle strength had been brought together into this relatively small area. If this massive concentration could be annihilated, it would have meant a severe blow for the Russian war effort. For once the high command could not deny the wisdom of Hitler's analysis of the operational situation but they were united in their demands that the blow must be struck as soon as possible.

The Russians were renowned for their ability to construct huge defensive works of enormous strength and depth, this is precisely what was happening in the Kursk salient, and it was obvious that delays would be fatal to the offensive. If there was one dissenting voice to the clamour for an early offensive it was that of Guderian. Newly restored to favour, Guderian was now Inspector of Armour and as such, was acutely aware of the disparity in quality between the German tanks and those of the Russians. In order to rectify the situation, work was continuing at top speed to produce as many Tiger tanks as possible and to bring the new medium/heavy

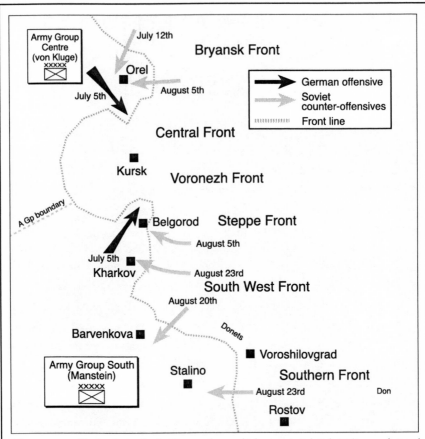

The two great offensive thrusts by the German forces which came on July 5th 1943 were designed to encircle the bulge into German lines continued onto the city of Kursk.

Panther tanks into action. In order to achieve this Guderian needed time, and the operation was frequently postponed and passed the favoured May date of the high command. Most of the high command would have settled for the earlier launch date for the offensive, if even without the benefit of the new heavy tanks, but Hitler had a childlike belief in the power of new weapons to achieve decisive and unexpected results. He had very high expectations of the effectiveness of the new battle tanks and it would appear that despite all his concerns he genuinely believed that the new tanks would be sufficient in themselves to bring him success in the battle which, even Hitler must have known was his last great gamble in the East.

The two army groups which were chosen to make the great offensive were drawn, one each, from Army Group Centre and Army Group South.

Drawn from Army Group Centre commanded by Field Marshal von kluge, was the 9th Army which was to be commanded by General Model. It was to attack the North flank of the great salient and drive on towards the town of Kursk, to meet up with the southern wing of the great offensive.

The southern wing of the offensive was drawn from Army Group South commanded by Field Marshal von Manstein, and was composed of the 4th Panzer Army along with Army Detachment Kempf. Commanded by a Colonel-General Hoth it was to strike from the town of Belgorod in the area just north of Kharkov and again drive towards Kursk where it was planned that the two pincers of the giant offensive should meet.

These meticulous preparations for Operation Citadel are an indication of just how important this offensive had become. Every tiny detail was worked out in advance and the forces which were deployed for this singled battle contained almost as many tanks and were supported by as many aircraft as those which had been assembled for the launch of Operation Barbarossa on June 22nd, 1941. Von Manstein's southern wing of the offensive had almost 1500 tanks and assault guns at its disposal and in the North von Kluge had almost as many.

Hitler was aware of the vital need for secrecy in the coming offensive. He is reported as telling his generals on July 1st "this time we must make absolutely sure that none of our intentions are betrayed again, either through our own carelessness or by neglect". In this respect Hitler was to be disappointed, thanks to their highly effective intelligence gathering network, the Russians had a complete knowledge of the timing and detail of the operation, which was to be ground to a standstill on the massive defensive works of the Red Army.

At first light on 5th July, 1943 the great offensive finally got underway. The northern wing made very little progress achieving a penetration of little more than six kilometres into the Russian defences. In the South the troops fighting under Hoth managed to drive some 25 kilometres into the Soviet defensive positions and extra Russian reinforcements had to be hurriedly thrown into position. It was on this sector of the front that the great tank battle of Prokhorovka took place. A gigantic collection of Russian and German armour which saw a huge swirling melee as the Tigers and Panthers clashed with the T-34s. Prokhorovka, like many of the actions in operation citadel proved bloody but indecisive, the sides were so finely balanced that neither could gain the decisive edge. At the tactical level on the battlefield, but strategically the losses suffered by the Germans, could never be made good and every tank destroyed brought the Russians closer to victory. The inability to achieve the decisive breakthrough and encircle the Russian forces was tantamount to a defeat for the Germans. The tenacity of the Russian resistance finally won the day and Hitler was forced to abandon the offensive on 22nd July. Even before that day Russian counter-offensives had begun both in the north and south.

German armour was certainly superior in quality but the Wehrmacht could never match the Red Army for the sheer numbers of machines which could be put into the field.

German infantry pass Tiger tanks in the build up to Operation Citadel.

5. THE TIGER

The armoured might of Hitler's Wehrmacht on the Russian Front will be forever associated with its most famous tank - the Panzerkampfwagen VI - better known to a fearful world, as the Tiger. Like its namesake, the Tiger was a rare beast and in its field, it was every bit as deadly. A hunter and killer of unmatched ferocity, it was born out of the urgent need to produce a counter to the Russian T-34 and KV-1, both of which were encountered in 1941.

The Tiger had been developed in 1940 and 1941, too late to benefit from all of the lessons from the Russian war, so it had the uncompromisingly flat-frontal armour, which didn't deflect shots away from the vehicle. But it was so very heavily armoured that the Tiger was almost impervious to most Russian guns at all but the closest ranges and it carried the deadly 88mm gun, then the best weapon on the battlefield. The makers manual proclaimed that the 88mm was one hundred per cent accurate at ranges of up to one thousand metres.

On the battlefield the Tiger soon proved its deadly efficiency, but there were never enough machines to equip all of the panzer divisions, so the Tigers were initially organised into special heavy tank companies of seventeen tanks, and later

The Tiger had uncompromisingly flat armour at the front of the vehicle. Sloped armour is much better for deflecting shots aiming for the vehicle. In the case of the Tiger however, the armour was so thick that it stopped most hits in any event.

into heavy battalions, called Shwere Abteilungs of forty five machines, which could be rushed from place to place on the hard pressed front, wherever they were most desperately needed.

The highly efficient Nazi propaganda trumpeted the arrival of the Tiger and, for once, the results justified the rhetoric. The training manual which dealt with the Tiger was very specific on the subject of how they were to be employed in battle.

"The terrific firepower, strong armour, high cross-country ability and high over-running power are the characteristics of the heavy Panzerkampfwagen in the TigerKompanie. They enable the company:

- to attack in the first wave against strong defences
- to destroy heavy enemy tanks and other armoured targets already at long ranges
- to decisively defeat the enemy defences
- to break through positions reinforced by defensive works

All German teachings stressed that the most important task of the Tiger companies was the engagement of enemy tanks, as the excellent combination of the 88mm gun and strong armour, matched by reasonably high manoeuvrability. This made the Tiger the strongest combat weapon available to the Wehrmacht.

The Tiger manual also pointed out that the unmistakable noise of the Tiger's engine, travelled long distances, especially at night. Care needed to be taken, therefore, with wind direction and the location of assembly areas, which, in order to preserve the element of surprise, were to be as far distant from the front as possible.

In combat, the Tigers were to be sent into action at the crisis points of the battle where their presence would be decisive. It was decreed that all other weapons were merely there to support the heavy tanks in the tasks allocated to them.

From experience of combat, the tactics which proved most successful were for the lighter tanks to engage the enemy with their fire, while the Tigers launched a flank attack, using their superiority in firepower against the enemy tanks weakest points.

During battles in built-up areas, it was stressed that the Tiger was not to be

A propaganda drawing of the first Tigers in action. For once the results justified at least some of the rhetoric.

Pz Kpfw Tiger model B (the King Tiger).

sent into house-to-house fighting because of its vulnerability to infantry at close quarters. There was also the danger that the long protruding gun, would cause the tank to get stuck in narrow streets."

The main drawback of the Tiger was its chronic mechanical unreliability which saw a depressingly high number of machines out of action at any given time. Its large size and weight also made it liable to bog down in difficult terrain and broken down vehicles were very difficult to remove.

The tactics set out in the manual certainly worked on the battlefield. Although only eighty Tigers had been delivered by the end of January 1943, they were already credited with over four hundred kills.

It is interesting to note that only a small proportion of Tiger tanks were actually destroyed by Russian tanks. The vast majority either fell victim to infantry tank buster teams or had to be abandoned and destroyed by their crews when they experienced mechanical difficulties, bogged down or, more frequently, ran out of fuel.

Before they were swept away, the small groups of Tigers performed heroically. One man will always be associated with the Tiger. He was Michael Wittman of the 1st SS Panzer Division. Wittman was responsible for a huge number of Russian tank kills. By June 1944, Wittman and his Tiger had been responsible for more than one hundred and thirty Russian tanks, when they were transferred to the

Michael Wittman, the extraordinarily successful Tiger tank commander.

Western Front.

Due to the huge maintenance requirements, during 1944, on average, there were never more than seventy Tigers available for action on any given day on the whole of the Russian front. The remaining machines were either under short or long term repair. It was this tiny force which forged a legend.

Russian troops enjoy a break in the main square after the recapture of Kharkov in February 1943. This success would be short lived however, as the city was retaken by the Germans again in March 1943.

5. KHARKOV

The Soviet winter offensive of 1942 came as an enormous blow to the southern sector of the Eastern Front. In addition to the disastrous loss of the 6th Army at Stalingrad, an even more dangerous new situation was developing, as the battered German divisions were driven back towards the Dnieper river.

At this desperate juncture, the newly formed SS Panzer Corps took field for the first time. Hitler ordered that the Corps should be rushed to the Eastern front with all possible speed. This new Corps comprised of three divisions, the SS Leibstandarte Division, the SS Das Reich Division and the SS Totenkopf Division. All three of these elite formations had been reinforced and were lavishly equipped with the very best of the new heavy weapons including, in the case of the Leibstandarte Division, an entire battalion of the formidable Tiger tanks which were still in desperately short supply. They were also given top priority for movement across the crowded Russian rail network. This was a vital consideration which was necessary to overcome the severe congestion which characterised the overstretched German transport system as it tried to meet the ceaseless demands of the Eastern Front.

The forceful contribution of the SS Panzer Corps was felt immediately, as almost from the rail head, a strong attack was mounted on the Russian salient in the Kharkov area. The Totenkopf Division was in action almost as soon as it had formed up for battle. However, even the presence of the SS Panzer Corps was not enough to guarantee the beleaguered city of Kharkov would remain in German hands. Although the initial actions by the SS Panzer Corps had met with success, by 15th February 1943, it was obvious that the new SS Panzer Corps was about to be surrounded in Kharkov. Once again Hitler issued one of his infamous "hold firm" orders. Had the defenders of Kharkov carried out their orders, it is likely that their fate would have mirrored that of the defenders of Stalingrad. The first SS Panzer Corps were fortunate in their Commander, Paul Hausser, who was prepared to disobey Hitler in order to save his Corps from certain destruction. Against the express order of the Führer, he withdrew his men from the City, Kharkov was re-occupied amid great rejoicing by Soviet troops on 16th February 1943.

When he heard the news, Hitler was incandescent with rage and he personally flew to the headquarters of Army Group South in order to extract an explanation from Field Marshal von Manstein. The reputation of his own personal favourite formation had been tarnished, and during a long, furious rant, Hitler demanded the immediate recapture of Kharkov. It was now a matter of honour, the City had to be retaken in order to restore the reputation of the SS. Over the next few weeks, that was exactly what the SS Panzer Corps was able to deliver. Despite the prevailing operational situation, which was rapidly moving against the increasingly hard pressed German forces, the first SS Panzer Corps was able to execute an audacious counter-offensive. This involved a three pronged attack by each of the divisions in the Corps, which saw Kharkov firmly back in German hands by March 16th 1943. The fighting which led to the capture of Kharkov saw some of the most bitterly contested actions which the Leibstandarte was to encounter, in a career marked by extraordinarily bitter and vicious fighting. With the Soviet troops still elated from their capture of the city, it proved to be a difficult task to drive the determined defenders from the ready-made defensive positions amidst the rubble of the city, which had now changed hands twice in the space of as many months. The fierce battles which took place, often at suicidally short ranges, proved the mettle of SS Panzer Corps in their Führer's own eyes.

The recapture of Kharkov was to prove to be the last real success for the German arms on the Eastern Front. At the same time, the SS Panzer Corps had proved beyond doubt that it was a capable and potent battlefield formation. But the success at Kharkov also served to create a dangerous precedent. Hitler now became convinced that his Waffen SS formations were capable of achieving almost any task assigned to them. In the coming months and years, these already difficult tasks, would become increasingly impossible, as the thinly stretched resources were called upon to rescue situations which would have been beyond the ability of far larger formations. In the coming months and years, the SS Panzer Corps would continue to fight with bravery, but the road ahead now lay only downwards into defeat.

German troops march into captivity. It would be twelve years before the last survivors would see their homeland again.

CHAPTER 7
TURNING THE TIDE

Having enticed the Germans into the disastrous commitment to their armoured forces, and nullified their threat, the Red Army swiftly exploited the advantage. Even while the gargantuan tank struggle was still being bitterly contested, on the 12th July, the Russians counter- attack towards Orel was a mirror image of Kursk itself, a Russian salient project into territory in German hands. The redoubtable Army Group Centre, reinforced by units from the 4th Panzer Army which had broken off its attack on Kursk, attempted to check the advance.

But by now the Eastern Front was not the only theatre of disaster for the German armies. On the 10th July Allied Forces had invaded Sicily. By the 25th Mussolini had been arrested and a provisional Government set up in Italy. Fearing the defection of his Mediterranean ally Hitler desperately needed to make troops available for the defence of the Italian peninsula. In marked contrast to his previous orders to hold fire at all cost, he ordered an immediate withdrawal from the Orel Salient on August 1st 1943. By the 5th August the provincial capitals of Orel and Belgorod had been liberated by fresh Soviet thrusts.

Near Belgorod the Germans attempted a major counter-attack with sixty thousand troops.

At first, the unexpected German counter stroke succeeded in pushing back the Red Army, but the Russian tide of resurgence was irresistible. After clawing their way forward for ten days the German advance was again flung backward towards the Dnieper, and the great retreat was begun.

The all conquering German Army, which had disdainfully swept aside the Russian border defences only two years previously, was now struggling to maintain a presence in the field of battle. The Panzer units which had sliced the Red Army to pieces in the dazzling pincer movements of 1941, now hung on in the grim defensive battles of 1943 in the desperate hope of slowing the Russian progress. For the ordinary German soldiers the notion of victory ceased to have meaning, the survival became the central concern of their lives.

On the Russian side the liberation of the cities and towns was proving a bittersweet experience. In Orel the Soviet troops arrived to find half the town destroyed and all its bridges destroyed by the retreating Germans. Of the pre-war population of one hundred and fourteen thousand, only thirty thousand haggard souls survived to greet their saviours. Twenty five thousand had been sent as slaves to the labour camps of the Reich, twelve thousand had been murdered by their German overlords, and thousands had died from disease and starvation.

As the German forces began to move back, the Russian Partisan movement which had always been active, now really exploded into life. The partisans used demolition and harrying operations to draw thousands of German troops from the hard pressed front. The partisans now operated in military bands of thousands of resistance fighters which kept close communication ties with the army and the civilian population. Huge swathes of what was nominally German controlled territory were effectively reclaimed by the partisans.

One of the most constant and rewarding targets of the partisan operations were the German rail connections with the frontline. No matter what precautions the German army took, the partisans somehow managed to outwit them. Besides the actual damage they inflicted on German troops and their morale, the partisans offered hope and example to those still in the midst of Nazi tyranny. Zoia Kosmodemianskaia, an eighteen year old member of the Moscow Komsomol was caught setting fire to German stables in the village of Pestriehevo. Although tortured, she revealed nothing about her comrades to the German interrogators. As she was led to the gallows with a placard around her neck describing her crime, she turned to her German captors and

Confident smiles as the Red Army prepares to turn the tables on Hitler.

proclaimed defiantly "You can't hang all 190 million of us!"

The story of Zoia was circulated widely and she became a national heroine. Zoia grew to be a symbol not only of partisan resistance but of Russian defiance in the face of the most terrible adversity.

Despite the suffering which the German invasion had brought, the people of the Soviet Union had taken everything that the Germans could throw at them and the nation had held. By now the majority of the population were willing cogs in a gigantic war machine. Civilians and soldiers alike seemed to grasp a new awareness of their role in the bitter conflict which raged all around them.

The authorities continuously attempted to control the morale and attitudes of the front line troops by the almost obsessional production of reading matter. Newspapers were printed on a portable plant which moved around with the troops. Each Front, each army and each division produced its own newspaper. The Moscow Defence produced the Red Star paper and the national newspapers were also distributed to the soldiers.

The mood of the retreating Germans was one of intense frustration and manic desperation, each man knowing he was staring death in the face. Their fury at certain death was unleashed towards civilians and soldiers alike. The Germans had been decisively defeated but the brutality was far from over.

The only hope for the armies of the Reich in the midst of this desperate retreat now lay in holding the line of the River Dnieper. "Sometimes we would try to run away; but orders, adroitly worded and spaced soothed us like shots of morphine. On the Dnieper we were told "Everything will be easier. Ivan won't be able to force the barrage, so courage and do your best to hold him, if you want everyone to get through. The Russian counter-offensive will be crushed on the Dnieper and then we will resume our push to the East."

Even though a strategic withdrawal to the Dnieper seemed the only possible option for the ragged German formations, Hitler initially stuck to his policy of holding territory to "the last man". von Tippelskirch, one of the German generals in the East, summed up the helpless rage of the Field Commanders forced to sacrifice men and material to a principle of no withdrawal, which had now been elevated to a moral necessity. "A series of withdrawals by adequately large steps would have worn down the Russian strength, besides creating opportunities for counter strokes when the German forces were still numerous enough to make them effective..... The root cause of German defeat was the way her forces were wasted in fruitless efforts and above all, fruitless resistance at the wrong time and place."

By the 23rd of August, Kharkov was once again in Russian hands, by the 30th Taganrog had fallen. The capture of Donbass was followed by Novrossisk and by the

25th September Smolensk had also been re-taken. In the face of this depressing string of defeats, the waters of the Dnieper represented the only possibility of regrouping the decimated German divisions.

For the pursuing Red Army the liberation of the towns and villages east of the Dnieper continued to fill the hearts of its soldiers with a succession of contrasting emotions, the scenes of devastation and cruelty on a scale never even considered before, pits full of dead children and the starved remains of whole families could only make their determination to totally crush their opposition complete.

Even in retreat the élite units of the German Army, such as the Gross Deutschland Division, managed to maintain something of their reputations by mounting a ferocious defence of the German rear.

But the Dnieper was not to prove the refuge the battered German troops had been promised. Even as their defensive perimeter finally withdrew to the rivers edge, they found the Russians already established there. Goaded onwards by their commanders, by the atrocities they had witnessed, and the prospect of sweeping the enemy from the Motherland, the Russians swiftly overcame the German rear guard and immediately prepared to continue their pursuit. Between the 22nd and 30th September the Russians had forced numerous crossings of the 300 mile stretch of river between the Pripyat Marshes and Zaporozhe.

Further south by 23rd October, Zaporozhe and Melitopol were taken by the Russians and the 17th Army was isolated in the Crimea, reducing the dwindling strength of the German eastern forces by a further quarter of a million. To the north Kiev fell on 6th November threatening the northern flank of Army Group South's defence of the Dnieper bend. This Soviet pressure continued throughout November and December. Despite von Manstein's pleas to abandon what was now a vulnerable salient, Hitler remained adamant that the Dnieper bend was to be held at all costs.

By the New Year of 1944 the line of German resistance, from the Baltic to the Black Sea, had either collapsed, or was suffering such Russian pressure as to make it untenable.

To compound matters, in Italy the allies had landed on September 3rd and were battling their way up the peninsula.

Back in Germany, the Reich was experiencing destruction from the air on a scale never before experienced by any nation at war. In the first major blow against Hamburg, thirty thousand people perished in a series of raids which left many more scarred and burned. Hamburg was swept by a holocaust which created such intense firestorms that tornadoes were formed which sucked living people into the flames.

By late 1943 the concept of fortress locations which could be held to the last man had become a fixture in Hitler's warped outlook. By the end of December 1943 - with Kiev retaken by the enemy and a Russian bulge extending as far west as Zhitomir - the German forces in the Dnepr bend were ordered to hold their positions at all costs. XLII Corps (Map 4), on the right flank of First Panzer Army, had been under persistent enemy attack since 26 December when some of the Russian forces recently engaged in the battle for Kiev were shifted south and renewed their pressure against the corps sector. To the right, Eighth Army's XI Corps, the 5th SS Panzer Division *Wiking* as its left flank, was likewise engaged in heavy defensive fighting along its entire front. Both corps had the specific mission of continuing to hold their front lines against superior Russian forces in order to assure a favorable base for a projected German counteroffensive. To the left of XLII Corps, VII Corps had been operating against the flank of the Russian bulge. Since about 20 December the corps had been attacking in a westerly direction, but without achieving any significant results.

The situation of XLII and XI Corps, their most advanced elements fighting along the Dnepr and their long exterior flanks inadequately secured, was certain to invite attempts by the enemy to encircle and annihilate both corps. As early as mid-December the commander of XLII Corps had requested authority to fall back behind the Ross River. This would have meant that, instead of having to defend a frontage of seventy-five miles with two divisions, the corps would have been able to occupy a shortened defensive position behind a natural obstacle. However, that request was turned down.

Nevertheless, XLII Corps had taken a few precautionary measures during December. Two rear positions had been prepared north of the Ross River, east of Boguslav, which were to prove very useful later on in the withdrawal of the corps toward the south. Also, all food stocks of the former German civil administration in the corps area had been evacuated south of the Ross River, a move that turned out to be of decisive importance as these provisions soon became the sole source of supply for the German pocket forces.

Day after day, from the end of December 1943 until 24 January 1944, Russian infantry, often supported by tanks, attacked the positions of XLII Corps. From mid-January on the enemy's main effort was clearly directed against the left flank of the corps. On 25 January Soviet forces launched a large-scale attack against the adjacent VII Corps whose right flank division fell back toward the south-east and south, so that by the end of the same day the roads leading to the flank and rear of XLII Corps were open to the enemy. Over these roads the pursuing Russians pressed forward via Medvin toward Boguslav and Steblev.

Simultaneously, XI Corps had suffered enemy penetrations on the right boundary and at the center of its sector. To escape the danger of envelopment and keep its front intact, the corps withdrew its right wing and center toward the west and northwest

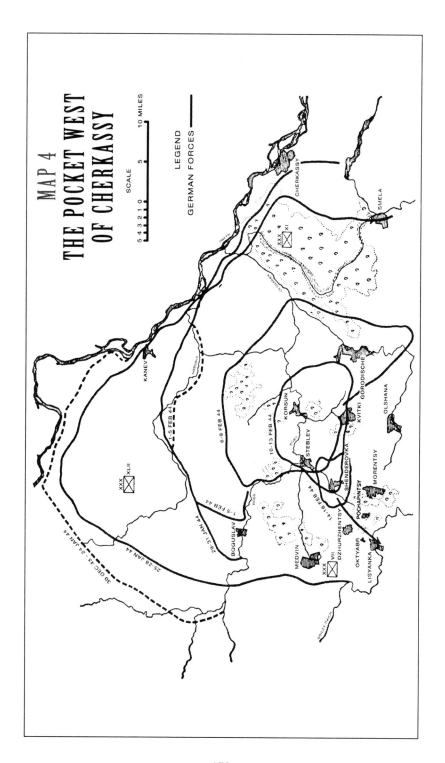

MAP 4
THE POCKET WEST
OF CHERKASSY

SCALE

5 4 3 2 1 0   5   10 MILES

LEGEND

GERMAN FORCES

CHERKASSY

SMELA

XI

KANEV

XLII
XXX

BOGUSLAV

1-5 FEB 44

6-9 FEB 44

10-13 FEB 44

KORSUN

STEBLEV

SHENDEROVKA

14-16 FEB 44

GORODISCHE

KVITKI

OLSHANA

MORENTSY

POCHAPINTSY

OKTYABR

LISYANKA

MEDVIN

DZHURZHENTSY

VII
XXX

1-5 FEB 44

25-29 JAN 44

29-31 JAN 44

30 DEC 43 - 24 JAN 44

173

where it, was eventually to form the eastern front of the German pocket.

Before 24 January most enemy attacks against XLII Corps were blocked or repelled. These engagements, both in terms of battle casualties and lowered physical resistance of individuals, drained the fighting strength of the German forces. Their commanders were under constant pressure, trying to seal off the daily penetrations by virtually uncovering other sectors which were not under heavy attack and by using all available trucks, horses, and horse-drawn carts to shift their units to the threatened points. Initially, each of the two divisions on line with a troop strength of six battalions had to defend a frontage of 35 to 40 miles, with weak artillery support and without tanks. Except for the Ross River sector, the area in which they were committed was almost completely flat and offered few terrain features favoring the defense.

From mid-December 1943 until its breakout from, the pocket on 16 February 1944, XLII Corps was actually never in a position to offer effective resistance to a far superior enemy who attacked with numerous tanks; if it could not dodge enemy attacks by timely withdrawal, it was constantly threatened by Russian penetrations of its lines. Authority for any withdrawal, however, could only be granted by Adolf Hitler in person, and no such decision could be obtained in less than twenty-four hours. One can easily visualize the difficulties, mounting from day to day, which the corps had to face under these circumstances.

The Russian attacks on 25 January and the following days had produced a deep penetration separating XLII and VII Corps. With its left flank and rear threatened by the enemy, XLII Corps was forced to establish a new front along the general line Boguslav-Steblev. For a short time it appeared that VII Corps would be able to close the gap and restore the situation, but after a few days, as the Russians succeeded in widening their penetration, it became evident that VII Corps was rapidly withdrawing toward the southwest. At this stage the German forces east of the Russian salient were ordered for the first time to make preparations for fighting their way out of the encirclement that was now taking shape. A breakout toward the west was clearly out of the question, thus southeast or due south were the only possible directions. During the first few days of February, however, another Russian penetration turned the right flank of XI Corps and made its position untenable. With its center withdrawing west and its right wing northwest the entire corps was rapidly moving away from its neighboring units adjacent to the southeast. In that area, too, a continuous German front had ceased to exist, and a breakout in that direction was no longer possible.

Moreover, since 28 January the sole supply roads leading to XLII and XI Corps (via Shpola and Zvenigorodka) had been cut. Supply by air was requested and furnished. By 6 February, XLII and XI Corps were completely encircled.

In shifting its main effort toward the south, XLII Corps had been forced to weaken its northern and western fronts which were now slowly giving ground. This development, together with the withdrawal movements of XI Corps on the right, led to a gradual shrinking of the pocket, which in turn resulted in greater concentration - an important prerequisite for the eventual breakout from encirclement.

At the same time, it had become evident that the surrounded German units could escape annihilation only if they succeeded in breaking through the enemy lines on the southern front of the pocket. In weeks of defensive fighting, however, they had suffered excessive casualties, and the forces that would have to be used for such an operation were obviously incapable of getting through the Russian encirclement on their own; it was clear that the breakout attempt would have to be supported by a relief thrust from the outside. Accordingly, the encircled units were informed that III Panzer Corps, located about twenty-five miles southwest of the pocket, would launch an attack toward Morentsy in order to establish a forward rescue position. Simultaneously, another panzer corps at about the same distance due south of the pocket was to thrust north in the direction of Olshana.

On 6 February, in a radio message from Eighth Army, D Day for the breakout and rescue operation was set for 10 February. Because of the sudden start of the muddy season, however, the date had to be postponed for nearly a week. In order to establish unity of command inside the pocket, the two encircled corps were placed under the control of General Stemmermann, the commander of XI Corps, and designated Force Stemmermann.

Meanwhile, repeated Russian attacks - from the southeast against Korsun and Shenderovka, and from the west against Steblev - had threatened to split up the German pocket. Although all of these enemy thrusts were repelled, they further reduced the forces available for the breakout and had a detrimental effect on the morale of the encircled troops.

On 14 February elements of XLII Corps succeeded in taking Khiiki and Komarovka (Map 5), two to three miles west of Shenderovka, and thus reached a favorable jump-off line for the final breakthrough. It was high time indeed: The gradual restricting of the pocket had resulted in a dangerous massing of troops. The entire German-held area was now within range of the Soviet artillery; volume and intensity of enemy fire seemed to be merely a question of how much ammunition the Russians were willing to expend. It was feared that at any moment German casualties might amount to an unbearable level. The Russians themselves, however, were hampered by snow-storms and poor road conditions and could not use their artillery to full advantage. Thus the German troops inside the pocket were able to rally for their last effort.

The breakout began, as ordered, on 16 February at 23:00. Jumping off from the line Khilki-Komarovka, three divisional columns struck in a southwesterly direction; their mission was to reach the forward rescue position established by the leading elements of III Panzer Corps at Lisyanka and Oktyabr, and to join forces with First Panzer Army.

The composition of the two German corps encircled in the pocket west of Cherkassy was as follows:

XI Corps consisted of three infantry divisions, the 57th, 72d, and 389th Divisions, each without tanks, assault guns, or adequate anti-tank weapons. Of these only the 72d Division was capable of aggressive combat. The two other divisions, with the exception of one good regiment of the 57th, were unfit for use in the attack. The 5th SS Panzer Division *Wiking* was part of XI Corps until the end of January. Corps troops comprised one assault gun brigade of two battalions totaling six batteries, and one battalion of light GHQ artillery.

XLII Corps included Task Force B, the 88th Infantry Division, and, from the end of January, the SS Panzer Division *Wiking*. Task Force B was a cover name given to the 112th Infantry Division to hide its identity. Although the unit carried a corps standard, it was an ordinary infantry division consisting of three regiments, the normal complement of artillery, a strong antitank battalion, but no tanks or assault guns. Now at about four-fifths of its authorized strength, Task Force B had the combat value of one good infantry division. The 88th Division had been badly mauled during the preceding engagements. It consisted of two regiments totaling five battalions and its artillery was seriously depleted.

In terms of personnel, weapons, and equipment the 5th SS Panzer Division *Wiking* was by far the strongest division of XLII Corps. It was fully equipped as an armored division and consisted of two armored infantry regiments, one tank regiment with a total of 90 tanks, the Belgian volunteer brigade *Wallonien* organized in three battalions, and one replacement regiment of about 2,000 men. Accurate strength reports from that division could not be obtained; its effective strength before the breakout was estimated at about 12,000 men.

On the evening of 15 February, at his command post at Shenderovka, the commander of XLII Corps had issued verbal and written instructions to his division commanders. The breakout order for XLII Corps read, in part, as follows:

For days the enemy has been attacking continuously along our entire defense perimeter, with tanks and infantry, in an attempt to split up the pocket and destroy our forces.

At 23:00, on 16 February, Task Force B, 72d Division, and 5th SS Panzer Division *Wiking* will attack in a southwesterly direction from the line Khilki-Komarovka,

The joy of these Russian civilians was in marked contrast to the scenes of despair which also filled the liberated cities where the Einsatztruppen had been at work.

break the enemy's resistance by a bayonet assault, and throw him back in continuous attack toward the southwest, in order to reach Lisyanka and there to join forces with elements of III Panzer Corps. Compass number 22* indicates the general direction of the attack. This direction is to be made known to each individual soldier. The password is: "Freedom" (Freiheit).

For the attack and breakout each division will be organized in five successive waves, as follows: First wave: one infantry regiment reinforced by one battery of light artillery (at least eight horses per gun, plus spare teams) and one engineer company. Second wave: antitank and assault gun units. Third wave: remainder of infantry (minus one battalion), engineers, and light artillery. Fourth wave: all our wounded that are fit to be transported, accompanied by one infantry battalion. Fifth wave: supply and service units.

The rear guard, under the direct command of General Stemmermann, will be formed by the 57th and 88th Divisions, which will protect the rear and the flanks of the forces launching the breakout attack. By 23:00 on 16 February, the rear guard divisions will withdraw from their present locations to a previously determined defense

---

*Ed. : The magnetic compass carried by the German soldier had 32 consecutively numbered gradations. Number 22 equals an azimuth of about 236°.

line; further withdrawals will be ordered by General Stemmermann, depending on the progress of the breakout.

The entire medium artillery and certain specifically designated units of light artillery will support the attack. They will open fire at 23:00 on 16 February, making effective use of their maximum range. Subsequently, all artillery pieces are to be destroyed in accordance with special instructions.

The radios of each division will be carried along on pack horses. To receive signal communications from corps, each division will, if possible, keep one set open at all times, but in any event every hour on the hour. The corps radio will be open for messages from the divisions at all times.

The corps command post will be, until 20:00, 16 February, at Shenderovka; after 20:00, at Khilki. From the start of the attack the corps commander will be with the leading regiment of the 72d Division.

The order was explained orally to the division commanders, and all details of the operation were carefully gone over, especially the difficult relief of the SS Division near Komarovka by the 57th Division, whose G-3 was present during the briefing conference.

Despite persistent enemy attacks against the pocket perimeter, constant Russian shelling of Komarovka, Khiiki, and Shenderovka, churned up roads, and numerous traffic bottlenecks, the German forces inside the pocket were able, by 20:00 on 16 February, to report their readiness for the breakout. Determination was the prevailing mood. Apparently the large majority of the troops was not influenced by Russian propaganda, nor by the hundreds of leaflets dropped from Russian planes on behalf of the Free Germany Committee (General von Seydlitz)—they wanted to fight their way through.

Shortly after 20:00, the commander of XLII Corps appeared at the command post of the 105th Grenadier Regiment which was to spearhead the attack of 72d Division. He was on horseback, accompanied by members of his staff, several aides, and radio operators with their equipment. The events that followed are illustrated by a personal account of the corps commander, written from memory at a later date, and presented here in his own words:

"By 23:00 the regiment - two battalions abreast - started moving ahead, silently and with bayonets fixed. One-half hour later the force broke through the first and soon thereafter the second Russian defense line. The enemy was completely caught by surprise. Prisoners were taken along. Not until the following day did it become evident that the Russians, under the protection of heavy snowfall, had pulled out most of their troops from the south front of the pocket in order to use them in an attack, on 17

February, from the area west of Steblev.

The advance toward the southwest continued. No reports from either Task Force B on the right or the 5th SS Panzer Division on the left. That they were making some progress could only be inferred from the noise of vehicles due north and south of us, and from the sounds of firing that indicated the location of their leading elements. Over roadless, broken terrain traversed by numerous gullies, our march proceeded slowly. There were frequent halts. Here and there, men and horses suddenly disappeared, having stumbled into holes filled with deep snow. Vehicles had to be dug out laboriously. The slopes were steeper than could be presumed from looking at the map. Gradually the firing decreased until it broke off entirely by 02:00. About two hours later the leading elements of 72d Division were approximately abreast of Dzhurzhentsy. Still no reports from *Wiking* and Task Force B. I could not give them my position by radio because by now my headquarters signal unit was missing and could not be located.

Shortly after 04:00 enemy tanks ahead opened fire. They were joined by Russian artillery and mortars operating from the direction of Dzhurzhentsy, at first without noticeable effect. The firing increased slowly but steadily, and was soon coming from the south as well. We began to suffer casualties. The advance, however, continued. By about 06:00 the leading units reached a large hollow southeast of Dzhurzhentsy. Enemy fire, getting constantly heavier, was now coming from three directions. Elements of *Wiking* could be heard on the left, farther back. No message, and not a trace of Task Force B. Day was dawning. The difficult ascent out of the hollow began. The climb was steep and led up an icy slope. Tanks, guns, heavy horse-drawn vehicles, and trucks of all kinds slipped, turned over, and had to be blown up. Only a few tanks and artillery pieces were able to make the grade. The units lapsed rapidly into disorder. Parts of the *Wiking* Division appeared on the left.

Between 07:00 and 10:00 the 72d Division made several attempts to mount a co-ordinated attack toward southwest. It did not succeed. The few guns and most of the tanks that were still firing were soon destroyed by the Russian. Armoured cars and motor vehicles suffered the same fate. Except for a few tanks that had managed to keep up, there were now only soldiers on foot and on horseback, and here and there a few horse-drawn vehicles, mostly carrying wounded.

In the protection of a ravine I was able to collect a small force of about battalion size, mainly stragglers from Task Force B and the *Wiking* Division. With them I moved on toward the line Hill 239-Pochapintsy, which was visible from time to time despite the heavy snowfall, and from where the enemy was firing with great intensity. Russian ground support planes appeared, opened fire, and disappeared again. They were ineffective, and did not repeat their attack, probably because of the difficult weather

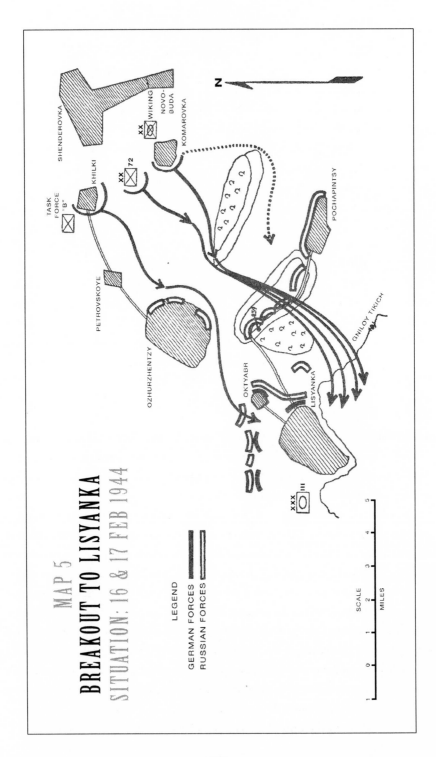

MAP 5

BREAKOUT TO LISYANKA

SITUATION: 16 & 17 FEB 1944

LEGEND

GERMAN FORCES

RUSSIAN FORCES

SCALE

MILES

SHENDEROVKA

WIKING
NOVO-
BUDA

KOMAROVKA

KHILKI

72

TASK
FORCE
"B"

PETROVSKOYE

OZHURZHENTZY

POCHAPINTSY

GNILOY TIKICH

OKTYABR

LISYANKA

Z

Some of the 50,000 German prisoners described by Alexander Werth are paraded through the streets of Moscow.

conditions.

There was no longer any effective control; there were no regiments, no battalions. Now and then small units appeared alongside us. I learned that the commanding general of the 72d Division was among the missing. My corps staff still kept up with me, but the aides who had been sent on various missions did not find their way back. On the steep slope northwest of Pochapintsy, defiladed from enemy fire, I found the G-3 of the 72d Division. He reported that infantry units of his division had penetrated the enemy line along the ridge south of Hill 239. Nevertheless, enemy fire was still coming from there, maintained principally by about ten Russian tanks.

Behind and alongside me thousands of men were struggling south-west. The entire area was littered with dead horses, and with vehicles and guns that had either been knocked out by the enemy or simply abandoned by their crews. I could not distinguish the wounded; their bandages did not show, as we were all wearing white camouflage clothing. Despite the general confusion and complete lack of control one could still recognize the determination in the minds of the troops to break through toward the southwest, in the direction of III Panzer Corps.

During a lull in the firing I readied my battalion for the attack across the line

181

Hill 239 - Pochapintsy which unfortunately could not be bypassed. My staff and I were still on horseback. After leaving the draw that sheltered us against the enemy, we galloped ahead of the infantry and through the gaps between our few remaining tanks. The enemy tank commanders, observing from their turrets, quickly recognized our intention, turned their weapons in our direction, and opened fire. About one-half of our small mounted group was able to get through. The chief of staff and the G-3 were thrown, but later found their way back to us. The greater part of the infantry battalion was still following behind me. While riding through the enemy sector, I noticed a few German soldiers surrendering, but the main body was pushing southwest without letup. Soviet tanks were now firing at us from the rear and quite a few men were still being hit. From the eastern edge of the forest south of Hill 239 came intensive enemy fire. I led my battalion in an attack in that direction and threw the Russians back into the woods. Rather than pursue them into the depth of the forest, we continued advancing southwest, still harassed by fire from Russian tanks.

Gradually, between 13:00 and 15:00, large, disorganized masses of troops piled up along the Gniloy Tikich River, east of Lisyanka. Units from all three divisions participating in the breakout were hopelessly intermingled. A few medium tanks had been able to get through to the river bank, but there were no heavy weapons and artillery pieces left. The river, below and above Lisyanka, was 30 to 50 feet wide, had a rapid current, and reached a depth of about 10 feet in most places. The banks were steep and rocky, with occasional shrubs and trees. Several tanks attempted to drive across, but the river was too deep and they failed to reach the opposite bank.

Heavy fire from Russian tanks located southeast of Oktyabr set the congested masses into forward motion. Many thousands flung themselves into the river, swam across, reached the opposite shore, and struggled on in the direction of Lisyanka. Hundreds of men and horses drowned in the icy torrent. An attempt by a small group of officers to create an emergency crossing for casualties succeeded only after several hours.

Toward 16:00 the enemy fire ceased. I crossed the Gniloy Tikich swimming alongside my horse, traversed the snowy slope southeast of Lisyanka which was covered with moving men, and finally reached the town. There I found the commander of the 1st Panzer Division, the forward element of III Panzer Corps. I learned that no more than one company of armored infantry and three companies of tanks of 1st Panzer Division were now at Lisyanka, while one armored infantry battalion consisting of two weak companies was established at Oktyabr, the village immediately north of Lisyanka.

A reinforced regiment of Task Force B had made its way into Lisyanka, and I received the report that the commander of Task Force B had been killed in action. Next, the chief of staff of XI Corps appeared; he had lost contact with General Stemmermann in the morning of 17 February, while marching on foot from Khilki to Dzhurzhentsy. He reported that the rear guard of the pocket force was in the process of withdrawal and that some of its units would soon appear

"I assumed command of what was left of Force Stemmermann. By now the situation was the following: The 72d and *Wiking* Divisions were completely intermingled. No longer did they have any tanks, artillery, vehicles, or rations. Many soldiers were entirely without weapons, quite a few even without footgear. Neither division could be considered in any way able to fight. One regiment of Task Force B was intact and still had some artillery support. However, this regiment also had no vehicles and no rations left. All wounded, estimated at about 2,000, were being gradually sheltered in the houses of Lisyanka, and later were evacuated by air.

For lack of vehicles and fuel, III Panzer Corps was unable to reinforce its units in the area of Lisyanka and Oktyabr. The corps commander, with whom I conferred by telephone, informed me that he had been forced to assume the defensive against heavy Russian attacks from the northwest in the area immediately west of Lisyanka. He had no extra supplies of any kind, and his forward elements were unable to provide rations for the troops emerging from the pocket. Thus I had to order the pocket force in its miserable condition to move on westward, while I requested supply, evacuation of casualties by air, and the bringing up of vehicles and weapons from the rear.

The march toward the main rescue area continued throughout the night, despite frequent bottlenecks, and was not completed until noon of 18 February. Renewed Russian flank attacks from the north endangered the roads to the rear and necessitated further withdrawal southwest and south during the following day. In the afternoon of 20 February, having clarified the question of food supply for the pocket force and dealt with a number of other problems, I was instructed to proceed to headquarters of Army High Command in East Prussia. From that moment on I had no further connection with XLII Corps or Force Stemmermann.

Of the 35,000 men launching the breakout from the pocket about 30,000 successfully fought their way out. 5,000 were killed or captured. The force lost all of its heavy weapons, artillery, tanks, vehicles, horses, equipment, and supplies."

The situation outside the pocket was less frought but still desperate. The second Russian winter offensive of 1943-4 was launched early in January 1944 against the German Eighth Army sector in the Dnepr bend. The First and Second Ukrainian Fronts - the latter consisting of four armies, including one tank army - attempted to cut off German forces deployed from a point southeast of Kiev to the Dnepr estuary. The Soviet offensive fell short of accomplishing its purpose, but in twelve days of fighting the Russians drove a deep wedge south-westward across the Dnepr and captured the

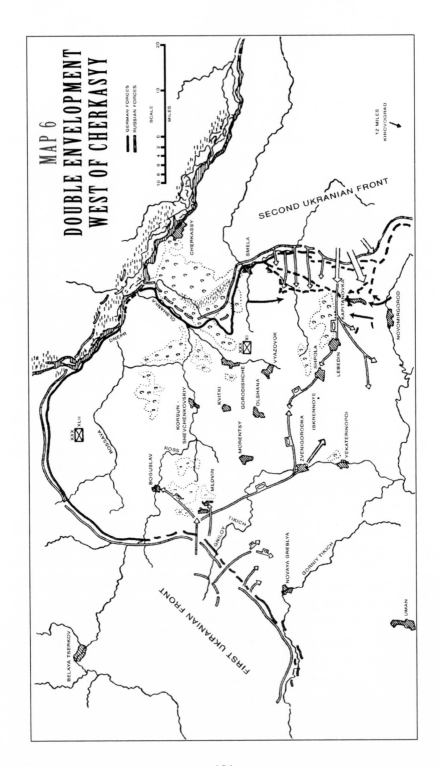

MAP 6

DOUBLE ENVELOPMENT
WEST OF CHERKASSY

GERMAN FORCES
RUSSIAN FORCES

SCALE

MILES

SECOND UKRANIAN FRONT

FIRST UKRANIAN FRONT

DNEPR

CHERKASSY

OLSHANKA

SMELA

XI

XXX XLII

ROSSAVA

ROSS

KORSUN-
SHEVCHENKOVSKIY

BOGUSLAV

MEDVIN

KVITKI

MORENTSY

GORODISHCHE

OLSHANA

VYAZOVOK

ISKRENNOYE

ZVENIGORODKA

SHIPOLA

LEBEDIN

KAPITANOVKA

NOVOMIRGOROD

YEKATERINOPOI

KIROVOGRAD

12 MILES

GNILOY TIKICH

NOVAYA GREBLYA

GORNIY TIKICH

UMAN

BELAYA TSERKOV

184

town of Kirovograd. Two large German salients remained, one to the northwest, the other to the southeast of the Kirovograd area.

Despite heavy tank losses, the Russians could be expected to re-organize their armored forces in the shortest possible time and continue their heavy attacks designed to push Army Group South farther back in the direction of the Romanian border. It was evident that the enemy would bend every effort to destroy the German bulge north-west of Kirovograd, held by elements of Eighth Army and First Panzer Army.

The commander of Eighth Army sent urgent messages to army group; he expressed grave doubts about continuing to hold the curving line of positions northwest of Kirovograd which committed an excessive number of men. Pointing out the Russian superiority in strength, he recommended withdrawal of the interior flanks of Eighth Army and First Panzer Army by retirement to successive positions, first behind the Olshanka-Ross River line, and eventually to the line Shpola-Zvenigorodka-Gorniy Tikich River. Permission for such a withdrawal, however, was denied on the grounds that the salient had to be held as a base for future operations in the direction of Kiev.

The expected attack was launched by the Second Ukrainian Front, on 24 January, against the right flank, and by the First Ukrainian Front, on 26 January, against the left flank and the rear of the German salient. By 28 January the armored spearheads of both Russian army groups met in the area of Zvenigorodka and thereby accomplished the encirclement of XI and XLII Corps. Having effected the original link-up with elements of two tank armies, the Russians rapidly committed strong infantry units from four additional armies which attacked toward the west, southwest, and south in order to widen the ring of encirclement and provide effective cover against German counterattacks from the outside.

In this situation the German Army High Command directed Army Group South to assemble the strongest available armored units along the boundary between Eighth Army and First Panzer Army. These forces were to execute converging counterattacks, encircle and annihilate the enemy units that had broken through, re-establish contact with the pocket force, and regain a favorable jump-off base for the projected counteroffensive.

Actually, the assembly of the German attack force presented the greatest of difficulties. Two of the panzer divisions of Eighth Army designated to take part in the operation were still in the midst of heavy fighting in the area of Kapitanovka. They had to be replaced by infantry units with frontages extended to the utmost. Two additional panzer divisions, recently engaged southeast of Kirovograd, were on the march toward the left flank of Eighth Army. Of these four armored units, only one was at full strength, while the others, after weeks of uninterrupted fighting, were actually no more than tank-supported combat teams.

German prisoners are made to confront the evidence of maltreatment of Soviet prisoners in German captivity. One Soviet guard recalled how the Germans marched slowly at first, but as more and more grisly remains were encountered, they began to move master and faster until they were virtually running through the camp.

The relief attack from the right flank of First Panzer Army was to be carried out by the four armored divisions of III Panzer Corps. They were still engaged in defensive operations on the left flank of the army sector, and could only be brought up after they had completed their previous missions. The two corps inside the pocket were to attack at the appropriate time in the direction of the Eighth Army and First Panzer Army units approaching from the south and west. It was clear that any build-up on the southern front of the pocket could only be accomplished at the expense of other sectors. Still, Army High Command insisted on holding the entire pocket area, and not until the situation of the encircled forces became far more critical was permission obtained for successive withdrawals on the northern sector. Even then, the pocket had to be kept sufficiently large to afford a certain freedom of movement. Also, despite the effort on the southern sector, adequate forces had to remain available to seal off enemy penetrations elsewhere.

The plan for a two-pronged drive by III Panzer Corps of First Panzer Army from the southwest and XLVII Panzer Corps of Eighth Army from the south, to coincide with an attack launched by the pocket force, was adopted on 1 February. The units concerned were ordered to complete their assembly for the proposed operation during the following two days. Then XLVII Panzer Corps was to jump off from the area of Shpola, thrusting into the rear of the Russian forces that were threatening the southern front of XI Corps. Simultaneously, III Panzer Corps was to launch a surprise attack in the general direction of Medvin, where enemy units were operating against the southwest front of the pocket defended by XLII Corps. After destroying these Russian units, III Panzer Corps was to pivot due east to effect close co-operation with the attacking elements of XLVII Corps coming from the south.

During a commanders' conference on 3 February, the Eighth Army commander voiced serious doubts whether, in view of the limited forces available and the muddy roads, this ambitious plan was practicable. He recommended instead that the attack by III Panzer Corps be led in a more easterly direction which would assure early co-operation with the advancing elements of XLVII Panzer Corps. This recommendation was turned down.

Meanwhile, the Soviets had committed strong infantry and armored units in an attack toward Novomirgorod, temporarily tying down two of the panzer divisions that were to take part in the relief operation from the south. The muddy season was rapidly taking effect and as the roads deteriorated all movements became extremely difficult.

Similar conditions prevailed in the area of III Panzer Corps. Engaged in continuous fighting on its left flank, this corps also suffered considerable delay in the assembly of its units for the projected relief thrust and could not be expected to launch its attack until 4 February.

The forces inside the pocket, in an attempt to keep the Soviets from separating XI and XLII Corps, had shifted their main effort to the south front of the perimeter. Despite heavy losses in defensive engagements they could not afford to give ground in that sector, as their only remaining airfield, at Korsun, had to be kept out of range of the Russian artillery. At the high rate of casualties, however, a continued stand along the entire perimeter of positions was obviously out of the question. To conserve its strength and reduce the threat of Russian penetrations, the pocket force eventually obtained permission to execute limited withdrawals on the northern and eastern sectors while bolstering its defenses to the south.

The full impact of the muddy season soon made itself felt on all fronts and, in addition to causing losses of motor vehicles and other equipment, began to endanger German air supply operations. The requirements of the encircled force called for supplies to be flown in at the rate of 150 tons daily. Despite the most determined efforts of the Luftwaffe units, this quota was never reached. Enemy anti-aircraft fire from at

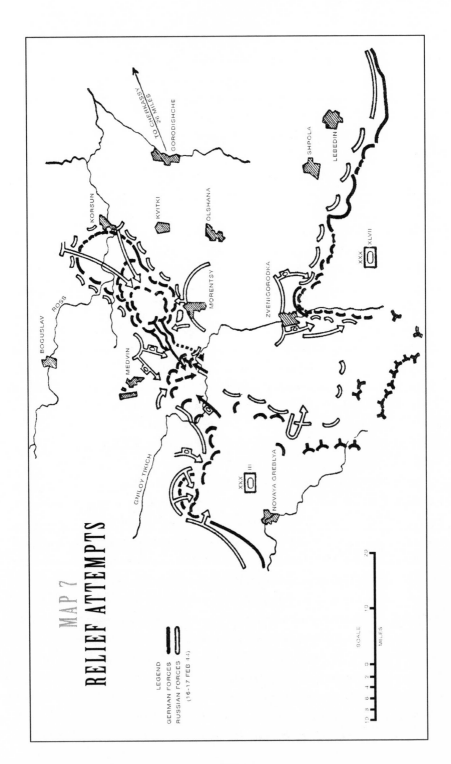

MAP 7

RELIEF ATTEMPTS

LEGEND

GERMAN FORCES

RUSSIAN FORCES
(16-17 FEB 44)

SCALE

MILES

TO CHERKASSY
20 MILES

GORODISHCHE

SHPOLA

LEBEDIN

KORSUN

KVITKI

OLSHANA

MORENTSY

ZVENIGORODKA

XXX XLVII

BOGUSLAV

ROSS

MEDVIN

GNILOY TIKICH

NOVAYA GREBLYA

XXX III

least three flak divisions in the Russian-held strip of terrain and interception by enemy fighter planes had seriously reduced the number of available transport aircraft. To prevent further losses, strong German fighter forces had to be committed in protection of the vital air supply line instead of supporting preparations on other sectors for the impending relief operation.

With the start of the muddy season, the lack of paved runways further aggravated the situation. One airfield after another became unusable, and even the Korsun field, the only one inside the pocket, had to be partially closed. Airdropping supplies, because of a shortage of aerial delivery containers, met only a small part of the actual requirements. Eventually, because of the road conditions, the two corps approaching from the outside also became dependent in part upon airborne supply, which forced a wide scattering of the air effort.

Time was obviously working against the Germans. As their difficulties continued to increase, it became clear that each day of delay further reduced their chances for success.

The assembly of an attack force on the western flank of XLVII Panzer Corps (Eighth Army) bogged down in a series of heavy local counterattacks south of Lebedin and Shpola. A small German force gained a temporary bridgehead at Izkrennoye and inflicted serious losses on the enemy. In all these engagements, however, the strength of XLVII Panzer Corps was constantly being whittled down until, by 3 February, it had only 27 tanks and 34 assault guns left. At that point it became clear that Eighth Army could do no more than to tie down enemy forces by continued holding attacks. Thus the original plan which provided for two converging relief thrusts had to be abandoned.

Neverthless, on 4 February, First Panzer Army attacked toward the north in order to take advantage of favorable tank terrain, achieve surprise, and avoid any further loss of time. Successful during the first day, it was, however, unable to maintain this direction of attack, as terrain and road conditions grew worse by the hour.

Meanwhile, the situation inside the pocket had become more critical and made it imperative to establish contact with the encircled forces over the shortest possible route. Therefore, on 6 February, Army Group South issued new orders to First Panzer Army. After regrouping its units, III Panzer Corps was to attack due east, its right flank advancing via Lisyanka toward Morentsy. At the same time the encircled corps were ordered to prepare for an attack in the direction of III Panzer Corps, the attack to be launched as soon as the armored spearhead of the relief force had approached to within the most favorable distance from the pocket.

Planned for 8 February, the attack of III Panzer Corps, because of unfavorable weather conditions, did not get under way until three days later. It was initially successful and, by the end of the first day, led to the establishment of three bridgeheads across the Gniloy Tikich River. Concentrated enemy attacks, however, prevented any further advance. In the difficult terrain east of the Gniloy Tikich, the German armored units were unable to make any progress, and this attack also came to a halt in the mud.

Army group now realized that it could no longer accomplish a reinforcement of the pocket. The encircling ring, therefore, had to be broken from the inside. The divisions of III Panzer Corps were ordered to engage and divert the Russian forces located in the area of Pochapintsy-Komarovka-Dzhurzhentsy, and to establish on the high ground northwest of Pochapintsy a forward rescue position that could be reached by the units breaking out of the pocket.

By 11:05, on 15 February, the breakout order was transmitted by radio to General Stemmermann, the commander of the encircled German forces. It read, in part, "Capabilities of III Panzer Corps reduced by weather and supply difficulties. Task Force Stemmermann must accomplish breakthrough on its own to line Dzhurzhentsy-Hill 239 where it will link up with III Panzer Corps. The breakout force will be under the command of General Lieb (XLII Corps) and compromise all units still capable of attack."

Further instructions, radioed on 16 February, emphasized the importance of surprise and proper co-ordination: "During initial phase of operation tonight hold your fire so as to achieve complete surprise. Maintain centralized fire control over artillery and heavy weapons, so that in the event of stronger enemy resistance, especially at daybreak, they can be committed at point of main effort in short order. Air support will be available at dawn to protect your flanks."

During the operation that was to follow, two separate phases could be clearly distinguished. At first everything went according to plan. In the proper sequence and under perfect control, the troops moved into position at night, despite the most difficult road and weather conditions. As they were compressed into a narrow area, unit after unit had to be channeled across the only existing bridge at Shenderovka which was under heavy enemy fire.

The bayonet assault started on schedule. The complete surprise of the enemy demonstrated that the attack had been properly timed. Without much action, and suffering but few casualties, the German breakout force penetrated the enemy lines and in a relatively short time reached the vicinity of Lisyanka. On the opposite front of the pocket the rear guards held fast and thus assured the success of the initial breakout.

The second phase, the evacuation or the remaining pocket force, rapidly deteriorated into a wild surge toward the west. Following closely behind the successful spearhead, altogether about 30,000 men broke through the Russian lines in front of the pocket. At

Russian civilians greet their liberators. After three years of occupation by an inhuman regime, it is possible to understand the Red Army's drive for revenge. However the scale of the brutality, particularly with regard to sexual offences against the female population exceeded the bounds of the usual expectations of war.

daybreak, however, they ran into an unsuspected enemy front of antitank guns, tanks, and artillery, located on the line Dzhurzhentsy-Pochapintsy. Under massed enemy fire, enemy tank attacks, and infantry counter-thrusts, the German force was split into numerous small groups, each attempting on its own to get through to the west wherever there might be a possibility. Their guns, tank destroyers, and heavy weapons, which up to now had been dragged along laboriously through snowdrifts and over broken terrain, had to be left behind and were destroyed after the last round of ammunition had been fired. Here too, as the last vehicles were blown up, the wounded taken along at the insistence of their comrades had to be left to their fate.

Meanwhile a new complication arose that was to have disastrous consequences. Subjected to heavy enemy fire, counterthrusts, and armored attacks, the great mass of German troops breaking out of the pocket had deviated from their original direction of attack. No longer did they advance according to plan toward the area northwest of Pochapintsy. Instead of approaching the forward rescue position established by III Panzer Corps, they passed by at a considerable distance farther south. Here, their advance to the west was blocked by the course of the Gniloy Tikich, the enemy holding the near bank of the river. There were no crossings, nor had III Panzer Corps established any bridgeheads, since a link-up in that area had not been foreseen.

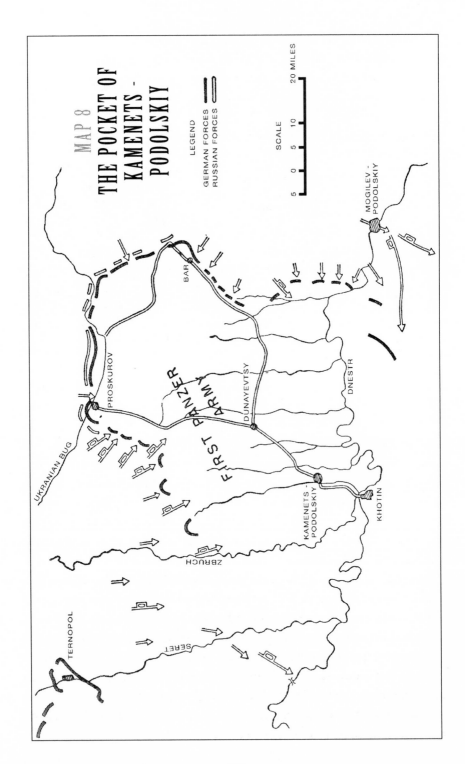

MAP 8

THE POCKET OF KAMENETS - PODOLSKIY

LEGEND
GERMAN FORCES
RUSSIAN FORCES

SCALE

5   0   5   10   20 MILES

MOGILEV - PODOLSKIY

DNESTR

BAR

PROSKUROV

DUNAYEVTSY

UKRANIAN BUG

FIRST PANZER ARMY

KAMENETS - PODOLSKIY

KHOTIN

ZBRUCH

TERNOPOL

SERET

192

Although greatly exhausted, the German troops were now forced to overcome the resistance of the Russian security detachments along the river and to swim across, leaving their last weapons behind. They suffered considerable losses as both banks of the river were under heavy enemy fire and not until they had placed this last obstacle behind them were they finally received by the forward elements of III Panzer Corps.

The German holding forces on the eastern sector of the pocket maintained contact with the enemy and successfully covered the breakout of the main body. This mission accomplished, they made their way westward according to plan and entered the lines of III Panzer Corps during the night of 17-18 February.

Contrary to expectations, the breakout had to be executed without air support. Unfavorable weather conditions during the entire operation made it impossible for the air force to play its part in the liberation of the encircled units.

The noose around Germany was tightening rapidly and the new year on the Eastern Front offered no relief from the process of strangulation. By 2nd January 1944 the Russians had advanced north of Kiev and were now just eighteen miles from the 1939 Polish border.

On the 14th of January, the offensive which came to be known as "The Liberation of Leningrad" was launched. Soviet forces smashed through the German defensive positions around the city, clearing the territory southwards as far as Novgorod. On the 17th January the besieged city was finally liberated. Leningrad had endured 900 days of isolation and unbelievable hardship: one million people had died.

Still the Russian momentum did not falter. On the 4th March, the northern flank of von Manstein's Army Group South was pierced by the First Ukrainian Front under direct command of Marshal Zhukov. By the 7th, after advancing one hundred miles, the Russians were astride the Warsaw-Odessa railway line and by the 28th, Nikolayev on the Bug had been captured. Further south the river Dniester was crossed and Kherson at the mouth of the Dnieper overrun. Eventually, the Red Army's overstretched supply lines and the spring floods brought an end to what was named the "Mud Offensive". In the Crimea however, the Russians continued to attack and Sevastopol was retaken on 19th May bringing the north shore of the Black Sea into Soviet hands once more.

As the Soviet armies surged forward the situation was becoming desperate. In mid-February 1944 the front of the First Panzer Army extended across the western Ukraine along a general line north of Vinnitsa and Shepetovka, northeast of Ternopol. To the right, north of Uman, was the Eighth Army; to the left, the Second Army. After the two corps encircled west of Cherkassy had made their way out of the pocket the front remained quiet until the beginning of March, while the Russians were reorganizing and regrouping their units. Then strong concentrations of Soviet tanks indicated that the enemy was getting ready to resume his attempts at forcing a decision.

The first large-scale Russian attacks, on 4 and 5 March, were directed primarily against the Shepetovka and Uman areas. Because of their great numerical superiority, the Russians succeeded in denting the overextended German lines in many places. While timely German counterattacks on the left flank eliminated the threat of a breakthrough aimed at Proskurov the enemy was rapidly gaining ground in the Uman area and succeeded, by mid-March, in pushing across the Ukrainian Bug River. Having driven a deep wedge into the German front, the Russians were in a position to threaten the right flank of First Panzer Army. Since there were no German reserves available to close the gap, First Panzer Army was forced to withdraw its entire right wing and establish a new defense line facing east. Under the pressure of continued Russian attacks, planned withdrawals were also carried out on the central sector until the right flank of First Panzer Army was finally anchored on the northern bank of the Dnestr River east of Mogilev-Podolskiy.

On the left boundary of First Panzer Army, west of Proskurov, strong Russian armored units soon accomplished another breakthrough. On 22 March five armored corps followed by infantry poured south between the Zbruch and Seret Rivers, and two days later crossed the Dnestr in the direction of Chernovtsy. Since the enemy had also pushed across the river farther east, in the area of Yampol and Mogilev-Podolskiy, First Panzer Army was now contained in a large semicircle north of the Dnestr. Hitler's explicit orders prohibited any further withdrawal and eliminated the possibility of a more flexible defense which might have established contact with other German forces to the east or the west. As could be expected, the two Russian forces, after crossing the Dnestr, linked up under the protection of the river line in the rear of First Panzer Army. By 25 March the encirclement was complete.

As in all similar situations, the first threat to make itself felt came when the last supply lines into the German saliest were cut. Until 25 March First Panzer Army still had one supply route open, which led south across the Dnestr bridge at Knotin and was protected by a strong bridgehead on the southern bank of the river. Over this route all staffs and units that could be dispensed with were moved to the rear, and every nonessential user of supplies and equipment was taken out of the pocket before the ring was actually closed. As soon as it became evident that no more supplies could be brought up, stock was taken inside the pocket. While ammunition and rations were sufficient to last for about another two weeks, fuel reserves were found to be critically low. First Panzer Army therefore immediately requested supply by air and restricted the use of motor vehicles to a minimum.

All measures taken inside the pocket were made extremely difficult by unfavorable

Even the much vaunted SS formations could not prevent the collapse of Army Group Centre.

MAP 9
BREAKOUT TO THE WEST

LEGEND
GERMAN FORCES
RUSSIAN FORCES

TERNOPOL

ZBRUCH

SERET

CHORTKOV

SKALA

KAMENETS - PODOLSKIY

DNESTR

KHOTIN

SCALE

5   0   5   10   20 MILES

weather. At first snowstorms and snowdrifts hampered the air supply operation and obstructed movements on the ground. Then, practically over night, the snow began to melt, and the roads quickly turned into bottomless morasses. The supply of motor fuel, which was flown in over a distance of 125 miles from the nearest German airfield, fell far short of requirements. Time and again vehicles had to be destroyed when they blocked the roads in long, immobilized columns. Finally, only combat vehicles, prime movers, and a few messenger vehicles were left intact.

Having completed the encirclement the Russians, as expected, decreased the intensity of their attacks. Only on the eastern sector Soviet pressure remained strong; there was no more than moderate activity in the north; and from the west no attacks were launched against the defense perimeter of First Panzer Army. Apparently the continuous movements of German service units southward across the Dnestr had led the Russians to believe that the First Panzer Army was in full retreat toward the south. The Russians, in an effort that turned out to be a serious mistake, moved more and more units in the same direction on both sides of the pocket. Their lines of communication grew longer and longer, and they began to face difficulties of supply similar to those of the encircled German force.

In response to enemy pressure from the east and north, First Panzer Army deliberately shortened its front until it ran along a much smaller perimeter north of Kamenets-Podolskiy, assuring a greater concentration of the defending forces and a more efficient use of the limited ammunition supply. Local Soviet penetrations were sealed off more easily and break-throughs could be prevented altogether. At the same time First Panzer Army deceived the Russians into believing that by day and by night large-scale evacuations across the river were taking place.

Even before it was completely cut off, First Panzer Army had requested authority to conduct a defense along mobile lines. When this request was turned down and the encirclement became a fact, a breakout remained the only possible course of action short of helplessly facing certain annihilation. Because of unfavorable weather conditions, the quantities of supplies that could be flown in were entirely insufficient to maintain the fighting power of the encircled troops. Relief of the pocket by fresh forces from the outside could not be expected. In this situation the enemy sent a terse demand for surrender, threatening that otherwise all soldiers of the encircled German army would be shot.

The reaction of First Panzer Army was to immediately make all necessary preparations to enable its total force of eight divisions to break out. Once more, in a systematic culling process, the divisions were relieved of all unfit personnel and superfluous equipment, while special arrangements were made with the Luftwaffe to assure that the transport planes bringing in supplies were used to evacuate casualties on their return flights.

The question of the direction in which the breakout should be launched played an important part in all considerations. Was it more advisable to strike toward the west, along the Dnestr, or toward the south, across the Khotin bridgehead? An attack in the latter direction would involve the least difficulties, be opposed by the weakest Soviet forces, and perhaps permit the withdrawal of the entire German force into Romania. In this case, however, there would be one less panzer army fighting the Russians, at least for some time. West of the pocket several successive river lines constituted natural obstacles in the path of an advance. There, too, the Germans had to expect the strongest concentration of enemy forces along the ring of encirclement. Breaking out in several directions at once was another possibility under consideration; this would have forced the enemy to split his strength in numerous local countermeasures and might have enabled some small German groups to make their way back to the nearest friendly lines with the least fighting.

The final decision was to break out to the west, in the direction involving the greatest difficulties, yet assuring a maximum of surprise. Simultaneously, on the outside, another German force was to attack from an area southwest of Ternopol (over 125 miles from the scene) in the direction of First Panzer Army.

Another highly important question was the formation to be adopted for the breakout. Desirable as it might have been to lead off with a strong concentration of armor, it was to be feared that these armored units, intent on making rapid progress, might outrun the infantry and thus break up the unity of the command. The plan of attack, therefore, provided for a northern and a southern force, each consisting of two corps and specifically ordered to form an advance guard of tank-supported infantry and combat engineers, while the main body and the rear guard were to be composed of mobile units. This meant that the entire panzer army would be committed in two parallel formations attacking abreast, with units in column. Control over the operation, of course, could only be exercised from inside the pocket; evacuation of an operations staff via Khotin to the south, in order to direct the breakout from the outside, was out of the question.

On 27 March, having regrouped it's forces according to plan and completed all preparations for the thrust across the Zbruch River, First Panzer Army launched its breakout toward the west. Simultaneously, the rear guards on the eastern and northern sectors of the pocket switched to delaying tactics.

In the zone of the northern attack force, the enemy along the Zbruch River was overrun with surprising speed, and three undamaged bridges fell into German hands.

MAP 10
THE POCKET MOVES WEST

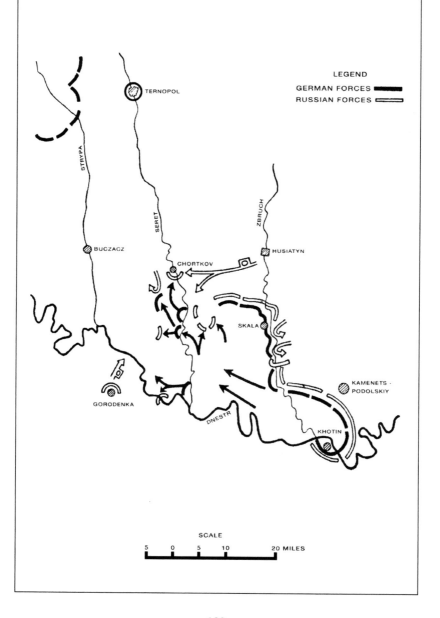

LEGEND
GERMAN FORCES ▬▬▬
RUSSIAN FORCES ▭▭▭

TERNOPOL

STRYPA

SERET

ZBRUCH

BUCZACZ

CHORTKOV

HUSIATYN

SKALA

KAMENETS -
PODOLSKIY

GORODENKA

DNESTR

KHOTIN

SCALE

5   0   5   10   20 MILES

The advance of the southern attack force met greater resistance, and considerable difficulties arose as the enemy launched a counterthrust from the west across the Zbruch and was able to force his way into Kamenets-Podolskiy. The loss of this important road hub made it necessary to reroute all German movements in a wide detour around the city, an effort that required painstaking reconnaissance and careful traffic regulation. It was not long, however, until the enemy penetration was sealed off, and in this instance the Germans, themselves surrounded, were able in turn to encircle a smaller Russian force which was not dependent upon air supply and could no longer interfere with subsequent operations. As soon as several strong bridgeheads had been established across the Zbruch River, new spearheads were formed which attacked the Seret River Line. Thus the panzer army maintained the initiative and kept moving by day and night.

Apparently the enemy was still uncertain about German intentions. Instead of combining all his forces from the eastern and northern sectors in an attempt to pursue and overtake the Germans pushing west, he persisted in atttacking the pocket from the east and north, in some instances striking at positions already vacated by the German rear guards. His units southwest of the pocket actually continued to move farther south. Meanwhile, First Panzer Army kept up its westward advance; on 28 March the southern force was able to cut the road leading to Chortkov, severing enemy communication lines in that area; one day later German spearheads reached the Seret River, which they crossed during the following night.

The Russians then began to react. They recalled elements of their Fourth Tank Army from south of the Dnestr and, by 31 March, launched a strong armored thrust toward the north from the area of Gorodenka. As a countermeasure, the southern attack force of First Panzer Army, deployed mainly between the Zbruch and Seret Rivers, assumed the defensive and was able to break up the Russian armored attack. Thereafter, since their supply lines had meanwhile been cut, these Russian units no longer constituted a menace to the German left flank.

A more serious threat existed in the north where Russian forces moving west could have overtaken and blocked the entire right wing of First Panzer Army. However, the enemy did not choose to do so, and the northern attack force continued to advance and was able to cross the Seret without major difficulty.

The last week in March was marked by heavy snowstorms. A rapid thaw followed early in April, with the effect of seriously hampering all movements. Supply during this period continued to be the greatest problem. As the German force kept moving, the planes bringing in supplies had to use different airstrips every night. In the final phase of the operation supplies could only be dropped by air, a procedure that proved wholly inadequate to satisfy the requirements of an entire army. Despite the daily moves of the pocket force, the maintenance of adequate signal communications was assured at all times, primarily by the use of conventional and microwave radio sets.

Since the troops were constantly on the move, launching successive attacks toward the west, they never developed the feeling of being trapped in the slowly tightening grip of an encircling enemy force. Consequently, there were no signs of disintegration or panic, and the number of missing during the entire operation remained unusually low. By 5 April the leading elements of both the northern and the southern attack forces reached the Strypa River. On the following day, near Buczacz, they were able to link up with other German units coming from the west.

In two weeks of heavy fighting, but without suffering severe casualties, First Panzer Army had freed itself from enemy encirclement. Rear guard actions continued for a few days and then the Germans succeeded in establishing a new, continuous defense line running from the Dnestr to the town of Brody, which prevented any further advance of the Soviets. Moreover, despite their considerable losses in materiel, elements of First Panzer Army were still able to launch an attack southeast across the Dnestr to break up an enemy force which had appeared in the Stanislav area. Soviet equipment captured and destroyed during the entire breakout operation amounted to 357 tanks, 42 assault guns, and 280 artillery pieces.

While the Russians were threatening the southern sector of the Eastern Front with collapse, events were unfolding off the South Coast of England which would completely alter the complexion of the war in the East. The long awaited Second Front was about to be created. Until now the Allied practical support had been limited to sending vehicles to support the Russians and fighting a slow campaign in Italy.

By the first week in July one million Allied soldiers had been landed. With the arrival of the third battle front in Europe, German military resources were more stretched than ever.

While the attention of the world focused on the D-Day landings, the Red Army launched a fresh offensive against Army Group Centre in Belorussia. It was this offensive more than any other which was to do most to win victory for Stalin.

The destruction of Army Group Centre moved at lightning speed. After two years of stubborn resistance, most of the 3rd Panzer Army was destroyed within a few days. At the beginning of July 1944, one hundred thousand German troops were encircled at Minsk. Within the week Army Group Centre had been effectively destroyed. A gap two hundred and fifty miles wide had been ripped in the German Front and German casualties were estimated at thirty thousand. The Russian Army now had a clear pathway to East Prussia and the Baltic. The failure of the Germans to deal with

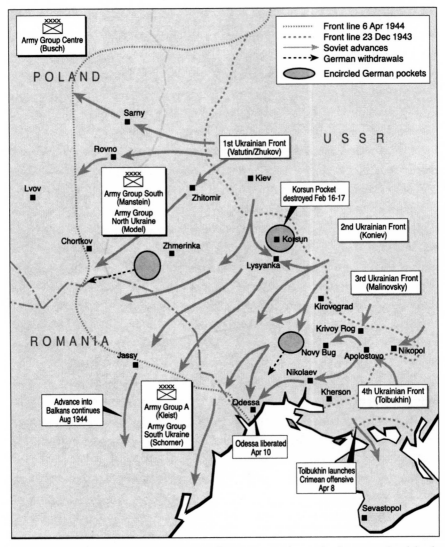

the summer offensive was emerging as a disaster on such a scale that even the debacle of Stalingrad paled in comparison.

The war correspondent, Alexander Werth, reported from the Russian capital, "In Moscow today all hearts are filled with joy. Every night, a familiar deep male voice, speaking like a man giving orders to soldiers, announces a new major victory. The new places now being captured by the Russians are in distant Lithuania or in Western Belorussia. Division after division has been encircled and wiped out, hundreds of thousands killed and about one hundred thousand taken prisoner. Even the score of generals captured is about twenty-five. Of these one hundred thousand or so prisoners,

202

fifty seven thousand were paraded through the streets of Moscow with their Generals at their head. The Moscow crowd was remarkably disciplined. They watched the Germans walk or rather shuffle past, in their dirty grey-green uniforms - this grey-green mould which had rotted away half of European Russia and was still rotting a great part of Europe. The Moscow people looked on quietly without booing or hissing, and only a few youngsters could be heard shouting "Hey, look at the Fritzes with their ugly snouts", but most people only exchanged remarks in soft voices. I heard a little girl perched on her mother's shoulders say "Mummy are these the people who killed Daddy?" And the mother hugged the child and wept. The Germans had finally arrived in Moscow. When the parade was over Russian sanitation trucks disinfected the streets."

By the middle of July the Germans had been swept from Belorussia and the Russians held much of North East Poland. As they drove northwards into Lithuania, Army Group North was threatened with en-circlement.

South of the Pripyat Marsh the Russians were making faster progress. Army Group North Ukraine was flung back beyond Lvov and Lublin. By the end of July 1944, units of the Red Army had reached the Vistula and were attacking the Warsaw suburbs.

On the 1st August the Polish Home Army command in London, anxious that the Polish capital should not fall into the hands of the advancing Soviets, ordered the Warsaw Partisans to rise against their Nazi oppressors. It was to prove a tragic mistake. The Wehrmacht was on the road to defeat, but it was not beaten yet.

The 20,000 insurgents held only enough ammunition for seven days fighting. By the end of the battle after two months of bitter struggle, nine tenths of the city had been destroyed, 200,000 people had been massacred and the rest deported to extermination camps. The SS had organised an orgy of savagery, dousing suspects with petrol and setting them alight, gassing them in the sewers and subjecting them to a nightmare regime of torture and summary execution. During this period the Red Army remained inactive on the outskirts of the city. With good reason, Stalin was accused of standing by, while this barbarous German campaign of reprisal wiped out any opposition to the future Russian domination of Poland.

Although they did nothing in the Warsaw sectors, on the 20th August the Red Army unexpectedly launched a huge offensive against Rumania, a major headache for Hitler. The Rumanian oilfields produced the last significant supplies for the hard-pressed German army, and was a major issue for Hitler. By the 23rd, twenty divisions of the German 6th Army had been encircled in a giant pocket between the rivers Dnestr and Prut. The skill of the Russian advance was admired by the eminent military historian Ziemke who noted "In executing their breakthroughs, the Russians showed an elegance in their tactical conceptions, economy of force, and control that did not fall short of the Germans' own performance in the early war years."

The effect of these reverses on Hitler was catastrophic. Increasingly he retreated into a semi-fantasy world which did not correspond to the realities of the battlefield. It seemed that he hoped to hide from the public eye until he could once again force events to conform to the pattern he had enjoyed until 1942. So he continued to hide himself away in his headquarters, embarrassed to face up to the hollowness of his boasts. Hitler's ostensible reason for shutting himself away was the demands made on him by the war, in reality he was hiding from the humiliating pattern of failure. He now lived in a private world of his own from which the ugly and awkward facts of Germany's situation were excluded. He refused to visit the bombed towns, just as he refused to read reports which contradicted the picture he wanted to form.

The commanders in the east nevertheless had to deal with the realities of orders issued by this shambling recluse, who was now a pathetic shadow of the decisive, intuitive and supremely arrogant leader who had launched Operation Barbarossa.

Stalin sent the Red Army of Liberation northwards into Rumania and by the 31st August Bucharest had been entered. An essentially Communist Government was formed and Rumania was compelled to ratify its 1940 loss of territory to Russia. It was also forced to pay the Soviet Union a financial indemnity and use its army to fight against its erstwhile allies. The Red Army had advanced two hundred and fifty miles in twelve days. In the next six days it dashed a further two hundred miles to the Yugoslav border at Turnu Severin. From here the Soviets launched a giant flanking manoeuvre against the Axis defenders of Hungary. By 24th September the south east salient of Hungary had been removed and the Russians advanced to within a hundred miles of Budapest.

Further south the Yugoslav capital, Belgrade, was liberated with the aid of the Yugoslavian resistance under Tito. Bulgaria, until now at war only with Britain and the United States was pressurised by Germany into declaring war on the USSR as well. Four days after this declaration of 5th September, the Bulgarians surrendered. Further west, Slovakia, formally a co-belligerent of Germany, had been in a state of upheaval since the previous year. A general uprising began in the second half of 1944 but a Russian advance which began in September was held up in the Carpathians by a stiff German resistance and failed to reach Slovakia before the middle of October. By then the sixty five thousand strong uprising had been quelled. The results of Nazi barbarity, by now sickeningly familiar, greeted Russian liberators and more than two hundred mass graves had been filled with slaughtered Slovaks.

The unremitting pattern of bad news continued on all fronts. In the north an armistice was concluded with Finland and the Germans driven back into Norway before climatic conditions put an end to the fighting there. The Baltic States of Estonia, Latvia, and Lithuania were overrun and the German Army Group North isolated in the Kurland Peninsula.

When the Russian armies poured across Germany's eastern borders in the beginning of 1945, the Army High Command introduced a major improvisation, the Leuthen Project, which constituted a radical change in the Army's replacement and training polity. To the German mind Leuthen, a small town in Silesia where Frederick the Great had won a major battle with the improvised forces, was the symbol of a victorious last-ditch stand. It was probably for this reason that the Army selected the term Leuthen to designate this project. The plan foresaw that all training units of the entire Replacement Army were to be transferred and assigned to the field forces as soon as the code word Leuthen was transmitted to them.

The exact operation of these desperate measures were later described for a US Army pamphlet.

"In immediate proximity of the front these training units were to be subjected to a more realistic combat training than they could possibly receive in the zone of the interior. Moreover, they were to serve as security forces in rear area positions or defence lines. The original idea was therefore both sound and practical, but it should have been put into effect much sooner, when the front was still stable. What actually prompted the execution of the Leuthen Project at that late stage, whether it was still the original intention as officially proclaimed, or rather the steadily deteriorating situation on the fighting fronts, must be left to conjecture. In reality, all the Leuthen units were immediately committed and thrown into the thick of fighting in critical situations.

What did the Leuthen units look like? In every Wehrkreis there were a number of training and replacement units of various arms which were under the command of division staffs. The men who had completed their training and were ready for combat duty were in the replacement units. The training units were composed of recently inducted recruits who were to be prepared for combat by undergoing an eight-week basic training course. Upon receiving the code word Leuthen, the division staffs were to move out with all training units that had completed one to seven weeks of training.

One of the units alerted in this manner was the Special Administrative Division 413, which consisted of several training battalions, a regimental headquarters, an artillery battalion with an odd assortment of guns, and elements of an engineer and a signal battalion. As a tactical unit, the division was really no more than a reinforced infantry regiment, commanded by an elderly general with a small staff. Needless to state, is was absolutely incapable of any combat assignment. The cadre up to the division commander consisted of personnel unfit for combat because of sickness, injury, or for lack of tactical qualifications. Most of the non-commissioned officers had suffered combat injuries of such severity that they were barely fit for garrison duty. Some of the men were entirely untrained, others had completed one half to three quarters of their basic training. Some of them were unarmed because the number of weapons provided for training units did not suffice to arm every soldier. In addition, the various formations had absolutely no organic transportation. There were no more horses than those needed for the normal garrison functions and the division had no field kitchens since the food had always been prepared in the permanent garrison kitchens. The clothing and equipment were equally defective. Quite a few soldiers, for instance, could not be issued garrison belts. In general, everything was in exactly the condition to be expected from a home station in times of stress, where shortages have become the rule rather than the exception.

When the Leuthen division moved out it was therefore no more than an improvisation of the poorest sort. This might not have mattered so much had the division undergone a rigid training schedule far behind the lines. But even while it was on the approach march to its destination, one of its battalions was shifted from the Main River Valley to Hammelburg where a small enemy armoured force had broken through. The remainder of the division was immediately sent into combat and annihilated.

In summarising, one may state that the Leuthen Project was doomed from the outset because it was applied in a situation for which it was entirely unsuited."

In view of the extremely heavy losses of manpower, the shortage of weapons, and the precarious condition of the transportation system, the situation of the German Army became so critical that the need for improvisations grew even more urgent during the last few weeks of the war. The organisational improvisations of that period were a far cry from those introduced during earlier stages. In many cases the selection and training of replacements was makeshift. Equipment of all types was totally inadequate and consisted of whatever was left over or could be picked up. Since no guns were available, the organisation of new artillery units was practically impossible. Whatever new infantry units were organised during this period were of limited capability in the field. In Bavaria, for instance, the last regular activation of a new infantry division took place in November 1944. What followed thereafter was pure improvisation, not so much because of the shortage of trained replacements, but because of the inadequate supply of weapons and equipment.

Although the organisation of new divisions had become impossible, replacement units were sent to the front until the beginning of March 1945. Then, even this function could no longer be accomplished. Each Wehrkreis assumed command over its replacements, organised a few emergency infantry battalions and transferred them to the nearest tactical command. Many well-trained soldiers were still available but

War weary Grenadiers crawl through the wreckage of another destroyed city.

because of the serious shortage of infantry heavy weapons, it was no longer possible to organise entire machine gun companies. The battalions were therefore composed of a small battalion staff and four rifle companies. Each company had one machine gun platoon with two heavy machine guns and a few locally requisitioned would-be-artillery battalions organised during this period were composed of a great variety of guns. No two batteries were alike and every section had guns of different calibre.

During that period, occurred a very significant incident which demonstrated the effects of the improper utilisation of administrative personnel. Several first-rate panzer battalions were in the process of rehabilitation at the Grafenwoehr troop training grounds in Bavaria. When enemy armoured spearheads approached the area, a corps commander responsible for a near-by sector of the front, who was well along in years but had always handled administrative assignments very competently, but had never during his long career commanded a panzer unit, ordered the staff of the training centre

In the closing stages of the war, the Luftwaffe had practically disappeared from the skies above Germany, so the troops had to remain on constant vigilance for air attacks.

to assume the tactical command of the panzer battalions and stop the enemy. His staff was composed of elderly reserve officers and ordnance specialists. Their leadership spelled disaster for the panzer battalions.

The numerous organisational improvisations introduced during that period were only stop-gap measures applied in time of extreme emergency. Since most of them were adopted to overcome purely local critical situations, they are of little consequence in a study of this type.

During the years proceeding the outbreak of the war, civilian labour procurement had to be improvised on a large scale for the construction of fortifications. Even at the time when the West Wall was under construction, the allocation of manpower was essentially an improvisation of gigantic proportions. Receiving unusually high pay and enjoying a variety of other benefits, hundreds of thousands of men were employed by the Todt Organisation and moved from one building project to the next. Not everything that was built at that time was beyond criticism, yet some of the achievement of the years 1938-39 would not have been possible without these improvisations. Toward the end of the war another improvised labour force was formed to construct additional fortifications in the west. This time it consisted of entire Hitler Youth units, of men who were in age groups subject to labour conscription but too old for military service, and of men who were no longer fit for combat.

The improvisations introduced during that period had highly political aspects. They were directed by laymen, some of whom had never seen military service and whose technical knowledge was very limited. They were unaware of the major importance of material in military planning and were inclined to confuse a temporary surge of enthusiasm - such as undoubtedly existed among the Hitler Youth Combat Units - with real fighting ability. These party functionaries were under the erroneous impression that their own fanaticism was shared by everybody and that this alone would make up for all the shortages and deficiencies which characterise all last-minute improvisations. On the other hand, there was little opportunity for preventive measures at a time when only painstaking efforts could conceal the existing chaos. The Volkssturm might perhaps have presented such an opportunity, if only it had been drawn up as a levée en masse with long-range material preparations and if an entirely different slogan had been used for the mental and spiritual conditioning of the people.

The most extensive improvisation undertaken by the National Socialist Party was the mobilisation of the Volkssturm during the last few months of the war. The idea was to call on the last forces of resistance the German people were capable of mustering. A misunderstood and misinterpreted tradition built on memories of 1813 may also have played its part in the minds of some Party officials.

The Volkssturm included all men up to the highest age groups, as long as they were capable of bearing arms and were not already serving with the armed forces. This might have provided a broad basis for successfully mobilising whatever fighting strength had not yet been tapped, if there had not been a complete lack of weapons, clothing and equipment. Whereas clothing and equipment might conceivably be improvised, this does not hold true of arming hundreds of thousands or even millions of men. The Wehrmacht could spare nothing. At the same time it became more and more obvious that the paramilitary Party formations had hoarded and hidden weapons and ammunition, but in view of the large number of Volkssturm draftees these weapons were of little help. Then, a Party official had the idea of manufacturing simplified Volkssturm rifles with barrels he could "procure" from some factories in Saxony. This plan was also of little consequence. Thus the whole project of staging an armed levée en masse was doomed from the very outset.

Leadership and training were two of the other problems to be solved. Among the men of the Volkssturm were many veterans of World War I. Although there had been many changes in the field of tactics, these men had sufficient military background to cope with the simple missions of which the Volkssturm was capable. To provide adequate training was a more difficult matter. Men who differed widely in age, former branch

Russian tanks roll into an Austrian town.

of service, or type of training, as well as men without any training whatsoever, were attending military drill period in their spare time as a rule on Sundays. Occasionally, in towns with local garrisons, one or two instructors were provided by regular army units. That was all the assistance the Wehrmacht could give because it had no men to spare. Moreover the Volkssturm was a Party improvisation and probably deliberately kept apart from the Wehrmacht from its initial organisation.

Only when actually committed in combat was the Volkssturm to be placed under the tactical control of the Wehrmacht and fight in conjunction with the regular field forces. There was no reason for great expectations. The call to arms for an extended tour of duty was to be locally restricted. The men were to be called upon only if the enemy threatened their home county and even that was almost too much to expect. When, towards the end of the war, entire Volkssturm battalions were committed far away from their homes on the Eastern Front, this emergency measure was contrary to the spirit and original mission of the Volkssturm and could only lead to failure.

Guard duty and local security assignments were practically the only missions for which the Volkssturm was really qualified. Its composition, its limited training, and the fact that no more than rifles and in some cases only pistols and hand grenades could be issued as weapons, precluded its commitment in real combat operations.

Since it was incapable of withstanding critical situations, the Volkssturm could only become a liability and threat to the troops it was to join in battle. Its proper mission was to construct and guard road blocks. Important psychological considerations spoke against restricting Volkssturm units to purely local commitments. Often the primary interest of the men resided in inflicting a minimum of war damage to the home towns where their families lived. Thus, it was safe to assume that the Volkssturm men would prefer to avoid any last-ditch stand in the immediate vicinity of their home towns. The tactical commanders therefore took the precaution to suggest that road blocks and fortifications should be erected at a sufficient distance from any community, in order to spare it the effects of combat action. The orders from higher headquarters specified that no Volkssturm units should be committed any closer than thirty miles to their immediate home towns. This, however, meant a complete reversal of the basic principle of restricting the Volkssturm men to the defence of their immediate home territories.

In East Prussia, the Volkssturm did a better job than anywhere else. It was here that the idea of the Volkssturm levy had originated. Since East Prussia was the first German province directly threatened by the enemy. There the organisation and training of the Volkssturm made the greatest progress.

East Prussia alone raised thirty-two Volkssturm battalions. All of these remained in that province even when, in November 1944, the civilian population from the northern districts had to be evacuated. After that, most of the Volkssturm units were used to prepare reserve battle positions in the rear area for a possible withdrawal of the combat troops who in turn provided instructors for the Volkssturm battalions. Months of continuous instruction raised their standard of training to such a degree that a number of Volkssturm battalions were able to carry out limited combat missions. A few of these so-called special employment units were equipped with a sufficient number of modern weapons such as the most recent 75mm anti-tank guns, the latest model machine guns, and some older-type small-calibre anti-aircraft guns. Some of them even had adequate motor transportation. The units were composed of a small percentage of World War I veterans, with the rest about equally divided between sixteen and seventeen year old youngsters and elderly men from sixty to seventy-five. Some of the battalions were under the command of former staff officers who had distinguished themselves in World War I but were now afflicted with various physical disabilities. The majority of the battalions were short of weapons, equipment, and training, and their employment in actual combat operations was out of the question. It was planned to integrate them into the field forces only in case of a general withdrawal of the lines.

From the outset this was recognised as a serious handicap which, however, could not be corrected since the army had no jurisdiction over these formations. Time and again, the Army requested that the battalions be immediately disbanded and all Volkssturm men fit for combat duty be transferred to the field forces. Yet every one of these requests was flatly rejected by the Party. Thus, during the latter part of January 1945 when the front began to give way, most of the Volkssturm battalions employed in East Prussia were of no use to the army. Wherever they did not disintegrate altogether, they suffered heavy casualties. But contrary to standing orders, a few battalions had been moved up into combat alongside seasoned field units during the proceeding weeks and these battalions gave a good account of themselves. An example of this rare breed is the Volkssturm Battalion Libau which fought as part of a division improvised from service troops. Three times the battalion was dislodged but in every case it launched fierce counter-attacks. In this bitter struggle the battalion commander and most of his troops remained on the field of battle.

Other times the Volkssturm performed less well. Showing much zeal in military matters, Party Headquarters in East Prussia produced its own 75mm anti-tank guns with iron-wheeled gun mounts and conducted short training courses to familiarise members of the Volkssturm organisation with the weapon. By the end of January 1945 the situation near Tapiau east of Koenigsberg was obscure. There, the personnel of an army ordnance school were engaged in bitter fighting against advancing enemy armour. The commanding officer of the ordnance school had been killed and Tapiau had changed hands several times but was held by German troops at that moment. Rumour had it that enemy tanks had broken through and were advancing on Koenigsberg. Thereupon, Party Headquarters improvised an anti-tank gun battalion with twenty new 75mm anti-tank guns from its training school and dispatched it to the area east of Koenigsberg, to take up positions for the protection of that city. At sundown strong armoured formations suddenly came into sight opposite the anti-tank gun position. This impressive spectacle caused such a state of terror among the inexperienced gun crews, that they left their guns and ran for cover in all directions. Their leader, a young first lieutenant, tried in vain to stop them. Assisted by a few instructors he succeeded in getting some of the guns ready for action and was just about to open fire when he realised to his surprise that he was facing German tanks. It was the 5th Panzer Division which, after heavy tank fighting in the area east of Tapiau, had succeeded in breaking through the enemy lines and was now assembling in this area in compliance with its orders. For once the failure of an improvisation was of distinct advantage.

Towards the very end of the war, the Party organised certain tactical units which were to be committed in the field. Political considerations predominated and outweighed all others. For some time past, elements of the Reich Labour Service had served as anti-aircraft units. Since there were absolutely no other forces available, elements of

A lend-lease Sherman tank with its Russian commander in the streets of Vienna.

labour service battalions were employed to defend the road blocks they had previously constructed.

Hitler Youth Combat Units, organised during the last weeks of the war, were assigned to the field forces on various sectors of the front. Their special task was the pursuit and destruction of enemy tanks, with the help of bazookas and Panzerfausts. Just before the end of the war, Party Secretary Bormann attempted to organise an Adolf Hitler Volunteer Corps.

By January 1945, with all German troops finally driven from the holy soil of Mother Russia and Stalin in control of the Balkans and the Baltic States, the Red Army prepared for its final drive towards the Reich. Between June and November, the German Army in the East had suffered two hundred and fourteen thousand men killed in action, and six hundred and twenty nine thousand missing in action or held prisoner. Another approximately six hundred thousand men had been seriously wounded. 1944 had proved Germany's most disastrous year of the War in the East, one hundred and six divisions had been destroyed, three more than the total number mobilised in September 1939. German intelligence estimated that in the assault on the Reich, the Red Army would possess a superiority of eleven to one in infantry, seven to one in tanks, and twenty to one in guns. Hitler dismissed such estimates as "bluff".

On the 12th January the Soviets launched their expected offensive from the Vistula against the German Central Front. The seventy divisions of Army Group Centre and Army Group A were pierced over an area of two hundred miles and almost two hundred

Red Army divisions poured through the breach. By the end of the month Soviet Forces reached the lower reaches of the River Oder and were now only forty miles from Berlin. The remnants of Army Group Centre had been encircled in East Prussia. Falling back on the ancient city of Koenigsberg, they desperately attempted to carry out Hitler's order to defend the region to a man. The Soviet tide was finally halted on the line of the River Oder and Neisse in February; now the limited German counter stroke was merely postponing the inevitable. A fresh Russian offensive in Hungary progressed to the borders of Austria by April 1st and six days later the outskirts of Vienna were coming under Soviet fire.

The situation was clearly deteriorating fast for the German forces, who were now being hard pressed from both East and West, but even in these last desperate months, the German Wehrmacht continued to function as a fighting force.

Army Group Centre was a case in point. As most of the seasoned veterans of the Eastern Front had been lost in the great encirclement battle of the 19th June 1944, for the final defence of Germany in 1945, a new 'Army Group Centre' was thrown together under the command of General Schorner. Although the men of the new Army Group Centre fought with great courage, there was little that they could do to prevent a second and final collapse. In January 1945, elements of Army Group Centre was again trapped and surrounded in East Prussia with the pocket centred on the town of Kustrin, where they continued to offer resistance until April 1945.

Under General Heinrici, the surviving elements of Army Group Centre were ordered to join in the last gasp defence of Berlin. Eventually, even here, sanity prevailed and in direct opposition to Hitler's orders, Heinrici moved his men away from Berlin and certain destruction. It saved at least some lives. The brave survivors of Army Group Centre deserved no less.

As the Reich disintegrated around them, and the overwhelming might of the Red Army began to grind Germany into submission, the last surviving elements of the army were finally trapped by the Red Army in Konigsburg, where they surrendered on May 8th 1945. The name of Army Group Centre was associated with the very highest fighting spirit to the very last.

The survivors of the old Army Group North, now Army Group Kurland, maintained their cohesion and fighting ability until the final surrender on May 8th 1945, almost four years since they had first moved into Russia. On that day, two hundred and three thousand men began the long march into Soviet captivity. Many would never return and others were held as slave labourers until 1955. A high price to pay for their long defiance.

Of the three huge army groups which Hitler sent into Russia, it could be argued that Army Group North was the most successful in carrying out the tasks assigned to it. Although the campaign ultimately ended in failure for them, the men of Army Group North retained their military cohesion, with some units achieving the rare distinction of serving for the whole four years of the Russian war in the same army group.

From 1944 onwards, only bitter fighting retreats awaited Army Group South. They still put up some incredible resistance. The dogged fighting retreat which allowed 30,000 trapped German soldiers to escape from a pocket near Korsun, is a lasting testament to courage in adversity. General Hube's famous fighting withdrawal in March 1944, was another stirring feat of endurance and tenacity, but the writing was on the wall for the Wehrmacht in Russia.

The destruction of Army Group Centre in June 1944, created a huge gap in the German front in Russia. In order to manage the over stretched forces of Army Group South, it was again divided into two separate commands, Army Group North Ukraine under Model and Army Group South Ukraine under Schorner. The net effect was the same, the Russian advance was now a headlong dash. Despite some tenacious resistance during the fierce summer battles of 1944, there was little that could now be done to prevent the final defeat.

On the 20th September, 1944 the Army Group South title was again revived and bestowed on a scratch group of formations, fighting under General Freissner but the inevitable could not be delayed much longer.

For a time, the rather pathetic rumour that Army Group South was about to join forces to fight with the Americans against the Russians, gained currency. But by now, they were clutching at straws.

Operation Spring Awakening, designed to roll back the Red Army, proved to be the final offensive by the Wehrmacht in the East. The last remaining forces of Army Group South, under their last commander General Rendulic, surrendered near Vienna in May 1945. The long struggle was finally over.

Shortly after the war, Colonel General Rendulic, the last commander of Army Group South, gave a long account of these final few weeks of fighting to his American captors, which still survives in manuscript form.

"On 6th April 1945, I received orders to take command of Army Group South, which had retreated from Hungary to bring it to a halt, and to hold Vienna whatever the cost. In any event, however, I was to stop the Russians from penetrating into the Alps and advancing in the Donau valley.

To my question of 6th April 1945, as to how the continuation or the termination of the war was envisaged, I received the answer that the war was to be ended by political measures. I could not get more detailed information, however, and had to assume that

The Panzer IV was the only German tank which entered service before the war which was still operational in 1945. By then, its limitations were obvious and the attrition rate was high.

the statement had some basis in truth.

By ferocious fighting, it was possible to bring the Second Panzer and Sixth Armies south of the Schemering Pass, and the Eighth Army north of the Donau, to a halt and to form a new and reasonably firm defensive front. From the start, Army Group South was eager to move forces into the area between the approaches to the mountains west of Vienna, for it was conceivable that the Russians, after the fall of Vienna, would press their attack westward in the Donau valley. We succeeded in constructing along the line Kaumberg-Neu Longback - the Donau a very weak front, which gradually grew in strength and which was under the command of General of Infantry von Buenau.

In view of the impending cessation of hostilities, Army Group South refrained from destroying bridges and roads in its area."

There was now a widespread, if rather forlorn hope, among the German forces, who had seen the Russian advances, that it might be possible to join forces with the Americans and British to continue the common struggle against the Red menace. Although some later writers have tried to give serious credence to this theory, Rendulic himself makes it clear that no real prospect of this existed at the battlefield level, although doubtless, a number of German commanders contrived to hold on to this last pathetic straw of hope.

"Army Group South were aware of the possibility that, upon reaching our sector, the Americans and the British might join us against the Russians. This possibility had now become essential, and the final moment to discover the truth had finally arrived. Above and beyond the attitude and demeanour of the Americans, there were other facts which made the idea seem possible. For example, many telephone lines and installations in upper Austria were still intact, although they were now behind the American front lines. Also, supply columns of the Army Group and of the American forces drew rations from the same ration supply depots in northern Austria and drove along together on the same roads leading to the East.

The advance of the Americans offered the first opportunity to clarify the situation. On the morning of 6th May 1945, the Army Group Commander sent Major General Caedcke with a letter to the Commanding General Third US Army General Patton. The letter asked General Patton to allow the movement of medical supplies from the area south of Salzberg by the road through Linz. General Caedcke was also instructed to ask for authorisation to move troops from western Austria, through the American lines, to the Eastern Front. For the American forces, negotiations were handled by the Commanding General XX Corps, General Walker.

General Caedcke returned to Army Group Headquarters on the evening of 6 May 1945 and brought with him refusals to both requests, with the comment that it could hardly be expected that U.S. forces would allow the movement of German troops (which would have to be disarmed anyway), through an American controlled area, to bolster the German front against an ally of the U.S.A. It was now obvious that the hopes for a political solution of the war were false. On the same evening, prior to the return of General Caedcke, Field Marshal Kesselring (who now held supreme command in the south) issued the following order, by telephone to the Army Group Commander.

"It is essential for the salvation of the Reich that the Eastern Front be held. Effective immediately, strong resistance is to be offered to the Americans along the Enns."

After the arrival of General Caedcke with his clarification of the situation, the Army Group Commander considered it irresponsible to ask for further sacrifice in a battle which had become completely senseless. During the night of 6th May 1945, he ordered the cessation of hostilities on the Western Front, facing the U.S. forces, from 0900 on 7th May 1945. At the same time, he commanded the armies on the Eastern Front to disengage at dark on 7th May 1945 and to retreat westward. At that time nothing was known at Army Group Headquarters about the armistice negotiations between OKW and the Supreme Commander of the U.S. forces.

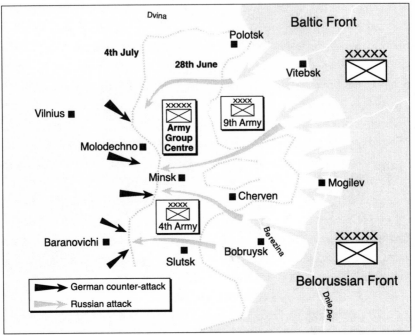

The bulk of the forces of Army Group Centre were trapped and destroyed between the city of Minsk and the river Brezina in a victory of such finality it is often compared to the destruction of the Roman army at Cannae.

6. THE DESTRUCTION OF ARMY GROUP CENTRE

The defeat of the Army Group Centre in the summer of 1944 must rank as one of the most sudden and complete military disasters in history. It was a remarkably brief and complete battle of annihilation which made Stalingrad pale into insignificance.

As supreme commander, Adolf Hitler must shoulder the blame for the catastrophic defeat which befell Army Group Centre in June 1944. It was his policy of holding on to territory at all costs which contributed more than any other single factor to this cataclysmic defeat. In the Führer's order of 8th March 1944,

(Order number 11) Hitler expanded upon his concept of a "fortified locality".

"The fortified localities are intended to discharge the same function as fortresses in the past, the day must prevent the enemy from taking possession of strategically vital localities, they must allow themselves to become encircled, and in this way tie down the largest possible number of enemy forces. In this way they will also play a part in creating the prerequisite for successful counter-operations."

The fortified localities were intended to be supported by a number of smaller positions which would be known as local strong points. Obviously Hitler had given a great deal of thought to the matter and his Führer's order expanded upon the expected roles of the troops trapped in what were "fortresses" only in the deranged mind of the Führer. His order number 11 continues-

"The 'Local strong points' are envisaged as stubbornly defended strong points in the depth of the battlefield, in the event of any breakthrough. By incorporation in the main defensive line, they are to provide the backbone of defence in the event of any penetration, and the pivot points, and corner posts of the front, as well as jumping off basis for counter-attacks. The Commandant's of the fortified localities should be specially selected from the very toughest soldiers, if possible of generals rank. His appointment will be made by the army group concerned and the commandant of a fortified locality is to be personally entrusted with his task by the Commander in Chief."

signed Adolf Hitler.

Despite the repeated lessons which had time and time again shown that tactical withdrawals could often avert a dangerous situation, Adolf Hitler clung to the concept of "fortified localities". In his increasingly deranged imagination, the concept of allowing formations to be first surrounded and then used as spring boards for a counter-offensive, represented sound military logic despite all evidence to the contrary. Hitler had never enjoyed a trusting relationship with the army high command and favoured the Counsel or only the most sycophantic officers among his immediate retinue. Unfortunately none of the generals in the field had sufficient influence to overcome the stubborn will of Adolf Hitler. The fate of Army Group Centre was sealed.

On 22nd June 1944, the same date as that on which Hitler had originally launched Operation Barbarossa, the Red Army launched its own all out offensive against the salient held by Army Group Centre. Hitler immediately declared that the garrisons of the "fortified localities" should prepare to allow themselves to be cut off. Effectively this meant that the troops stationed in Vitebsk, Mogilev and

Bobruysk, who could have been of enormous value in a fighting retreat, would become encircled in a futile attempt to complete a ludicrous mission.

The forces fighting in Army Group Centre had been drained by two years of constant combat, losses had not been made up and the strength of the divisions fighting in the field had been constantly diluted. Now as the Soviet forces swept through the crumbling German front, defenders could no longer produce the strength to provide the ferocious resistance which had been its hallmark in previous years. In consequence, the Red Army continued to sweep onwards towards the West, leaving the "fortified localities" so deep in Russian territory that they were soon beyond help. By refusing them the right to make even a tactical withdrawal, Hitler had signed the death warrant for many of the divisions which formed Army Group Centre.

The bulk of the German 4th Army and 9th Army were trapped in the area between the City of Minsk and the river Berezina. The newly appointed Army Group commander, General Model, tried in vain to stabilise the situation. He even attempted to scrape together a new defensive front and managed to bring up some extra divisions to go over to the counter-offensive. But the German counter-attacks were brushed aside by the oncoming Russian forces. Only five weeks after the start of the offensive, the Russian armies were already on the border of East Prussia, Poland. Army Group Centre had effectively ceased to exist. A gap of two hundred and fifty miles now existed between the forces of Army Group South and Army Group North, held only by scattered remnants of a once proud fighting force.

A section of the German prisoners who were paraded through Moscow after the collapse of Army Group Centre.

THE KEY BATTLES

7. THE FALL OF THE REICH

During 1944 with the tides of war running inexorably against Germany, it seemed there was a very real prospect of an end to the conflict in that year. The Russians had christened 1944 as the year of ten victories, in honour of the unbroken stream of successes which had begun with the lifting of the siege of Leningrad. By October, the commander of the first Baltic front could report to Moscow that Army Group North had been driven apart from Army Group Centre and that large elements of the 16th and 18th German armies were now trapped in the Kurland Bridgehead. In fact these two armies, supplied by the valiant efforts of the Kreigsmarine, managed to hold out against overwhelming odds, until the final German surrender in May 1945. The unflagging resistance of the men trapped in the Kurland Peninsula is typical of the dogged resistance which German forces continued to offer in the last days of the War. In the face of continued resistance like this, the drive for Berlin could not begin in earnest until April 16th 1945.

The final assault on Germany itself began at the southern end of the front on 12th January 1945, when the massed tanks and infantry of the first Ukrainian Front under Marshal Koniev moved against the German lines. By now the German army was massively outnumbered and the best estimates are that they possessed one tank for every sixteen which the Russians could put into battle. The advance of the first Ukrainian Front swept through Poland and saw the Russian armies on the border with Czechoslovakia by the end of March.

Farther north, the first Belorussian Front under Zukhov swept aside the newly formed German Army Group A and, by the end of March, Zukhov's troops were positioned at Kustrin only fifty miles from Hitler's capital. Further north, the last remnants of Army Group Centre were trapped in a huge pocket centred around Konigsberg by the combined forces of the second Belorussian Front advancing from the North of Warsaw and the third Belorussian Front which had launched its offensive from Lithuania.

By the first week of April, German resistance in the east of the country was limited to a few "fortresses" on the Baltic coast including Konigsberg, Kolburg and the valiant remnants of the 16th and 18th armies which continued to resist in their

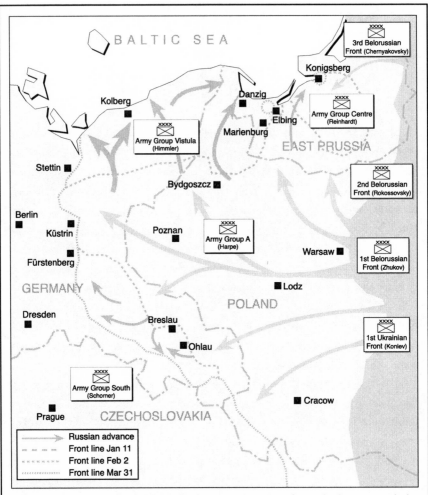

BALTIC SEA

3rd Belorussian
Front (Chernyakovsky)
XXXX

Konigsberg

Kolberg

Danzig

Elbing

Army Group Centre
(Reinhardt)
XXXX

Marienburg

Army Group Vistula
(Himmler)
XXXX

EAST PRUSSIA

Stettin

2nd Belorussian
Front (Rokossovsky)
XXXX

Bydgoszcz

Berlin

Küstrin

Poznan

Army Group A
(Harpe)
XXXX

Warsaw

1st Belorussian
Front (Zhukov)
XXXX

Fürstenberg

GERMANY

Lodz

POLAND

Dresden

Breslau

Ohlau

1st Ukrainian
Front (Koniev)
XXXX

Army Group South
(Schörner)
XXXX

Cracow

Prague

CZECHOSLOVAKIA

Russian advance
Front line Jan 11
Front line Feb 2
Front line Mar 31

isolated positions around Kurland. The enormous sacrifices which were made by
men fighting in what were obviously lost causes, was justified by both the men and
their commanders, on the grounds that the continued resistance against the Soviet
thrusts had allowed thousands of refugees to escape from the terror of the Red
Army advance. With the blessing, and in many cases actual participation of, their
officers, the men of the Soviet forces in Germany, embarked on an unrestrained
orgy of looting, murder and mass rape which, given all that had occurred in Russia,
was to an extent predictable.

As they advanced into Germany, the Red Army had the opportunity to
demonstrate that the forces of barbarism could be replaced by humanity. They
chose instead to behave in a manner which aped the vile excesses of the regime

A German soldier has paid the ultimate price for Hitler's greatest gamble.

against which they fought.

All that remained for the ordinary German citizen was to wait for the Red Army to regroup and gather its huge strength for the final assault on Berlin.

Soviet fighter bombers over Berlin in the last days of the war.

CHAPTER 8
THE BATTLE FOR BERLIN

On April 16th 1945, the final thrust toward Berlin was begun. On the first day of the assault alone, twenty two thousand artillery pieces and mortars fired two thousand four hundred and fifty freight car loads of shells toward the German lines. Zhukov, excited at the prospect of being the first Soviet Commander to reach Berlin, opened the attack, lighting up the battle field with searchlights to blind the enemy.

Having retreated to the capital, Hitler alternated between vitriolic outbursts about betrayal and demonic delight in the holocaust which was descending on Germany. In the words of Albert Speer he "deliberately attempted to make everything perish with him".

Army, state and economic leaders tried to mediate Hitler's destructiveness with varying degrees of success. By 22nd of April, with Russian troops now fighting on the streets of the German capital, the insanity was about to end. But the street warfare

Soviet infantry storm the steps of the devastated citadel. It is highly likely that this picture was specially staged for the camera.

in Berlin was bitter. The threat of a Bolshevik invasion had been hyped by the nazi propaganda machine as the end of Germany and the German people. Even in the last chaotic days of the Reich there was a common joke, "Enjoy the war while you can, the peace will be terrible."

Amidst the smoking ruins of Berlin a remarkably cohesive defence was maintained by the remnants of those German armies which were still capable of offering resistance. The main defenders of Berlin were the 9th Army under Buss to the south of Berlin and the 11th Army under Steiner, fighting to the north of the city. Since mid-January when Hitler returned to Berlin, he had ensconced himself in the Führer bunker. In the city proper, there was by now, no electricity, gas, water, or sanitation, and Hitler had intended to leave Berlin immediately after his 56th birthday on 20th April, in order to move to his summer retreat in the Bavarian Alps around which, it was planned, that diehard Nazis would establish a "national redoubt" where they would make a heroic last stand. The use of the word heroism in relation to Adolf Hitler raises a number of unresolved issues with regard to his personal courage. For a man so full of bombast and rhetoric, Hitler does not appear to have been possessed of much bravery at a personal level. Throughout his political career he certainly evidenced no great willingness to expose himself to danger. As events began to turn against him, Hitler appears to have behaved in a cowardly manner. In the light of his almost complete retreat from any form of contact with the public which he had led into this fiasco, it could be fairly alleged that he lacked the personal courage to face the victims of his actions. This was certainly not a man who was prepared to face the music.

Once inside the bunker, Hitler was to prove to be as unpredictable as ever, and he became mesmerised, once more, by the arrows on the situation map in the bunker. Now reduced to clutching at straws, he began to believe once again that the flags on the map represented real military forces. In particular he began to believe that Steiner's 11th Army could somehow link-up with the surviving German forces north of Berlin and strike a decisive blow against the Russians. In reality the grand sounding title of "army" was as illusory as the title of "fortress", which Hitler was notoriously inclined to bestow upon hopeless defensive positions, in the hope that they might miraculously be transformed into impregnable defensive positions by the power of words alone. The rag-bag of forces at Steiner's disposal could only be described as an army in the mind of Adolf Hitler. In fact the depleted forces available to the German commanders still fighting on the outskirts of the city had no real prospect of halting the Soviet advance, never mind any question of reversing the tide.

Against this gloomy scenario, matters took a further turn for the worse when Steiner's 11th Army was brushed aside to allow the Russians to complete the

Soviet tanks and other heavy equipment in front of the Brandenberg Gate.

encirclement of Berlin. Hitler was once again beside himself with rage. In a pointless gesture, he removed the hapless Steiner from his command over an army which had, to all intents and purposes, ceased to exist. Any prospect of a wholesale evacuation for the Führer and his entourage, had now disappeared and a radio broadcast on 22nd April announced that the Führer would stay in his capital to the very last.

The final Russian assault on Berlin began on 26th April, it was preceded by very heavy air attacks and, as always, a thunderous artillery barrage. Despite all of the enormous difficulties under which they now laboured, the logistical services of the German armed forces continued to produce minor miracles of supply, which allowed some fairly formidable formations to enter the final battle for Berlin. One such example is the 503rd heavy tank battalion equipped with the mighty King Tiger tank. These impressive machines fought alongside the 11th SS division "Nordland" and even more remarkably, a battalion of French volunteers which had formed a part of the "Charlemagne" division, at the beginning of the third week of April there were still three hundred men available for combat in the French volunteer battalion. Together these formations played a key role in the defence of the government buildings in the centre of Berlin. In many respects the Frenchmen had nothing to lose and there was even less at stake for their German Masters. The SS in particular knew that they could expect no mercy from the Red Army which had long since adopted the practice of shooting SS prisoners out of hand as a response to the brutal treatment of the commissars. Perhaps

The famous image of the Reg Flag being raised over Berlin had to be re-staged for the camera after the results of the first shoot proved to be unsatisfactory.

it was this knowledge which kept many formations at their post during the dark days of the battles for Berlin, but just in case, the military police remained vigilant to the last, ready to hang or shoot suspected deserters.

Whatever the reason, as late as 26th April, the commander of the Tigers in the 503rd heavy tank battalion was able to report that he still had six tanks ready for active service in the defence of the routes leading to the centre of Berlin. Even more remarkable they also had stocks of fuel and a plentiful supply of ammunition, including the bulky 88mm ammunition for the massive high velocity guns which were carried in the turrets of these formidable machines. Backed up by the Panzerfausts of the French and Norwegian volunteers, this small battle group claimed dozens of Russian tanks during the bitter street fighting which marked the last days of the Third Reich. Incredibly, even the back-up and repair services of the tank battalions continued to function and by May 1st the number of tanks available to the 503rd heavy tank battalion had actually increased, and there were now five King Tigers and six Panzer IV's ready for action.

In addition to the foreign volunteer forces there were, of course, substantial Wehrmacht elements who fought to the bitter end. In many cases they were assisted by the men of the Volksturm battalions, who were now literally fighting to defend their own homes and families. Given the barbaric behaviour of the men of the Red Army this was to prove a forlorn hope indeed. After the surrender, the city authorities estimated that there were something like 90,000 instances of rape which were in the last few days before the surrender of the city. Spurred on by outrages on this scale, the men of the Volksturm had become highly proficient in the use of the Panzerfaust, which was a weapon of deadly effectiveness at short range. One additional obstacle which the Russians now had to overcome, were the wrecks of their own tanks which frequently formed a convenient barricade across many of the streets where they had come to grief.

Just as the ruins of Stalingrad, created by the aerial bombardment of the Luftwaffe, had once produced ideal defensive positions for the defenders of that city, so too did the ceaseless bombing of Berlin by the allied air forces. The cumulative effect of years of bombing and the devastation caused by the heavy Russian artillery barrage, had created a wilderness of rubble full of ready made strong points, which naturally favoured the defender in the fierce street fighting which continued to rage unabated, as the Red Army fought bitterly all the way to the Reichstag.

Stalin himself had recognised that the battle for Berlin was likely to be a severe test and he had opened the final planning session for the battle with the ominous words "I have the impression that a very heavy battle lies ahead of us". In his memoirs, Marshal Koniev admitted that the Soviet army had lost eight hundred tanks in the fighting for Berlin, in many respects this last nut was the toughest that the Red Army had to crack. The Russians had announced that they would capture Berlin on May 1st but the beleaguered defenders took perverse pride in the fact that by the morning of May 2nd, there was still fierce resistance in some sectors of the city. Although the official surrender took place on the afternoon of May 2nd, a number of German units nonetheless attempted to break out of the Soviet sector and make their way towards the Western allies, with the result that Berlin was not finally pacified until May 3rd. On the night of 28th April, with the Russian forces grinding ever closer to his headquarters, Hitler married his mistress, Eva Braun. After the wedding meal he retired to write his last will and testament. He defiantly reaffirmed his belief in Liebensraum and indulged in one vitriolic attack on the Jewish race. On the afternoon of 30th April, having made his farewells, he poisoned his wife and his dog and shot himself. Then their bodies were burned on a petrol soaked pyre to be joined the following night by Dr. and Frau Goebbels and the six children they had poisoned. On the same evening that Hitler committed suicide, Sergeants Yagorov and Kantariya planted the Victory Banner of the Soviet flag on the Reichstag at 22.50 hrs. It symbolised the triumph of the Soviet Union over Nazi Germany.

But the cost had been horrendous. By May 8th, when the German act of surrender was ratified at Russian Headquarters in Berlin, twenty eight million Russians, one in seven of the population, had died as a direct result of the war. They had died as soldiers, partisans, prisoners of war, slaves, or innocent civilians. They had met their end through bombs, bullets, hunger, torture, burning and exposure. Less than five per cent of the young people aged between seventeen and twenty one had survived. For each of the one thousand four hundred and eighteen days of the war, almost nineteen thousand Russian people had perished. The German invaders destroyed or burnt seventeen hundred towns and more than seventy thousand villages and hamlets; decommissioned sixty per cent of the steel works and sixty per cent of the coal mines; destroyed sixty five thousand kilometres of railway lines and four thousand one hundred stations; thirty six thousand communication centres and tens of thousands of State farms. They looted and demolished forty thousand medical establishments, eighty four thousand schools and forty three thousand public libraries. Twenty five million people had been left homeless. But in the end the forces of National Socialism had been defeated.

Throughout Western Europe, Germans from the SS, the army and the civilian administration, were put on trial for offences committed during the Nazi occupation. However, the number punished and the severity of their sentences was astonishingly limited given the massive scale of the crimes against humanity which had occurred. Even though the Russian Government had the right to hold its own trials under Article Ten of the Four Power Ordinance, none took place. Stalin was far more concerned about taking vengeance on traitors to the Soviet Union. Some two hundred and fifty thousand prisoners of war, now in allied hands, were Soviet citizens who had been captured in German uniform. Under agreements affirmed at the Yalta Conference in 1945, those accused of treason or desertion were to be returned to their native countries for judgement. Those who had fought for the Germans were now forcibly repatriated. Some took the only escape route open to them and committed suicide. The Soviet authorities regarded these traitors as human scum and treated them with a barbarity which reflected their hatred.

Keitel (bottom right) signs the final German surrender document in May 1945. Zhukov is on the extreme left of the picture.

Another five million plus Soviet prisoners of war had been captured or had surrendered on the fields of battle. Tragically, Russian administrators seemed to view their very survival as an act of treachery. Many who had lived through years of gruesome warfare and the savage inhuman degradation of the German work camps, were now to spend the remainder of their time in the penal colonies of their own motherland.

Inside Russia the pre-war status quo was rapidly re-established and strengthened. The cult of Stalin as a personalisation of victory, ensured that his position as dictator of an authoritarian, centralised society was unassailable. The reforms and liberalisations which had occurred during the organised chaos of the war years were gradually retracted. Religious toleration, a greater modicum of popular involvement in civilian administration, and the virtues of individual and collective initiative became incompatible with the need for the entrenched elite to control all aspects of social development.

But none of this should detract from the awesome achievement of the Soviet people. Through their bravery, their labour and their sacrifice, they managed to halt and eventually crush a seemingly invincible war machine which, with chilling efficiency, had conquered almost the entire Western European continent in a matter of months. They annihilated a German army which had unleashed in its wake, a regime of apocalyptic terror, a tyranny which had turned vast tracts of Europe into a surreal playground of sadists and perverts. The victory of the Soviet people may not have ensured an era of justice and democratic ideals but it rid the world of the cancerous malignancy of National Socialism which had for long periods threatened to engulf it.

The victory parade held in red Square to mark the end of four years of hardship and misery on a scale which defies comprehension.

APPENDIX 1

THE STALIN LINE

The 'Stalin line', in no sense a single unbroken line, was the name the German Army gave to the fixed fortifications built between 1931-34 to protect the old pre-1939 frontiers of the Soviet Union. This defensive system consisted of eleven 'fortified districts' and two less well fitted out, extending from the north in the Leningrad Military District, through the Belorussian Military District (subsequently the Western Special Military District) and southwards to the Kiev Special Military District and the Odessa Military District. The areas of heaviest concentration were around Minsk in the north and Kiev in the south, together with special defensive zones to cover the roads leading to Moscow and Kiev.

The 'Stalin line' consisted of 3,324 planned defensive positions, of which 228 had yet to be completed in 1941. The German Army in Russia discovered and carried out a detailed survey of 142 casemates for heavy guns, 248 anti-tank positions, 2,572 machine-gun posts and 134 command posts or battle stations.

STALIN LINE	GUN EMPLACEMENTS	ANTI-TANK EMPLACEMENTS	MACHINE GUN POSITIONS	COMMAND POSITIONS	TOTAL
Lenningrad & Karelia MD	16	34	88	13	302
Special Western MD	39	160	871	62	2264
Special Kiev MD	114	90	909	56	2338
Special Odessa MD	39	24	773	36	1744
Total (minus Karelia)	208	208	2641	167	6648

APPENDIX 2

5/6TH DECEMBER 1941
RED ARMY STRENGTH INCLUDES ALL FRONTS

The battle for Moscow is often depicted, particularly from German sources, as an unequal struggle between exhausted German units and a numerically superior Red Army. Given the enormous losses so recently suffered by the Red Army, this scenario is unlikely to say the least. As far as can be accurately assessed, the actual numbers in the field, taking into account the right flank of the Salhurst front, suggests that the Wehrmacht enjoyed both a numeric and a material advantage over the Russians.

MOSCOW 6.12.41

TOTAL FORCES	RED ARMY	WEHRMACHT
Manpower (Divisions & Brigades)	approx 718,000	801,000
Guns and Mortars	7,985	14,000
Tanks	721	1,000
Aircraft	11,170	1,615 (1st Jan 1942)

KALININ FRONT 1.12.41

TOTAL FORCES	RED ARMY	WEHRMACHT
Manpower	approx 100,000	approx 153,000
Guns and Mortars	980	2,198
Tanks	67	60
Aircraft	83	-

WESTERN FRONT 6.12.41

TOTAL FORCES	RED ARMY	WEHRMACHT
Manpower	approx 558,000	approx 590,000
Guns and Mortars	4,348	7,440
Tanks	624	900
Aircraft	199	-

SOUTHWESTERN FRONT: Right Flank 6.12.41

TOTAL FORCES	RED ARMY	WEHRMACHT
Manpower	approx 60,000	approx 29,000
Guns and Mortars	388	745
Tanks	30	up to 40
Aircraft	79	-

APPENDIX 3

CANNIBALISM AND THE SIEGE OF LENINGRAD

Starvation drove the population not only to extreme measures but to the horrifying excess of cannibalism, the first cases of which occurred at the beginning of December, 1941. The Soviet criminal code made no mention of such a crime as cannibalism. Soviet officials could only define it at first as an extreme form of 'banditry'. According to the top-secret report of the Military Procurator of Leningrad, A.A. Kuznetsov, dated 27th February, 1942, investigations of cannibalism led to criminal charges against twenty-six individuals in December, 1941, 366 in January, 1942 and 494 in the first two weeks of February, 1942. Investigation revealed that not only was human flesh consumed by individuals but it was also sold to other citizens. By 20th February 1942, 866 individuals were under criminal investigation or actual indictment for suspected cannibalism. Only eighteen per cent of this number had any previous criminal record. Of the 886 suspect individuals, 322 were men and 564 women, almost thirty per cent (255) were aged over 40, the next largest group being in their thirties. More ghoulish still was the discovery of extensive intrusions into cemeteries and the mutilation of the recent dead. One evening in March 1942, the watchman at the Bogoslovskii cemetery detained a woman with a sack. Once opened the sack revealed the bodies of five infants. The increase in cannibalism forced the city authorities to set up police guards at all the major cemeteries.

(Documents Nos. 180 and 153 respectively, Leningrad v Osade)

APPENDIX 4

THE INITIAL COMPOSITION OF ARMY GROUP NORTH AT THE TIME OF OPERATION BARBAROSSA JUNE 22ND 1941.

APPROXIMATELY 700,000 MEN IN TOTAL

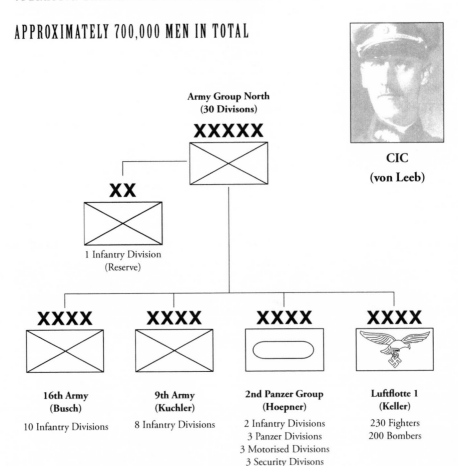

Army Group North (30 Divisons)

XXXXX

CIC
(von Leeb)

XX

1 Infantry Division
(Reserve)

XXXX	XXXX	XXXX	XXXX
16th Army (Busch)	**9th Army** (Kuchler)	**2nd Panzer Group** (Hoepner)	**Luftflotte 1** (Keller)
10 Infantry Divisions	8 Infantry Divisions	2 Infantry Divisions 3 Panzer Divisions 3 Motorised Divisions 3 Security Divisons	230 Fighters 200 Bombers

The bitter cold of the Arctic forests outside Leningrad was where the men of Army Group North fought and died, constantly short of manpower and material, they considered themselves to be the forgotten men of the Russian Front. It is no surprise that they christened the pitiless war they were fighting, "the eternal war of the poor man".

Most of the "poor men" of Army Group North were destined never to return to Germany. The ceaseless demands of the cruelest conflict in history would ultimately claim the whole Army Group as its victim.

As the name suggests, Army Group North formed the northern wing of the German attack on Russia. In June 1941, the time of the attack, Army Group North was commanded by Field marshal Ritter von Leeb and was composed of two subsidiary armies, the 16th army initially commanded by Field marshal Busch and the 18th army commanded by General von Kuchler. For the initial thrust into Russia under the Barbarossa directive, Army Group North enjoyed the support of a powerful tank force designated as Panzer Group 4, under the leadership of General Hoepner. For air support, Army Group North could call upon Luftflotte One, commanded by General Keller. The Stukas of Luftflotte One were to provide the flying artillery for the lightning attack of June 22.

Source - US Dept of the Army Pamphlet 20-261(a) Halder/Heinrici et al

Men of Army Group North march into Russia during the summer of 1941.

APPENDIX 5

THE INITIAL COMPOSITION OF ARMY GROUP CENTRE AT THE TIME OF OPERATION BARBAROSSA JUNE 22ND 1941.

APPROXIMATELY 1,300,000 MEN IN TOTAL

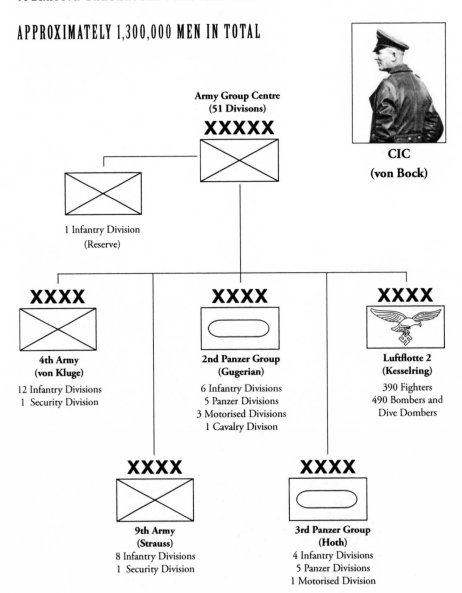

Army Group Centre
(51 Divisons)

CIC
(von Bock)

1 Infantry Division
(Reserve)

4th Army
(von Kluge)

12 Infantry Divisions
1 Security Division

2nd Panzer Group
(Gugerian)

6 Infantry Divisions
5 Panzer Divisions
3 Motorised Divisions
1 Cavalry Divison

Luftflotte 2
(Kesselring)

390 Fighters
490 Bombers and
Dive Dombers

9th Army
(Strauss)

8 Infantry Divisions
1 Security Division

3rd Panzer Group
(Hoth)

4 Infantry Divisions
5 Panzer Divisions
1 Motorised Division

During the titanic struggle between Hitler and Stalin there was always one prize which the Russian forces valued above all others. That prize was the destruction of Army Group Centre. This huge mass of men and equipment was aimed like a knife at the heart of Stalin's Soviet Union.

In December 1941, Army Group Centre came tantalisingly close to capturing the capital city of Stalin's empire, and it was to take years of bitter fighting before the men of the Red Army could claim victory. In that time they were to come perilously close to their own destruction.

As its name suggests, Army Group Centre was the force responsible for the middle sector of the front, formed by the three great army groups which Hitler unleashed upon Russia on June 22nd 1941. For the great offensive of June 22nd, Army Group Centre displayed two powerful Infantry Armies in the form of the 4th and 9th Armies under von Kluge and Strauss. Unlike the other army groups, Army Group Centre had not one but two Panzer Groups under the very capable leadership of Hoth and Guderian. Luftflotte 2 under Kesselring completed a powerful adversary.

Source - US Dept of the Army Pamphlet 20-261(a) Halder/Heinrici et al

The debris of war in the wake of the successful advance by Army Group Centre.

APPENDIX 6

THE INITIAL COMPOSITION OF ARMY GROUP SOUTH AT THE TIME OF OPERATION BARBAROSSA JUNE 22ND 1941.

APPROXIMATELY 1,000,000 MEN IN TOTAL

Army Group South
(48 Divisons)

XXXXX

CIC
(von Leeb)

1 Infantry Division
2 Mountain Divisions
(Reserve)

XXXX

XXXX

XXXX

6th Army
(von Reichenau)

11 Infantry
Divisions

17th Army
(von Stülpnagel)

5 Infantry Divisions
2 Mountain Divisions
2 Security Divisions
3 Light Divisons

Luftflotte 4
(Loehr)

210 Fighters
490 Bombers and
Dive Dombers

XXXX

XXXX

11th Army*
(von Schobert)

15 Infantry Divisions
1 Cavalry Division
1 Motorised Division
3 Mountain Divisions
Includes 14 Rumarian Divisions

1st Panzer Group
(von Kleist)

5 Panzer Divisions
4 Motorised Divisions
1 Security Division

The dramatic events which were played out on the Russian Front during this terrible conflict, reached a peak of intensity and decisiveness on the Southern Front, the area of Army Group South.

It was this sector which witnessed the nightmare siege of Sevastopol, the disaster at Stalingrad, the fury of Operation Citadel, and the horrors of the Korsun pocket.

In 1941 Army Group South was ordered to drive into the southern part of the USSR, the initial targets were Odessa and the Crimea, but the final strategic objective was the capture of the oilfields in the Caucasus.

Army Group South was commanded by Field Marshal Gerd von Rundstedt, he had at his disposal three separate subsidiary armies, the 6th Army, initially commanded by von Reichenau, the 11th Army, commanded by von Shobert, and the 17th Army, under Stulpnagel.

They were supported by a powerful armoured formation known as Panzer Group One, under the leadership of von Kliest. Air cover was provided by Luftflotte 4, under General Loehr.

Source - US Dept of the Army Pamphlet 20-261(a) Halder/Heinrici et al

Rumanian troops from Army Group South during the early phase of Operation Barbarossa.

APPENDIX 7

DIARY OF THE COMMANDER OF XLII CORPS FROM THE CHERKASSY POCKET

The tactical situation between 28 January and 16 February, as described above, was modified by a number of developments inside the pocket. A record of these events is found in excerpts from the diary kept by the commander of XLII Corps up to the time of the breakout:

28 JANUARY

Communications to the rear along the road Shpola-Zvenigorodka have been cut. We are encircled. First Panzer Army to restore communication routes. Our defensive mission remains unchanged. Telephone request to Eighth Army: "Mission requires maintaining northeast front against strong enemy pressure. Russian advance against Steblev necessitates main effort on southern sector. Request authority for immediate withdrawal of northern and eastern fronts. This will permit offensive action toward southwest and prevent further encirclement and separation from XI Corps."

29 JANUARY

Radio message from Eighth Army: "Prepare withdrawal in direction Rossava up to Mironovka-Boguslav. Be ready to move by 12:00 on 29 January upon prearranged signal. Authority for further withdrawal likely within twenty-four hours. Report new situation."

Requested additional ammunition for artillery and small arms. Food supplies in the pocket are adequate. XI Corps under attack by strong Russian tank forces. Several of its regiments reduced to 100 men. Air supply beginning to arrive. Evacuation of casualties too slow. More than 2,000 wounded have to be removed.

31 JANUARY

Message from Eighth Army: XLVIII Panzer Corps will attack on 1 February toward Lozovatka (three miles northwest of Shpola) to relieve enemy pressure against XI Corps.

1 FEBRUARY

Daily losses 300 men. Fighter protection inadequate. Ammunition and fuel running low.

2 FEBRUARY

Air supply improving. Radio message from Eighth Army: "Withdrawal of north front approved. Prepare for main effort on eastern flank of south front. Vormann (general commanding XLVIII Panzer Corps) is continuing the relief attack from the south. Breith (general commanding III Panzer Corps) will attack 3 February from southwest."

3 FEBRUARY

Air supply continues to improve. Unfortunately several transport aircraft with wounded aboard were shot down on the return flight. Have requested that air evacuations be made at night only unless adequate fighter protection can be provided. Message from Army: "To strengthen southern sector, occupy proposed line without further delaying action at intermediate positions."

4 FEBRUARY

Made a determined effort to take Boguslav. Commander of Task Force B seriously wounded. Now all the division commanders are artillerymen, including the present SS big shot. The north front is tottering. Russian tanks today captured a medium battery of Task Force B that was firing from every barrel without being able to score a single hit. Evidently we have too few experienced gunners. By nightfall our line is restored. Daily ammunition expenditure of the corps 200 tons. Casualties still 300 per day. This cannot go on much longer. Have requested 2,000 replacements, also 120 tons additional ammunition per day.

5 FEBRUARY

Radio message from Eighth Army: "Prepare breakout for 10 February. Further instructions follow."

7 FEBRUARY

Radio message to Eighth Army: "Roads deeply mired. Will require more time for breakout preparations." Message from Eighth Army: "At time of breakout the following units will attack from the outside: XLVIII Panzer Corps toward Olshana, III Panzer Corps toward Morentsy. Pocket force will effect initial break-through and, covering its flanks and rear, concentrate its entire strength in attack across the line Shenderovka-Kvitki toward Morentsy, to link up with armored wedge of relief forces. Regrouping must be completed in time to permit breakout on 10 February. Final decision will depend on progress of armored spearheads. Situation does not permit further delay."

Stemmermann (general commanding Xl Corps) assumes command of both corps in the pocket. Report to Army that because of road conditions attack impossible before 12 February.

Had a look at the 110th Grenadier Regiment and Task Force B. Morale of troops very good. Rations plentiful. Enough sugar, sausage, cigarettes, and bread to last for another ten days. Army Group Commander radios that everything is being done to help us.

8 FEBRUARY

Radio message to Eighth Army: "Artillery, heavy weapons, and horse-drawn vehicles of 72d, 389th, and *Wiking* Divisions, as well as hundreds of motor vehicles of *Wiking* carrying many wounded, are stuck in the mud at Gorodishche. Withdrawal from line held today, to effect regrouping, would involve intolerable losses of men, weapons, and equipment. Line must be held at least twenty-four hours longer."

Today I saw many casualties, including four officers; ordered more careful evacuation of wounded, and destruction of all classified documents we can possibly get rid of.

9 FEBRUARY

Generals Zhukov, Konev, and Vatutin have sent an emissary, a Russian lieutenant colonel, who arrived with driver, interpreter, and bugler at the position of Task Force B to present surrender terms for Stemmermann and myself. He is treated to champagne and cigarettes, receives no reply. Ultimatum remains unanswered.

Forces for breakout dwindle from day to day. Inquiry from Army High Command about Leon Degrelle, commander of Brigade *Wallonien*. He is a young man, Belgian; I saw him a few days ago among his men. They are likeable fellows, but apparently too soft for this business.

Approach of relief forces delayed by necessary regrouping. Nevertheless Army now insists we break out on 12 February. Much as we would like to, we cannot do it by then. In this mud the infantry cannot possibly cover more than a thousand yards per hour.

10 FEBRUARY

My old division commander of 1940, General von Seydlitz* today sent me a long letter delivered by aircraft: He thinks I should act like Yorck during the campaign of 1812 and go over to the Russians with my entire command. I did not answer.

Army inquires whether breakout in direction Morentsy still feasible, or whether the operation should rather be directed via Dzhurzhentsy-Pochapintsy toward Lisyanka. Reply to Army: "Lisyanka preferable if Breith (III Panzer Corps) can reach it. Situation on east front critical. Several enemy penetrations. For the past forty-eight hours XI

Corps unable to establish new defense line. Troops badly depleted and battle-weary. XLII Corps front intact. We are attacking south of Steblev. Serious danger if east front cannot be brought to a halt. XLII Corps will break through in direction Lisyanka. The troops are well in hand. Early advance of Breith toward Lisyanka decisive."

Reply from Army: "Thanks for comprehensive information. In full accord concerning new direction of breakout. Breith will attack 11 February in direction of Lisyanka. Will do all we can. Good luck."

Seydlitz today sent me fifty German prisoners with letters to their commanders; in addition they are supposed to persuade their comrades to go over to the enemy. I cannot understand Seydlitz. Although the events at Stalingrad must have changed him completely, I am unable to see how he can now work as a sort of G-2 for Zhukov.

12 FEBRUARY

Breith has reached Lisyanka. Vormann is advancing in direction of Zvenigorodka. Our infantry has taken the northern part of Khilki. (Map 5) The regimental commander leading the attack was killed in action. So goes one after another. XI Corps has taken Komarovka. The Russians, according to intercepted signals, are about to attack our left flank. Radio message to Army: "Absolutely necessary that Breith advance to Petrovskoye as quickly as possible, in order to effect link-up. Speed is essential. Forward elements of XLII Corps now at Khilki." Reply from Army: "Vormann southeast of Zvenigorodka. Breith will attack 13 February with strong armored wedge in direction Dzhurzhentsy."

Was at Khiiki this afternoon. Things look bad. Our men are exhausted. Nothing gets done unless officers are constantly behind them. Am now keeping my horses inside the hut; they are in better shape than I. My orderly is burning my papers and giving away my extra uniforms.

13 FEBRUARY

Another message from General von Seydlitz, this time addressed to the commander of the 198th Division. Not bad: they think we are stronger than we really are. The letter was attached as usual to a black, red, and white pennant (German colors) and dropped from a plane. These people never fail to find my headquarters.

Breakout further delayed because of heavy enemy attacks against XI Corps' east front. Radio message to Army: "Concentration for breakout prevented by heavy Russian flank attacks and final mopping up at Shenderovka. Will shorten east front, involving evacuation of Korsun, during night of 13-14 February. Forces thereby released will not be available for breakout before 15 February. Intend to continue attack throughout 14 February. Breakthrough of Breith's armored force toward Petrovskoye indispensable to success."

Reply from Army: "Breith under orders to thrust toward Petrovskoye. His forward elements now on line Lisyanka-Khichintsy." Have requested strong fighter protection for 14 February, Russian strafing attacks are getting increasingly serious in view of the growing congestion in the pocket. I am most afraid that Army cannnot comply with this oft-repeated request.

14 FEBRUARY

Breith will have to arrive soon. Last night the Luftwaffe dropped ammunition over the Russian lines instead of ours. Now they are trying to put the blame on us claiming the drop point was inadequately lighted.

Stemmermann has just issued orders for the breakout. The date: 16 February. Radio message to Army: "North front will be withdrawn during the night of 14 - 15 February to the south bank of Ross Siver. Main attack ordered for 16 February. Further advance of tank force for direct support absolutely necessary."

We are destroying all excess motor vehicles and equipment. I have prohibited burning.

15 FEBRUARY

Our pocket is now so small that I can practically look over the entire front from my command post, when it is not snowing. Enemy aircraft are hard at work; lucky for us it is snowing most of the time. I was once more at Khilki to reconnoiter the terrain selected for the breakout. Then issued final order. Since this morning there is trouble at the SS Division. The Walloons and the *Germania* Regiment are getting fidgety. They must hold only until tomorrow night.

Final instructions from Stemmermann: We are to jump off on 16 February at 23:00, with Task Force B, 72d Division, and SS Panzer Division *Wiking* from Khilki-Komarovka across the line Dzhurzhentsy-Hill 239 to Lisyanka; 57th and 88th Divisions will cover the flanks and the rear.

With me, at my command post, are the three division commanders with whom I am supposed to perform the miracle tomorrow. One of them is doing this for the first time, the two others are old hands.

I left no doubt in their minds that, in my opinion, this is going to be one giant snafu, and that they should not get rattled, no matter what happens. You need a guardian angel to bring you through this kind of thing.

Have given my second mount to my G-3. His *Panje* horse will be used by the G-2.

16 FEBRUARY

Ample supply of ammunition dropped in aerial delivery containers as late as last night. In this respect we are now well off - if we can take it along.

After consulting Stemmermann I decided to hand over to the Russians some 2,000 wounded together with medical personnel and one doctor from each division. This is a bitter decision, but to take them along would mean their certain death.

Saw Stemmermann once more to say good-by. My orderly takes my diary; he is a crafty fellow and will get it through somehow.

BIBLIOGRAPHY

Bacon, Edwin, The GULAG at War. Stalin's Forced Labour System in the Light of the Archives. London 1994.

Barber, John and Harrison, Mark, The Soviet Home Front, 1941-1945:a social and economic history of the USSR in World War II. London 1991.

Bartov, Omer, The Eastern Front, 1941-45, and the Barbarisation of Warfare. London 1985.

Bellamy, Christopher, Red God of War: Soviet Artillery and Rocket Forces. London 1986.

Carell, Paul, Hitler's War on Russia. The Story of German Defeat in the East, Vol.1 London 1964 and Scorched Earth, Vol. 2, London 1970.

Chuikov, V.I., Marshal, The Beginning of the Road. London 1963. (Translation of 'Nachalo puti', Chuikov's personal account of Stalingrad)

Conner, Albert Z., and Poirier, Robert G., The Red Army Order of Battle in the Great Patriotic War. Novato, California, 1985.

Craig, William, Enemy at the Gates: The Battle for Stalingrad. New York, 1973.

Dunn, Walter S. Jr., Hitler's Nemesis. The Red Army 1930-1945. Westport, London,1994.

Dunn, Walter S. Jr., Kursk Hitler's Gamble. 1943, Westport, London 1997.

Dunnigan, James F.(ed.), The Russian Front. Germany's War in the East, 1941-1945, London- Melbourne 1978. (Organisation of German and Soviet Ground Forces, Tactics and Weapons, Orders of Battle)

Erickson, John, The Road to Stalingrad. Stalin's War with Germany. Volume 1. London 1998 and The Road to Berlin. Volume 2. London 1996.

Erickson and Dilks, David (eds), Barbarossa. The Axis and the Allies, Edinburgh 1998.

Garrard, John and Garrard, Carol (eds), World War Two and the Soviet People. London 1993.

Glantz, David M.(ed), The Initial Period of War on the Eastern Front 22 June-August 1941, London 1993.

Glantz, From the Don to the Dnepr. Soviet Offensive Operations December 1942-August 1943, London 1991.

Glantz, Stumbling Colossus. The Red Army on the Eve of World War. Kansas University Press 1998.

Glantz and House, Jonathan, When Titans Clashed. How the Red Army stopped Hitler. Kansas University Press, 1995.

Guderian, Heinz, General, Panzer Leader. London, reprint 1982.

Halder, Heinrici et al, Barbarossa, Planning and Operations. US Dept of the Army pamphlet.

Haupt, Werner, Army Group North/South/Centre. Atglen, PA 1998.

Irving, David, Hitler's War. London 1977.

Krivosheev, G.F., Colonel-General (ed), Soviet Casualties and Combat Losses in the Twentieth Century. London 1997. (See Soviet manpower and equipment losses, 1941-45)

Manstein, Erich von, Field Marshal, Lost Victories. Chicago, 1958.

Mellenthin, F.W., Major-General, Panzer Battles: A Study of the Employment of Armour in the Second World War. London, reprint 1984.

Milsom, John. Russian Tanks 1900-1970. London 1970.

Parrish, Michael (ed), Battle for Moscow. The 1942 Soviet General Staff Study, London 1989.

Rotundo, Louis (ed), Battle for Stalingrad. The 1943 Soviet General Staff Study, London 1989.

Ryan, Cornelius, The Last Battle. London 1966. (Berlin 1945).

Salisbury, Harrison S., The Siege of Leningrad. London 1969.

Seaton, A., The Russo-German War 1941-1945. London 1971.

Senger und Etterlin, F.M.von, German Tanks of World War II. The Complete Illustrated History of German Armoured Fighting Vehicles 1926-1945, London 1969.

Shukman, Harold (ed), Stalin's Generals. London 1993.

Trevor-Roper, H.R. (ed), Hitler's War Directives 1939-1945. London, reprint 1966.

Tsouras, Peter G. (ed) , The Anvil of War. German Generalship in Defence on the Eastern Front, London 1994.

Werth, Alexander, Russia At War 1941-1945. London 1964.

CPSIA information can be obtained at www.ICGtesting.com
Printed in the USA
LVOW061827290412

279596LV00002B/138/P